RESEARCH METHODS
FOR LIBRARIANS
AND EDUCATORS

RESEARCH METHODS FOR LIBRARIANS AND EDUCATORS

Practical Applications in Formal and Informal Learning Environments

Ruth V. Small and Marcia A. Mardis, Editors

LIBRARIES UNLIMITED™

An Imprint of ABC-CLIO, LLC

Santa Barbara, California • Denver, Colorado

Library of Congress Cataloging in Publication Control Number: 2017051876

ISBN: 978–1–4408–4962–6 (paperback)
       978–1–4408–4963–3 (ebook)

22 21 20 19 18   1 2 3 4 5

This book is also available as an eBook.

Libraries Unlimited
An Imprint of ABC-CLIO, LLC

ABC-CLIO, LLC
130 Cremona Drive, P.O. Box 1911
Santa Barbara, California 93116-1911
www.abc-clio.com

This book is printed on acid-free paper ∞

Manufactured in the United States of America

We dedicate this book to present and future librarians and teachers who currently
may be research novices but, we hope, have been inspired to become researcher-
practitioners in their libraries and schools. This book is intended to stimulate their
curiosity about research methodology and their desire to conduct, either alone
or in collaboration with other researcher-practitioners, meaningful research
that impacts their service and the people they serve.

We also wish to dedicate this book to those who have personally
inspired us along our research journeys.

Contents

Acknowledgments

We wish to acknowledge the participation of 18 research scholars who brought both their expertise and their experience to authoring their chapters and were willing to take a chance on a different approach to a book on research methods. We hope they and our readers are pleased with the results. We'd also like to thank the library and teaching practitioners who shared their real-life problem situations, written as research scenarios, for our authors to use as authentic contexts for their chapters. We'd also like to thank Danny Callison, who first approached us about this book, and Blanche Woolls of ABC-CLIO/Libraries Unlimited who worked so closely with us to make our manuscript the best it can be.

—Ruth V. Small and Marcia A. Mardis, coeditors

My co-editor, **Marcia Mardis**, a joy to work with. My dissertation advisor and professor (and a chapter author for this book), **Dr. Charles Reigeluth**, whose classes and collaborative projects ignited my interest in problem solving through research and sealed my lifelong love of the research process. **Dr. John Keller**, my professor, mentor, and role model who, more than anyone, has profoundly influenced my professional life and career by teaching and demonstrating, through word and deed, the critical importance of motivation in everything we do. My daughters, **Jacqueline Belen** and **Deborah Curtis**, who inspire me every day with the great work they do and the creative and ethical ways they approach their work in their respective fields. My grandchildren, **Carly**, **Zach** and **Phoebe**, who motivate me every day of my life to be the best and the most honorable person I can be.

—Ruth V. Small

My treasured colleague Ruth V. Small has opened many professional doors for me—this project among them. It has been a profound pleasure to work alongside her to prepare this volume. I would also like to thank my co-faculty at and the leadership of Florida State University' School of Information for allowing me the freedom to pursue my passions in research, teaching, and service. B. Glenn Rainey and Faye R. Jones tirelessly support me—I could not be as productive and inspired without your wisdom, humor, and ability to listen. Finally, the late Dr. Charles M. Achilles is in my heart in every research endeavor I undertake. Chuck, I miss you every day.

—Marcia A. Mardis

Chapter 1

Introduction to the Book

Ruth V. Small, Laura J. and L. Douglas Meredith Professor
School of Information Studies, Syracuse University

Introduction

Throughout their history, from ancient Egypt to modern times, libraries have been inextricably linked to scholarly research and librarians have been trained to support that research. Not long ago, those who typically used the library's resources to conduct research, we usually conjured up an image of doctoral students working on their dissertations, college professors preparing for publication, or high school students writing their term papers.

In recent years, however, librarians and teachers have counted themselves among those using information resources and conducting research studies to investigate important problems related to all aspects of their work—facilities, services, programs, collections, technologies, community needs, students, and other library users. The catalyst that, unfortunately, has increasingly motivated this growing interest in practitioner research over the past few decades has been rooted in the ever-present threat of looming cuts in staff and programs in schools and libraries, library mergers and closings, and a growing public perception that the library is no longer a critical player in serving today's information needs. Librarians, often in collaboration with other educators, are discovering that research provides them with a powerful tool for meeting these challenges.

Librarians as Practitioner-Researchers

"Practitioner-researcher" has become a title used by practicing professionals in a number of different fields, including education, to denote those who, in addition to their regular responsibilities, conduct research to investigate solutions to problems in or related to the workplace and to advance practice. Therefore, the role of today's librarian has evolved from simply supporting the research others are doing to a more proactive research role in actually conducting research to solve important problems in and related to libraries.

As a result, the term "practitioner-researcher" has begun to appear in the library and information science literature to describe one more critical role of today's librarian. In addition, courses on research methods in the curricula of many preservice library and information science programs in universities nationwide have also emerged or have enjoyed renewed interest. Many programs are adding research to their preservice program core course requirements, while other opportunities for preservice librarians to gain practical research knowledge and experience as budding library practitioner-researcher are also gaining in value, such as working alongside their professors in the conduct of funded research studies and choosing internships in libraries that promise active research experience.

In their 2009 *Core Competencies of Librarianship*, the American Library Association (ALA) lists research as one of the eight areas of basic knowledge for students graduating from ALA-accredited master's programs in library and information science. This demonstrates ALA's commitment to the importance of the role of practitioner-researcher and defines the Research competency as possessing knowledge of the following:

- The fundamentals of quantitative and qualitative research methods
- The central research findings and research literature of the field
- The principles and methods used to assess the actual and potential value of new research

The Ethics of Research

Before presenting any research methods, we would like to first call your attention to some basic ethical issues and concerns that must be considered and resolved before undertaking any research project. In the case of libraries, schools, colleges, and other formal and informal educational settings, one of the most important ethical concerns is what is referred to as "human subjects protection," which is a written plan that eliminates the possibility of conflict of interest and guarantees that all precautions have been taken to protect the rights and welfare of the people to be studied through the methods and procedures used in the research.

Today, many school districts, academic institutions, and library systems require that when conducting research that includes human participants (subjects), the researcher must submit a written plan, eliminating the possibility of conflict of interest and guaranteeing that all precautions have been taken to protect the rights and welfare of the people to be studied through the methods and procedures you intend to use. This plan protects those people who participate in research and also builds their trust in you, the researcher. Some examples are (1) using coding or pseudonyms for all data from minor participants, (2) providing evidence that the researchers are fully qualified to competently and ethically conduct the research, and (3) using noncoercive ways to recruit participants for a study. The plan is submitted to the researcher's institutional review board who will apply specific criteria to determine if the study may proceed or if changes in the plan are required.

In addition to the protection of people participating in your research study, there are other ethical considerations when conducting research. One of the most serious ethical breaches in research is the creation of fabricated data, such as when some or all of the data from a research study have been either made up or purposely misrepresented (often referred to as *false data*) or when some or all of the data from a research study have been either made up or purposely misrepresented. This may involve changing of data, the inclusion of data that did not come from the study, or the reporting of a study that was never conducted. Needless to say, this lapse of ethics can lead (and has led) to unfortunate, and sometimes disastrous, consequences.

An ethical issue of concern that is more commonly experienced in learning institutions is *plagiarism*—using someone else's work without citing it and representing it as one's own work as, for example, in a research report or professional publication or presentation or in a classroom report or presentation. Sometimes when plagiarism occurs, the offender is unaware of or has not learned about the need to cite one's sources and that copying someone else's words is inappropriate and unacceptable. Most librarians and teachers have had experiences with students who have plagiarized, although not all instances are intentional. Sometimes examples of plagiarism may be due to the students' lack of understanding of the term "intellectual property" and/or lack of knowledge as to appropriate methods for citing their sources. While this can become a teachable moment for the teacher or librarian, the teaching of appropriate citing of sources is an important part of any research or writing curriculum.

Other times, plagiarism is intentional, planned, and sometimes, if not properly handled, can become serial. When detected, the offender(s) is(are) often subject to a range of punishments, from receiving a failing grade for the plagiarized piece to suspension or expulsion.

Although there are a number of very effective computer-based tools for detecting plagiarism in electronic documents, these types of ethical offenses continue to occur and perpetrated by everyone from young students to adult professionals. Some of these ethical issues are addressed again in subsequent chapters of this book. As you read each chapter, we hope you will think about these ethical considerations in the context of each method described and the research you might plan to do.

Why This Book and Why Now?

In a project funded in part by the Institute of Museum and Library Services (IMLS), the American Association of School Librarians (AASL) in 2014 sponsored a national forum on research in school libraries, resulting in a white paper entitled, "Causality: School Libraries and Student Success (CLASS)," which concluded with a recommendation for three phases of causal research to be conducted by school library researchers and librarians. Efforts like this often arise from a need for evidence that demonstrates value, in this case the value of school librarians and libraries.

Today, however, librarians and other educators are finding that in order to prove their value, it is not enough just to conduct research that provides evidence, rather they must conduct *quality* research, using *rigorous* research methods and collecting *credible* data that demonstrate *valid* and *reliable* results. They also recognize the importance of sharing their findings not only with their administrators and supervisors but also with their users, their boards, and the general public. To do this, today's librarians must develop the knowledge and skills needed to become competent and proactive practitioner-researchers and seek collaborative research partners, such as classroom teachers, administrators, and community members, to add further power and credibility to their research efforts.

With this increasing need and support for research competency in the library profession, many excellent books on research methods in librarianship have become available to help librarians understand and learn about the research process. Some of those books focus in depth on one *type* of research (e.g., qualitative research and quantitative research) or on a *single research method* (e.g., the case study and participant observation), or they may target mainly university researchers and doctoral students as their reading audience. Some of these books cover the basics of research, often covering a few of the more common research methodologies, while others include more complex methods and data analysis techniques.

The goals for our approach to research in this book are for readers to:

(1) pique their curiosity and interest and build their research confidence of our primary target audience—librarians and teachers, particularly those who are novice researchers or have limited research knowledge and experience;
(2) stimulate their thinking about and exploring relevant issues and challenges that they face on the job through the use of authentic scenarios and examples;
(3) demonstrate the power of collaborative research for solving mutual or shared problems;
(4) present a variety of methods and tools for conducting research in the context of authentic library-related problems; and

(5) motivate the desire to learn more about one or more of those methods for developing a better understanding and investigation of those issues and challenges that they face on a daily basis.

How This Book Is Unique

Several factors make our approach to the design of this book creative and innovative, as well as uniquely designed to accomplish our goals. These include the following:

- Targeting librarians and other educators who wish to become practitioner-researchers, in order to demonstrate value, improve their library, identify paths to best practice, justify changes and innovations, and more. This book could also be useful as a textbook both in professional development and in-service training for librarians and teachers and in preservice professional programs in library and information science and in education.
- Selecting a range of chapter authors who are leaders and scholars in the fields of library and information science and education, representing universities nationwide. These authors not only have expert knowledge in their method, but they also have experience in applying that method in their own research, with their own unique perspective reflected in the style and focus of their chapter.
- Providing a variety of typical, real-world, practice-based scenarios, written by librarians and teachers in the field. Each scenario presents an authentic research problem facing today's librarian. In this way, not only do scenarios provide a real-world context for applying a research method that is relevant to the target reader population but also, by using them as context for multiple research methods, our chapter authors demonstrate how a problem might be viewed from different perspectives each using different research methods to solve the problem. You can read more about the role these scenarios play in this book in the Organization and Format section.
- Including 17 different, brief chapters that are dedicated to introducing readers to a specific research methodology and two additional chapters that describe the processes of determining a research question and conducting a literature review. Rather than covering a method in depth, each chapter is intended to provide basic information to help the novice researcher understand the thought processes for determining how and when that method might be appropriate for addressing a particular research problem and to motivate the reader to want to gain more in-depth knowledge of one or more methods in order to apply it to a current or future research problem.
- There is a thread running through the book, in both the scenarios and chapters, that highlights the importance of research in which educators work together to frame a problem, define the questions to be answered, and explore potential

solutions collaboratively. We hope to convey the importance of enriching the research conceptualization and processes through collaboration by (1) librarians from different, individual libraries or library systems; (2) librarians across different types of libraries (e.g., academic, public, and school); (3) librarians and classroom teachers or university faculty; (4) librarians and library or school administrators; (5) librarians and library paraprofessionals; and (6) librarians and community leaders or organizational representatives.

Each chapter includes a summary chart, summarizing the key information in the chapter and providing direction for obtaining deeper learning. The summary chart provides a type of research shorthand, allowing the reader, after reading the chapter, to refer back to the key points about a method without necessarily having to reread the chapter. A glossary of terms identifying the critical terms defined within the chapter and suggestions for "further reading" (those references the chapter author believes provide information needed for next steps in conducting the research that is important to them and their organizations) complete each chapter.

Our Target Audience

Our primary target audiences for this book are librarians and teachers in schools, colleges, libraries, and other institutions (e.g., museums) where formal and/or informal learning takes place. The book could be used as a guide or text for professional development programs and in-service training and/or for preservice library and information science and education students. These future educators are studying a variety of problems and issues, and this book provides a straightforward, easy-to-use textbook for beginning courses in research methods.

This book is intended to provide guidance to those with no research experience who may wish to learn how to conduct research to find answers to important problems related to learning outcomes and best practice in their organizations and are looking for guidance on where or how to begin or what research methods to use. It also supports those who have some experience with research but are looking for alternative methods that are likely to provide multiple perspectives and solutions.

Organization and Format

This book is divided into two main parts. Part I, "Framing a Study," sets up the research experience through Chapters 2 and 3. Chapter 2 describes the essential process of conceptualizing a research study, including identifying the issue or problem to be investigated and creating the appropriate research questions that need to be answered. Chapter 3 takes the reader through the process of creating a critical review and summary of relevant literature (scholarly work in the same or similar area of the research problem) and identifies existing gaps or weaknesses in current knowledge, justifying the need for future research.

Part II, "Research Methods," contains 19 chapters, each on a specific research method, and ends with a final chapter that offers a reflective look-back. The methods presented represent a wide range of qualitative, quantitative, mixed methods and online research methodologies. Chapters are clustered into groups of two or three; each cluster is preceded by a brief scenario that describes an authentic problem situation confronting practitioners. Each scenario also purposely contains some "noise" (distracting and irrelevant information) that both the author and the reader must identify and discard in order to determine the most appropriate research questions and, ultimately, methods. The scenario ends with a proposed, overarching research question related to the problem described in the scenario.

In addition to providing context, the scenarios demonstrate that any given research problem may be studied from a number of different perspectives, using one or more different research methods. For example, one of our scenarios describes a problem that is subsequently used by three chapter authors to form the context for three totally different studies using three totally different methods: phenomenological research, case study, and critical incident technique.

Readers will also discover that chapter authors were given the freedom to interpret and apply the scenario in their own way. As a result, some authors chose to do so in very different, and sometimes surprising, ways.

The chapters are purposely brief, in order to serve as an introduction to a method, rather than as a comprehensive, in-depth description of what it is and how to conduct that method. This allows the reader to enjoy a "taste" of a method and hopefully think about it as a potential method he or she wishes to master in order to solve important problems in his or her library or classroom.

The chapters cover a wide range of research methods. Some are more familiar methods, such as Interviews and Focus Groups, Survey Research, and Case Studies. Others, such as Action Research, Evidence-based Research, and Design-based Research, are gaining in popularity in schools and libraries because they fit well with the day-to-day work of practitioners. Yet others, such as Causal Research, Longitudinal Research, and Mixed Methods Research, may require more resources, time, and a higher level of research skill and experience by the practitioner-researcher than others.

Each chapter concludes with (1) a summary of key points in the chapter, (2) a glossary of terms used in that chapter, and (3) suggested further reading (i.e., specific sources providing in-depth coverage of the research method discussed in that chapter) that the author recommends for a more in-depth understanding of the method.

Finally, the book's back matter includes (1) practice scenarios, giving the reader an opportunity to apply what they have learned in the book to thinking about how to approach a variety of problems presented, (2) a list of references, and (3) an alphabetized, compiled list of glossary terms.

As you read this book, we ask you to think about your own work setting and the problems, issues, and questions that you face that might be resolved by quality, ethical research. Perhaps you may begin to identify your research questions and the research method or methods you will use to answer them. If so, you will be well on your journey toward becoming a Practitioner-Researcher.

PART I

Framing a Study

Part I of this book comprises Chapters 2 and 3 that focus on activities researchers often use to frame their entire research process. Typically, these activities are conducted at the beginning of the research process so that subsequent activities (data collection and analysis and presentation of the research findings) are aligned with this framework. These activities include (1) the theoretical basis and conceptualization of the study to be conducted, including the research problem and related questions, and (2) a thorough understanding of the relevant professional literature upon which you will be building or extending knowledge. However, it is important to be aware that for some research methods (particularly certain qualitative methods such as participant observation), the activities described in these initial chapters may be conducted later in the research process in order to help support the research findings.

As you begin, you will discover that these two chapters are preceded by Scenario I, entitled "Meeting the Needs of People with Disabilities," situated in a college library where members of the library staff are trying to determine how well their programs and services are meeting the needs of students with disabilities. The scenario provides the context and examples for the two chapters.

In Chapter 2, Sandra Hughes-Hassell focuses the reader's attention on the conceptualization of a study, including identifying the research problem and determining if that problem is not only *researchable* but also *worth researching*. That is, even if one can research a problem, is it worth the resources needed and is it important enough for the researcher? This leads to the formulation of the research question(s).

Conceptualizing a study is, perhaps, the most critical part of the research process because if this is not done thoroughly and appropriately, the eventual results of the study likely will not further our knowledge of the problem or provide a valid solution to it. Identifying a meaningful and researchable problem and relevant, precise, and robust research questions will help to guide the next part of the process, the review of related, existing literature, as well as provide a framework for every phase of the research, thereafter.

In Chapter 3, once the researcher has a solid understanding of the problem and the questions for which solutions will be sought, it is important to identify what work has been done in this problem area beforehand, through the literature of the field (and related fields) that provides the context of the study. This requires the researcher to make decisions about the scope and focus of the literature to be searched. In either case, carefully crafted research problems and questions and a relevant knowledge of prior research are critical aspects of high-quality research.

Coauthors Alison Brettle and Denise Koufogiannakis take the reader through the process of conducting a meaningful literature review, including three different review methods, ways to determine the scope and focus of a review, and a list of predetermined inclusion/exclusion criteria to be used to identify resources that may be useful for the study. The two chapters get readers off to a great start on their journey to become Librarian Practitioner-Researchers.

SCENARIO I

Meeting the Needs of People with Disabilities

Crystal Long, Head of Reference, Eugene P. Watson Memorial Library
Northwestern State University in Natchitoches, Louisiana

G lover College is a four-year, privately funded institution in Cooperville. Cooperville hosts two colleges, providing a home also to Fernard College. The two institutions of higher learning work together to create an atmosphere for inquiry and learning that is unique. Glover College offers 50 bachelor's degrees. Its population of 1,000 students is divided evenly between traditional, on-campus students and nontraditional, distance education students.

Within the past five years, Glover has hired a full-time director, Sheila Hatman, for its Disability Support Office. Sheila oversees the implementation of diverse teaching methods within classrooms and works with departments across campus to make students feel welcome. Grey Mathison came to Glover five years ago as one of three librarians; she maintains the library's website, creates instructional tutorials, and shares bibliographic instructions with her colleagues.

The Honore Library at Glover was constructed four years ago using universal design (UD) principles, so it is a natural place to implement universal design for learning (UDL) and instruction (UDI) methods. For three years running, Glover students on the autistic spectrum have been hired as library student workers. While no empirical data have been collected, anecdotal evidence supports the claim that these students' social skills have improved since working in the library. The anecdotal evidence does not indicate whether the results are related to the space design, continuous interaction with others, or the one-on-one library training that student workers receive.

In the fall of 2015, Sheila notified Honore Library that one of Glover's incoming students was visually impaired and would require across-campus adaptations, including bibliographic instructions. The UDL principles of representation, action and engagement, and expression needed to become part of the student's library experience. All incoming students go through a "Welcome to the Library" orientation, in the library, as part of their general orientation class. Glover's librarians removed handouts from their bibliographic instructions five years ago and moved everything to a web-based "course guide" model. To craft an active experience for the student within orientation and to give her freedom of engagement beyond orientation, multiple methods of navigation would be deployed: preparing a descriptive handout of the orientation instruction, partnering students for the in-library scavenger hunt, and preparing audio tutorials of the library's resources with accompanying handouts.

A descriptive handout of the library instruction was prepared and delivered to the student 24 hours in advance of the class session. Students were partnered for the in-house library scavenger hunt, so the student could participate and collaborate with her peers. Sheila also suggested implementing an alternative approach with the student with the ultimate goal of equipping her to undertake library research individually. Using a standard format of audio presentation and visually cued references like left column, right column, top, and bottom, Grey applied her limited knowledge of films for the visually impaired to create guided audio tutorials and handouts through the library's website and online resources as alternative methods of navigation.

Grey and Sheila await feedback from the student regarding the audio tutorials and handouts. Knowing that the library's sample size may stay small, that is, 1 or 2 students per 1,000, they are considering investigating the idea of a "one-size-fits-all" mentality regarding audio tutorials designed for students with visual impairments. They are fleshing out the following questions: "Is there a research question to be answered, and if there is, what is(are) the methodology(ies) to be used?" "What is the framework for this research study?" Their overarching research question is as follows:

How do standardized audio tutorials meet the distinct and unique instructional and learning needs of college students with visual impairments?

Chapter 2

Conceptualizing a Study

Sandra Hughes-Hassell, Professor
University of North Carolina

Introduction to Conceptualizing a Study

Before conducting a research study, you must first identify the problem to address and then develop a question, or questions, to ask regarding your selected problem. This chapter discusses the nature of a research problem, where you might get ideas for a problem to investigate, how to narrow down or focus on a particular problem, how to craft a strong **problem statement**, and the steps involved in writing good **research questions**. The Glover College scenario will be used to illustrate this process.

What Is a Research Problem?

Shoket (2014) defined a research problem as "an area of concern, a condition to be improved, a difficulty to be eliminated, or a troubling question that exists in scholarly literature, in theory, or in practice that points to the need for meaningful understanding and deliberate investigation" (512). Creswell (2012) identified two types of research problems—practical and research-based.

Practical research problems, referred to by Wildemuth (2009) as practice-based problems, originate from issues or concerns found in real-world settings, such as schools, libraries, or communities. For librarians and other information professionals, the goal of most practice-based research is to solve problems that arise in their daily professional practice (Wildemuth 2009). However, as Wildemuth (2009) pointed out, information professionals should not just focus on solving problems, but they should also "proactively question their current practices, constantly seeking ways to improve the resources and services they provide" (21). The exploration of practical research problems leads to evidence-based practice, "an approach to information science that promotes the collection, interpretation, and integration of valid, important and applicable user-reported, librarian-observed, and research-derived evidence" (Booth 2002, 53) to improve library services and programs. While practical research problems originate in a particular library, the findings often have important implications for other libraries or information settings (Booth 2002; Wildemuth 2009).

Research-based problems come from research and theory in a given field and are often based on gaps, conflicting or disputed findings, or the need to extend the research or theory to other areas or populations (Connaway and Powell 2010; Creswell 2012; Wildemuth 2009). Research-based problems are the kinds of problems most often explored by university faculty and doctoral students.

Where Do We Find Problems to Study?

Identifying a problem to study requires that you be curious, observant, and ask questions—questions about your environment, your practice, and/or the professional and scholarly literature (Connaway and Powell 2010; Creswell 2012; Wildemuth 2009). For many researchers, the first step in the process, identifying a problem, to study is the most thought-provoking and creative phase of the research cycle (Hernon and Schwartz 2016). If you work in a library, this is the phase where you get to look at your practice through new eyes, ask tough questions about why you do certain things, and dare to consider whether the library program is really making a difference in the lives of your patrons. This is the phase of the process where you are allowed to "think outside the box," be provocative, and consider all of your ideas without judging or critiquing them—that will come later.

One way to identify a problem for study is to examine your current practice (Creswell 2012; Wildemuth 2009). Turning to our scenario, when Grey and Shelia learned that one of the incoming students was visually impaired and would need adaptations across campus, they began to identify a number of concerns including (1) how the library's bibliographic instructional materials will need to change to meet the needs of the student with visual impairments; (2) how they will know what adaptations to make; (3) how they will know if the adapted materials are effective; (4) how instructional sessions, including the orientation, might need to be changed if they incorporate these materials into them; (5) whether the materials will need to be different if the student is enrolled in an online course versus a face-to-face class; and (6) what they can do to ensure that the materials are accessible to students with a broad range of visual impairments, not just those with the same impairment as this one student. In addition, they identified another concern not associated with the student with visual impairments—a lack of research-based evidence that explains why the social skills of the students on the autism spectrum who are employed by the library have improved.

Another practice-related strategy Grey and Shelia could use would be to talk to colleagues, library users (and nonusers), and library partners about their concerns, frustrations they are encountering, or problems they find perplexing (Creswell 2012). They might survey the library staff to learn about difficulties they currently experience in their work with students with disabilities and to discover their concerns and fears about meeting the needs of students with visual impairments. They might think about holding focus groups with university faculty to understand what issues they have faced or anticipate facing in engaging students with visual impairments. They might consider holding a forum with students with disabilities who currently attend Glover College to understand their perspectives and to uncover concerns they have about the current library services and programs. They might even reach out to other academic librarians to find out about their experiences of providing instructional materials for students with visual impairments.

Another strategy for identifying a research problem is to examine the professional literature for gaps or unresearched areas (Creswell 2012; Connaway and Powell 2010; Wildemuth 2009). In our scenario, Grey and Shelia want to explore a practice-based problem, but they will still need to review the professional library and information science literature (LIS) literature. The purpose of their review at this stage of the research process will be to see whether library interventions for college students with disabilities, especially those who are visually impaired, is an area that has already been well researched, one for which little is known, or if there are certain voids in the research. For example, past research may have looked at library interventions for college students with physical disabilities, but not for students with visual impairments. Or maybe past research has focused on library interventions for students with visual disabilities from the perspective of librarians, but not the students themselves. Maybe research on the topic is dated—perhaps conducted before the prevalence of web-based library services or the adoption of Universal Design for Learning (UDL) principles and Universal Design for Instruction (UDI) methods. They might also want to look at the professional literature in education, especially special education, since library instruction is informed by research on pedagogy in K–12 and university settings. As a result of their review of the literature, Grey and Shelia might refine or add to their list of potential research problems to study. The literature review might also provide Grey and Shelia with information they can use to justify studying the problem to the library director. Finally, the literature review might help Grey and Shelia select the research method they will use for their own study, a step that comes later in the research process.

Based on the scenario, Grey and Shelia might create a list of potential research problems to explore that includes the following:

- The relationship between library employment and the improved social skills of students on the autism spectrum
- The effectiveness of library interventions for students who are visually impaired
- The efficacy of audio library tutorials for college students with disabilities and those without disabilities
- The impact implementing library interventions for students who are visually impaired might have on library staff
- How changes in library materials that meet the needs of students with visual impairments might impact other students (those with and without disabilities)

How Do We Select a Specific Problem to Study?

Once you have generated a list of potential problems for study, the next step in the problem identification process involves choosing your focus. One recommended strategy is to rank order the potential problems, and to select the one that is of most significance or interest to you. Being clear about the problem you wish to address will assist in focusing your study and will also facilitate the process of developing good research questions (Hernon and Schwartz 2007, 2016; Wildemuth 2009). In the scenario, it appears that the problems of most interest to Grey and Shelia are developing and implementing effective library interventions for students who are visually impaired and then determining the efficacy of standardized library audio tutorials for college students with visual disabilities.

Selecting a problem to study consists of not only choosing an issue of interest but also justifying why that issue is worthy of study. In other words, you need to be able to articulate to your employer, your academic advisory, or a funding agency how studying a specific problem will benefit the organization, library users, the profession, or even the broader society. You also need to determine if the problem is researchable. As Busha and Harter (1980) pointed out, "Some problems are trivial; others are beyond the scope or talents of the investigator; still others are not amenable to research at all" (19). Table 2.1 summarizes the questions you must consider in selecting a research problem to study.

While Grey and Shelia will need to ask themselves each of these questions in order to move forward, we are only going to explore one: *Will studying this problem have implications for the field, not just my institution, and thus add to the knowledge-base of LIS?* (Hernon and Schwartz 2016)

Glover College currently has only one student who has a visual impairment. In order for their study to have implications beyond their own library, Grey and Shelia will need to extend their research to include students with visual impairments at other academic libraries. Otherwise, they will only be providing a snapshot of one student's experience, which while valuable is not a research study.

Table 2.1

Questions to Consider for Research Problem Selection

Determining if the problem should be studied	Ask yourself: • Will studying this problem have implications for the field, not just my institution, and thus add to the knowledge-base of LIS? (Hernon and Schwartz 2016) • Will studying this problem inform, and potentially improve, practice? (Connaway and Powell 2010; Creswell 2012) • Will studying this problem advance scholarly knowledge by filling a gap in the current literature or providing a more in-depth or nuanced understanding of a problem that has been previously studied? (Creswell 2012) • Will studying this problem replicate a past study in a different setting and/or with a different population? (Creswell 2012) • Will studying this problem include communities that are understudied or marginalized (Creswell 2012; Wildemuth 2009)
Determining if the problem is researchable	Ask yourself: • What will it cost to study the problem? Will the necessary funding and other resources be available? (Creswell 2012) • Can I gain access to the research site? Will I be allowed to contact and interact with the people I want to include in the study? Does my organization require permission from an Institutional Review Board? (Creswell 2012) • How much time will the study take? Do I have the time needed to complete all of the stages of the research process and produce a quality product? (Creswell 2012) • Do I have the research skills needed to study this problem? If not, is there someone else in the organization that can partner with me or is there funding to hire an external researcher? (Creswell 2012)

As Hernon and Schwartz (2016) pointed out, "There is a difference between shared experience and what knowledge might be gained by well-conducted research" (91).

Formulating the Problem Statement

Once you have identified the problem you wish to study, the next step is to formulate a problem statement that will guide the remaining steps of the research process. The problem statement must be "both specific and explicit" (Connaway and Powell 2010, 45). Hernon and Schwartz (2007, 2016), who have written extensively on writing problem statements, argue that they should "tell the reader about the value (and that value should extend beyond utility to an individual workplace)" and answer these questions: "Why does this research need to be done?

What is broken, why should the reader care if it gets fixed, and how does the planned approach differ from what others have done" (Hernon and Schwartz 2016, 91). In other words, the problem statement has to pass the "so what" and "how so" questions (Hernon and Schwartz 2007, 308).

Returning to our scenario, Shelia and Grey seem to be most interested in the relationship between standardized audio tutorials and the learning needs of college students with visual impairments. A possible problem statement then might be:

> While the interest in how academic libraries can best meet the learning needs of college students with disabilities is widespread, no study has looked at the usefulness of standardized guided audio tutorials as tools that enable students with visual impairments to independently use the library. This study will explore the potential benefits of standardized audio tutorials for college students by gathering and interpreting evidence from undergraduate students with visual impairments themselves. It fulfills an urgent need: to determine whether (and how) providing standardized audio tutorials for college students with visual impairments has a positive impact on their instructional and learning needs. Insights gained from this study would be useful to academic libraries that provide information literacy instruction for visually impaired students.

Framing the Research Questions

Once you have crafted a strong problem statement, it is time to formulate your research questions. Research questions narrow the problem statement to the specific questions you seek to answer and are usually found at the end of the problem statement. Depending on the complexity and breadth of your proposed study, you may have one or more research questions. Identifying the research questions provides greater focus to your research, clarifies the direction of your investigation, and often suggests appropriate research methods (Creswell 2012). Good research questions are specific, directly related to the problem, indicate a need for data collection, and designate the target population for the study.

For our scenario, Grey and Shelia might create three research questions their study will explore:

1. How do undergraduate college students with visual impairments perceive their experience of using standardized audio tutorials, and the impact these tutorials have on their use of the library and their ability to conduct research on their own?
2. What are the benefits that the students experience as a result of their engagement with standardized audio tutorials?

Table 2.2
Summary Chart: Conceptualizing the Study

	Overall purpose
Rationale	• Well-designed research studies require a strong problem statement and accompanying research questions. • There is a difference between sharing an experience and conducting a research study (Hernon & Schwartz, 2016). • Some problems can be solved without conducting research (Hernon & Schwartz, 2007). • Some problems are not researchable (Busha & Harter, 1980).
Steps in process	1. Outline areas of interest—examine current practice, talk to colleagues, library users/nonusers, and other stakeholders. 2. Select a specific problem to study (practice-based, research/theory-based, or a combination of both). 3. Determine if the problem will add to the body of knowledge, and is researchable, justifiable, and affordable. 4. Formulate the problem statement—make sure it tells "so what" and "how so" (Hernon & Schwartz, 2007). 5. Frame the research questions, making sure they are specific, refer to the problem, and indicate the target participants.

3. Which of these benefits are reported most frequently and therefore might be deemed to be most significant?

Conclusion

This chapter has focused on identifying research ideas, narrowing your problem focus, writing your problem statement, and posing your research questions (see Table 2.2). It is important to point out that research is an iterative process so that while these efforts are critical at the beginning of your research, you may revisit them later. That is, you may find yourself clarifying, or even redefining your problem statement or research questions later after you have conducted a formal literature search and review and selected your research design and method. Keep this thought in mind as you turn to the next chapters in this book.

Glossary of Key Terms

Practical research problems: These, as practice-based problems, originate from issues or concerns found in real-world settings, such as schools, libraries, or communities (Wildemuth 2009).

Problem statement: This is a specific and explicit statement of the problem to be studied that will guide the remaining steps of the research process (Connaway and Powell 2010).

Research questions: These questions narrow the problem statement to the specific questions you seek to answer and are usually found at the end of the problem statement.

Research-based problems: These problems come from research and theory in a given field and are often based on gaps, conflicting or disputed findings, or the need to extend the research or theory to other areas or populations (Connaway and Powell 2010; Creswell 2012; Wildemuth 2009).

Further Reading

Creswell, J. 2012. *Educational Research: Planning, Conducting, and Evaluating Quantitative and Qualitative Research.* 4th ed. Boston, MA: Pearson.

Hernon, P., and C. Schwartz. 2016. "Research May Be Harder to Conduct than Some Realize." *Library & Information Science Research* 38 (2): 91–92.

Shoket, M. 2014. "Research Problem Identification and Formulation." *International Journal of Research* 1 (4): 512–18.

Chapter 3

Creating a Meaningful Literature Review

Alison Brettle, Reader in Evidence Based Practice
University of Salford, UK
Denise Koufogiannakis, Collections and Acquisitions Librarian
University of Alberta

Introduction to the Literature Review

The literature review is a not always considered a research method but is almost always a precursor to doing research by understanding the topic of what the outcomes of previous research has been. Depending on the purpose, level of topic depth, and time, researchers may choose from many types of literature reviews. To ensure the literature review is meaningful, researchers must have a clear purpose for undertaking the review; this clarity is necessary for researchers to select the literature, themes, and extent of the review. Researchers conduct literature reviews to

- provide a context for a piece of research,
- demonstrate knowledge and understanding of the field of study,
- direct and provide ideas for your research,
- summarize the evidence in a particular area,
- highlight the gaps in the literature, and
- locate tools or methods which may be useful for your research or practice.

This chapter will first briefly explain the difference between three types of reviews: a **traditional narrative literature review**, a **systematic scoping review**, and a **systematic review** (see Table 3.1 for a comparison of similarities and differences between the three). Then, systematic reviews will be examined in more detail in the context of Scenario I, the Long case study, and from the perspective of applying systematic review methodology to the question raised in that scenario. Systematic review is a research method in its own right and can be used by researchers and librarians to find answers to questions that inform practice.

Traditional Narrative Literature Reviews

A traditional narrative literature review is usually part of a larger work, laying the groundwork to explain a research study, for example. Such a review should provide a synthesis of existing research that places the current study within the context of what has previously been published. Sometimes researchers, often considered to be experts on the topic, publish literature reviews as stand-alone articles in which they present overview of the state of the literature on a particular topic.

When part of a larger research report, the literature review should include thematic lines of argument that relate to the research question to demonstrate how the topic has been considered by other researchers or authors. In the research report's literature review, the researcher should also show where the study contributed the wider body of scholarly knowledge on the study topic. Researchers may present paper assessments at an individual level or in thematic groupings that identify gaps in the literature and critique what has gone before to demonstrate the value of the study.

When writing a traditional literature review, it is important to illustrate previous work in a balanced way, rather than selecting only research that demonstrates specific points that support the researcher's argument. Criticisms of traditional narrative literature reviews are that they are open to bias, and it is not always possible to tell what evidence has been considered when deciding what to include in the review (Rhoades 2011).

Systematic Scoping Reviews

Systematic scoping reviews seek to provide in-depth and broad results and take an iterative and reflexive approach (Arksey and O'Malley 2005). According to Arksey and O'Malley (2005), systematic scoping reviews are appropriate to

1. examine the extent, range and nature of research activity and provide a way of mapping fields of study;
2. determine the value of undertaking a full systematic review;
3. summarize and disseminate research findings; and
4. identify research gaps in the existing literature. (6–7)

Arksey and O'Malley (2005) developed a framework for undertaking systematic scoping reviews. Although the framework was developed in a health context, many health interventions are complex and can be seen as comparable to interventions in Library and Information Science (LIS) because the interventions have a number of interacting components, different behaviors are required from those delivering or receiving the intervention, there is variability in possible outcomes, and there is a degree of flexibility or tailoring of the intervention (Craig et al. 2008). An example would be the development and delivery of information literacy sessions. The framework involves a five-stage process and each of these is considered prior to beginning the review by drawing up a **protocol**. The protocol may be revised during initial literature searches but then is followed throughout:

1. identifying the research question;
2. identifying relevant studies;
3. selecting studies;
4. charting the data; and
5. collating, summarizing, and reporting the results.

Systematic Reviews

A systematic review is an overview of primary research studies on a specific topic conducted according to an explicit and reproducible methodology to give a summary answer; it provides a rigorous and unbiased way of summarizing research evidence related to a specific question. Systematic reviews originated in the healthcare field, initially including only research evidence from certain types of quantitative studies to provide evidence on whether healthcare interventions were effective or not. They have been adopted by other fields as a more rigorous means of summarizing research evidence, often incorporating multiple research designs. For practitioners, systematic reviews summarize evidence and keep them up to date (so they do not need to read all the individual studies) and provide a clear picture by collating results of research. Whether a systematic review incorporates only certain types of study design or is more inclusive, it follows the same process (similar to the previous systematic scoping review):

1. Define/focus the question.
2. Develop a protocol.
3. Search the literature (possibly scoping searches, then comprehensive searches).
4. Refine the inclusion/exclusion criteria.
5. Assess the studies using predefined data extraction tools and critical appraisal techniques (each study should be considered in the same way).
6. Combine the results of the studies to produce a conclusion (this may be a meta-analysis or a narrative synthesis).
7. Place the findings in context—provide details about the quality of the studies and whether they are similar to each other (or whether they are really examining different things), whether the findings are applicable to practice.

Table 3.1 summarizes and compares different types of literature reviews.

Table 3.1

Similarities and Differences in Different Types of Literature Review

Traditional narrative literature review	Systematic scoping review	Systematic review
Considers broad topic	Considers broad topic	Considers well-defined question—narrow topic
Includes wide range of studies and literature	Includes range of study designs	May include only certain study designs—appropriate to question or quality
Less specific questions	Less specific questions	Answers focused question
Review process not defined or made explicit; review conducted iteratively	Review process well defined, made explicit, and reported as part of review	Review process well defined, made explicit, and reported as part of review
Prone to bias Literature included according to interest or lines of argument	Less prone to bias Predefined inclusion and exclusion criteria to decide what literature is included	Less prone to bias Predefined inclusion and exclusion criteria to decide what literature is included
Topics considered thematically according to areas of interest	Arranged in themes to provide a "map" of the literature	Synthesized in themes to answer question; may include meta-analysis (statistical representation of conclusions across studies)
Individual papers may be discussed in-depth	Summaries across papers. All papers treated in same manner.	Summaries across papers; all papers treated in same manner
Draws subjective conclusions	Draws more objective conclusions	Draws more objective conclusions

Conducting a Literature Review

In Long's Scenario, librarians at Glover College are trying to determine how standardized audio tutorials meet the distinct and unique instructional and learning needs of college students with visual impairments.

As the librarians in the scenario consider a new approach to student learning, they would first want to learn from the research has already been done on this topic. They could conduct a traditional literature review to set the context and find out what has already been done on the topic. The types of themes they may want to consider may include libraries and instruction, libraries and the use of audio tutorials, standardized audio tutorials, personalized audio tutorials, and the instructional and learning needs of visually impaired students. Because the scenario covers a very broad topic, it may be difficult to cover every element of audio tutorials in depth.

A systematic review, however, would enable researchers not only to determine what has been done before but also to determine whether a particular approach is worth undertaking for their needs. The remainder of this section explores how the systematic review methodology might be used with Scenario I (Long) to assist the librarians with their decision making by following the steps of a systematic review process.

Step I. Define the Question

To begin, the librarians would need a focused question that looks at the intervention in which they are interested, and perhaps compares it with another method. This means they will need to narrow and refocus the question being asked, for example:

Are standardized audio tutorials better than personalized audio tutorials in meeting the instructional and learning needs of college students with visual impairments?

Mnemonics are sometimes used to help focus systematic review questions and provide a framework or standardized format for searching. There are several frameworks available for this purpose (Brettle and Koufogiannakis 2016a; Kloda 2008). For Scenario I (Long), use the **PICO framework** (e.g., Methley et al. 2014) from health science research to define the following:

Population—students with visual impairments
Intervention—standardized audio tutorials
Comparison—personalized tutorial
Outcome—meet instructional and learning needs

The concepts used in the PICO framework can be used to focus a search question and help think through the concepts or synonyms that need to be considered in a search. The concepts can be used as building blocks for the search strategy, often beginning with two concepts representing the population and intervention. A third concept can be added if there are too many search results. Alternatively, the additional concepts can be used to include and exclude papers to focus scanning through titles and abstracts to decide what should go in and out of the review. Table 3.2 illustrates an example.

As Table 3.2 suggested, this approach could lead to the search string:
(Visual impairment OR Blind) AND (Audio tutorial)

Table 3.2
Example of a PICO Framework

Population	Intervention	Comparison	Outcome
Students with visual impairments	Audio tutorial	Personalized tutorial	Improve knowledge of information literacy
Blind students	[focus of the search question]	Online tutorial	Improve search skills

Then, scroll through the results and look for articles that compare the audio tutorial with another type of tutorial and measure whether knowledge of information literacy or information literacy skills change.

Step 2. Develop a Protocol

A protocol is a plan for the review. It provides a map to follow and ensures that the systematic review is conducted in as rigorous way as possible. In the protocol, set out the background and objectives, define the question guiding the review, outline the resources to use, establish inclusion and exclusion criteria, and decide what and how data will be extracted and the detail the synthesis approach. For example, Long's Scenario includes background and context and the review question. A list of comprehensive resources to search should be drawn up, covering all perspectives of the topic area. Include specific journals to check and also websites or sources of **grey literature** (Bates and Maack 2010), which could inform the topic, considering the inclusion/exclusion criteria. Choose a critical appraisal tool (Brettle and Koufogiannakis 2016b) and decide what information and data are to be extracted from each study and how the findings will be synthesized and presented (e.g., narrative synthesis of particular themes or a meta-analysis; see Urquhart 2010).

Step 3. Search the Literature

The literature search should be done in two stages: (1) a scoping stage helps to determine the volume of literature available, helps to refine inclusion and exclusion criteria, and may refocus the review question; and (2) comprehensive searches conducted on a wide range of databases. The aim of the search is to be as comprehensive as possible; the more focused the question and inclusion criteria, the more likely it is for this to be feasible. Sampson et al. (2008) provide an in-depth overview of sources to consider and assist with systematic review searching within LIS.

The list of resources for searching may include education databases such as ERIC, library and information science databases such as LISA and LISTA, and health sciences databases such as MEDLINE. In addition, check selected websites of relevant organizations for any reports they may have produced, look at references within relevant journal articles, browse issues of the most relevant journals that seem to cover the topic, and contact experts for suggestions for additional sources of research evidence.

Reviewers often find it useful to download the results of their searches into reference management software (e.g., Endnote or Mendeley). The software can be used to manage the search results through the review process.

Step 3a. Refine the Inclusion and Exclusion Criteria

The initial inclusion criteria should be established in your protocol and can be derived from the review question and background. Some initial scoping searches will help to refine the criteria to make the task more manageable if the search retrieves many results or to widen the review if there is limited information on your topic. There is usually a balance to be considered: the tighter the criteria, the fewer papers to review; but the search needs to yield enough papers to review for meaningful conclusions. Some researchers adjust the criteria by more tightly focusing the question, whereas others narrow by using the quality of studies. Scoping the literature will help you decide which approach to take. For Long's Scenario, potential criteria would be the following:

Inclusion

- University, college, or higher education settings
- Library settings
- Students with visual impairments
- Audio tutorials

Exclusion

- Primary schools or workplace settings
- Instruction outside the library context
- Students with other disabilities

Adding a criterion such as requiring the included study to be a randomized controlled trials would likely reduce the number of papers to review, but it would ensure that only be looking at experimental studies that had really tested the approach would be included; however, in this case example, the criterion may be too specific, and there may not be any studies that meet this requirement.

Apply the criteria to the results of literature searches via a sifting or screening process in which the researchers examine the titles and abstracts of the located

Figure 3.1
Flow Diagram Illustrating Literature Search Process (Adapted from PRISMA 2009)

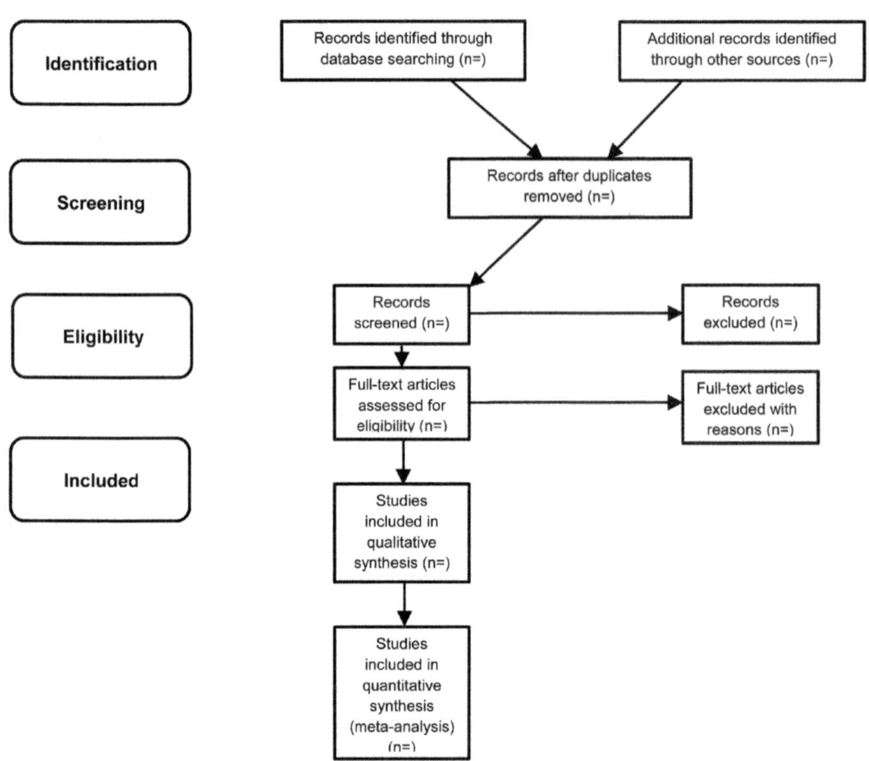

literature and decide whether the study matches the criteria. If the reviewer is unsure whether to include, the full text of the article can be checked. If reference management software is being used, articles can be separated into groups (initially as simple as include or exclude). This ensures that no material is lost and an audit trail of the process can be compiled. The full text of all articles to be included should be retrieved at this point (if not already). This stage is often represented by the process depicted in Figure 3.1.

Step 3b. Assess the Studies Found

At this point, there will be a much smaller batch of studies; assess each study in the same way, as well as extract the information that will be used to review findings and conclusions. Select your data-recording tool carefully to ensure it matches your needs, and think about what pieces of data from each study are important (i.e., what will help to answer the review question). There are a range of critical appraisal tools: some are study design specific, some cover a range of study designs (e.g., Glynn 2006), and in LIS there are some that have been created for particular types of studies

(Booth and Brice 2003; Koufogiannakis, Booth, and Brettle 2006). Ideally in a systematic review, each study should be appraised by two people (more rigorous) and the analysis for each study reached through consensus.

In this scenario, researchers may want to use the checklist by Glynn (2006) to determine the quality of the articles and also to develop other categories for data extraction based on the elements that they are interested in considering for their review of the literature related to their question—this would include elements such as type of study design, setting, country, type of library, type of tutorial, impact on learning need, and any specific data elements related to each study's results. Make a template with fields from the checklist or use a spreadsheet such as spreadsheet to record the information for each study.

Step 3c. Synthesize the Results

In a systematic review, the findings are reported across the studies to answer the review question. Studies are not considered individually. Begin with an overview, or summary, of the volume, nature, and quality of evidence. In a narrative synthesis, refer back to the review question and use it to generate themes. So, for example, include a section that examines the different types of audio tutorials and what the evidence says about these (which worked best, which did not, which were some better for particular types of users). Think about what the evidence says for each theme considered. Use evidence tables to summarize and synthesize the literature, as illustrated in Brettle et al. (2011). If the study findings are quantitative and the majority examine the same concept and measuring the same outcomes, consider a meta-analysis (see Urquhart 2010), which is a statistical summary of studies which looks at the size of the effect across the studies. An example is provided in Koufogiannakis and Weibe (2006).

Step 4. Place Findings in Context

The final stage of the review is to examine the findings and place them in your particular context. Examine the quality and heterogeneity of studies and consider whether the findings and the studies are applicable to the research question and context. Provide details about the quality of the studies and whether they are similar to each other (or whether they are really examining different things), whether the findings are applicable to practice. Be sure to review the studies' limitations.

Why Use This Research Method?

In a systematic review, a researcher systematically searches, critically appraises, synthesizes, and provides a detailed overview of the previously published literature pertaining to a specific question. This research-based approach to reviewing the literature allows for a deeper understanding of what research says at an aggregate level, providing a deep and meaningful way for past research to be understood and applied to decision making. The methodology limits bias, allows for conclusions to be more reliable and accurate, and assists with knowledge transfer (Greenhalgh 1997). Systematic reviews allow practitioners to know what the collective research evidence says on the topic, making the applicability of research on practice more likely (Brettle 2009; Koufogiannakis 2012; McKibbon 2006; Phelps and Campbell 2012). This methodological approach also shows research gaps in the existing body of research and points to areas where further research is needed (Koufogiannakis and Brettle 2015; Phelps and Campbell 2012).

Using a systematic review methodology is not always appropriate or possible, depending upon your circumstances. One of the biggest barriers to carrying out a systematic review is the amount of time required when taking this approach (Brettle 2009; McKibbon 2006; Phelps and Campbell 2012). The amount of time required often makes doing a systematic review unfeasible for librarian practitioners who also have full day-jobs and need to fit research in when they have time, not to mention that the time required to do the study may be beyond the time frame for when a practice-based decision needs to be made. Other barriers that often come into play include ensuring that librarians have the methodological skills to properly conduct a systematic review (Brettle 2009), often do not have good access to the LIS literature (Law 2005), and the complexity of the methodology itself when trying to apply it to a LIS context where the diversity of research methods is wide and not easily compared (Urquhart 2010).

The number of systematic reviews within LIS is small but growing, spurred on by the growth of evidence-based library and information practice (EBLIP), which urges greater connection between research evidence and practice, and has developed tools for critical appraisal and encouraged the adoption of systematic reviews within the field to assist with evidence based decision making. Prior to the year 2000, when the EBLIP movement began, there were only a handful of systematic reviews within LIS. Since then, there has been steady growth, and a range of topics covered, although the most significant area of coverage is within health sciences librarianship (Koufogiannakis and Brettle 2015).

Table 3.3 summarizes the steps in systematic literature review.

Table 3.3
Summary Chart: Systematic Review of the Literature

Overall purpose	A systematic review is an overview of primary research studies, on a specific question, conducted according to an explicit and reproducible methodology to give a summary answer. It seeks to provide a rigorous and unbiased way of summarizing research evidence related to a specific question.

Table 3.3
Summary Chart: Systematic Review of the Literature (Continued)

Advantages	• Rigorous method that controls for bias • Provides deeper understanding of research at an aggregate level • Allows for the application of research to practice • Uncovers gaps in existing research
Disadvantages	• Amount of time required • Need comprehensive access to literature • Methodological complexity
Steps in process	• Define/focus the question. • Develop a protocol. • Search the literature. • Refine the inclusion/exclusion criteria. • Assess the studies using predefined data extraction tools and critical appraisal techniques. • Combine the results of the studies to produce a conclusion. • Place the findings in context.
Data collection methods	• Comprehensive literature searching • Inclusion/exclusion criteria • Critical appraisal and data extraction from included studies
Data analysis methods	• Quantitative and/or qualitative analysis of aggregated data • Meta-analysis or meta-synthesis where able
Support technologies	• Bibliographic databases • Reference management software • Software for data gathering and analysis • Statistician for help with meta-analysis

Glossary of Key Terms

Grey literature is research produced by organizations outside of the traditional commercial or academic publishing and distribution channels. Common grey literature publication types include reports, working papers, government documents, white papers and evaluations. The standard of quality, review and production of grey literature can vary and it may be difficult to discover, access, and evaluate without sound search strategies (Bates and Maack 2010).

PICO framework: This is a framework for developing quantitative research questions that includes population, intervention, comparison, and outcome.
Protocol: A protocol is a plan for conducting research.
Systematic review: A systematic review is an overview of primary research studies, on a specific question, conducted according to an explicit and reproducible methodology to give a summary answer.

Systematic scoping review: Systematic scoping reviews seek to provide in-depth and broad results, and take an iterative and reflexive approach (Arksey and O'Malley 2005).

Traditional narrative literature review: This review is a synthesis of existing research that places the current study within the context of what has previously been published.

Further Reading

Brettle, Alison, Maden-Jenkins, Michelle, and Anderson, Lucy. 2011. "Evaluating Clinical Librarian Services: A Systematic Review." *Health Information and Libraries Journal* 28 (1): 2–32.

CASP (Critical Appraisal Skills Programme). (2017). "CASP Tools & Checklists." Accessed June 29, 2017. http://www.casp-uk.net/casp-tools-checklists.

Greenhalgh, Trisha. 1997. "How to Read a Paper: Papers that Summaries Other Papers (Systematic Reviews and Meta-Analyses)." *British Medical Journal* 315 (672): 672–75. doi:10.1136/bmj.315.7109.672.

Koufogiannakis, Denise, and Natasha Wiebe. 2006. "Effective Methods for Teaching Information Literacy Skills to Undergraduate Students: A Systematic Review and Meta-Analysis." *Evidence Based Library and Information Practice* 1 (3): 3–43. doi:10.18438/B8MS3D.

McKibbon, K. Ann. 2006. "Systematic Reviews and Librarians." *Library Trends* 55 (1): 202–15.

Urquhart, Christine. 2010. "Systematic Reviewing, Meta-Analysis and Meta-Synthesis for Evidence-Based Library and Information Science." *Information Research* 15 (3). Accessed June 29, 2017. http://www.informationr.net/ir/15 -3/colis7/colis708.html.

PART II

Research Methods

P art II of this book comprises 19 chapters that respond to seven different scenarios.

Scenario II, "Serving the Oral Tradition" by Lynn Hoffman, concludes with the question "How have libraries traditionally reflected the diversity of their communities through their programs and services, and how can they continue to do so today?" In response to this scenario, in Chapter "How have libraries traditionally reflected the diversity of their communities through their programs and services, and how can they continue to do so today?" instead? 4, Amanda Waugh and Mega Subramaniam discuss how interview and focus group research might be used to explore the efficacy of the audio tutorials. Action research may offer another viable option for documenting the usefulness of various supports for visually impaired learners, as Lesley Farmer details in Chapter 5. Suzanne Stauffer offers another approach in Chapter 6 by positioning how historical methods can shed light on the community's successes and challenges with strategies to support visually impaired learners that have been used in the past.

Scenario III, "Teaching Research Skills" by Angela Branyon, illustrates a situation to be addressed by the question "What instructional factors are most effective for improving research skills acquisition?" Joette Stefl-Mabry also focuses on assessment in Chapter 7 by detailing how formative assessment can be used to solve the mystery of what students are learning. In Chapter 8, Melissa Gross describes how the method of participant observation can be used to identify promising instructional practices. Chapter 9 details a different approach, with Megan Oakleaf focusing on assessing learning with well-designed rubrics; Joette Stefl-Mabry also focuses on assessment in Chapter 9 by detailing how formative assessment can be used to solve the mystery of what students are learning.

Scenario IV illustrates Heidi Neltner's take on "Games as Learning Tools" and is anchored by the question "Are games effective learning tools?" In Chapter 10, Minkyoung Kim and Charles Reigeluth consider how formative research techniques can be used to document games' role in learning. Nelson Maylone addresses a technique that educators may be tempted to use that is unsuitable for exploring games as learning tools: correlational research.

In Scenario V, Bree L. Ruzzi addresses the "Impact of Collaboration and Scheduling on Learning" at Red Pond school by proposing that researchers investigate "How have librarian-teacher collaboration and flexible scheduling impacted student achievement at Red Pond?" Ross J. Todd looks "Through the Lens of Evidence-Based Practice" in Chapter 12, while Shana Pribesh and Kristen Gregory propose causal research designs that may be used to document the benefits of collaboration.

In Scenario VI entitled "Co-Teaching, Student Learning, and Faculty Collaboration," Mirah J. Dow addresses a related question "How does co-teaching impact student learning and faculty?" Jenny Bossaller proposes the methodology and research methods of phenomenology as a means to characterize the relationship between collaborative teaching and learning in Chapter 14, while in Chapter 15, Maria Cahill and Kyle A. Lee suggest case study approaches that may also be effective strategies to explore educators acting together. In Chapter 16, Critical Incident Technique, Audrey P. Church illustrates the ways in which researchers can identify key occurrences in teaching and learning that can document the contributions of co-teaching to student learning.

The next set of research methods respond to Scenario VII, "Engaging the At-Risk Student" by Sarah A. Chauncey and H. Patricia McKenna, and its question "What is the impact of collaborative 'Smart Teams' on student engagement in technology-rich, cross-curricular experiences?" In Chapter 17, Marilyn P. Arnone and Susan Rothwell propose that Design-Based Research offers tools for examining smart teams, while in Chapter 18, Carol Collier Kuhlthau, Leslie Maniotes, and Jannica Heinstrom position longitudinal research as a useful approach to discerning smart teams' impact.

The final methods examined in this volume pertain to Scenario VIII, "Envisioning the Library of the Future" by Charles O'Bryan and Molly Brown; they wondered about the future of New York College and "What is the vision for the college library of 2020, and what are the implications for space utilization?" In Chapter 19, Rebecca Teasdale describes how survey research might be used to gather information about the future, and Jami Jones discusses how the Delphi method might lend insight in Chapter 20. Dabae Lee, author of Chapter 21 concludes the methods described in this book by showing how mixed methods research design could be used to document current phenomena and inform priorities for the future.

SCENARIO II

Serving the Oral Tradition

Lynn Hoffman, Director of Operations
Somerset County Library System of New Jersey

The Middle City Public Library (MCPL) serves a population of just over 100,000 people from a large central library and four branches. Middle City is at the center of its own metropolitan statistical area and is surrounded by several smaller communities, each with their own municipal public library. With an annual budget of approximately $5,000,000, MSEPL is moderately well-funded.

Middle City has seen a major demographic shift over the past 10–15 years. The Hispanic population has grown from 7.5% in 2000 to 15% in 2010, and projections are for that percentage to continue to grow. MSEPL's two smallest branches are located in neighborhoods with high concentrations of new residents and immigrants for whom Spanish is their first language.

Library staff have worked hard to develop programs and collections that will bring this population into the library and begin to see MSEPL as a supportive resource. They have had some success with Spanish language and bilingual storytimes for preschoolers, and their conversation groups for new English speakers have a small but enthusiastic following. Circulation of materials, however, has been lackluster. From bilingual picture books to Spanish translations of best sellers, Spanish language materials have a relative use rate well below that of their English-language counterparts.

MSEPL's most recent strategic planning process, completed four years earlier, included some data gathering in regard to library nonusers and what might get them to become library customers. In looking at the survey that was used, however, MSEPL's library director Karen Smith realized that some of the questions may not have captured the true needs and expectations of the total community. In order to learn more about how the library might be able to better serve specific populations, Karen would have to completely rethink her methods for gathering information.

As the new library director, Karen Smith has spent her first six months on the job getting to know the library and her community. At a literacy fundraiser event, she met the Middle City School District's English language learner coordinator Jennifer Jones, who made a comment about the importance of the oral tradition in the cultures of many immigrant families. This got Karen thinking: libraries have faced new and changing needs within their communities for centuries. How have they accomplished this, and have they been successful? Do longstanding library policies and procedures somehow hinder the ability of MSEPL to institute the types of changes needed to better serve the library and information needs of their entire, and increasingly diverse, community?

Karen has asked Jennifer Jones from the school district to help a team of library staff—including Karen, MSEPL's public services manager, and two Spanish-speaking frontline staff members—to develop a research plan, the results of which she hopes will lead to more responsive programs and services. Jennifer has agreed to help, especially if they can design their research in a way that will also help the school district find out if there may be better ways to engage non-English-speaking parents in their children's literacy development.

Karen and Jennifer have created the following overarching question for their research:

How have libraries traditionally reflected the diversity of their communities through their programs and services, and how can they continue to do so today?

Chapter 4

Interview and Focus Group Research

Amanda Waugh, Doctoral Candidate
College of Information Studies, University of Maryland
Mega Subramaniam, Associate Professor
College of Information Studies, University of Maryland

Introduction to Interviews and Focus Groups

This chapter will provide an overview of interviews and focus groups, imagine their use in light of Hoffman's Scenario, present some advantages and disadvantages, and share some ideas for further reading.

Perhaps no data collection methods are more heavily associated with qualitative research than interviews and focus groups. When gathering data "in the wild," one of the most obvious ways to collect data is to simply ask the people involved, either through an interview or through gathering a group together to share their experiences and ideas. However, this familiarity with interviewing and focus groups can obscure the challenges in using these methods and the importance of careful planning and experience. Furthermore, some will challenge the validity of findings when they are based on the impressions of a handful of people, no matter how integral those people might be to the problem covered by the research question.

When conducting qualitative research (broadly defined as research that answers questions of how and why), rigor in planning and executing the study is of paramount importance. Qualitative research uses the skills of the researcher in combination with established and rigorous methods to explore questions that cannot be answered numerically. Researchers talk about **rich** data and data that are **thick**. These terms mean that there is a lot of information contained in an observation or interview and that this information encompasses details about the environment, demeanor, social interactions, and so on (Creswell 2007).

To define terms, Yin (2014) described an interview as a "guided conversation." An interview can be structured (all the questions are scripted) or semi-structured (there are questions and a list of topics, but the researcher uses tangents and follow-up questions to gather a fuller picture.) Interviews can take place in person, via telephone, through video calling (Skype, Google Hangout, etc.), though in our experience, face-to-face interviews are almost always preferable. **Focus groups**, according to Yin (2014), involve gathering a small group of people to discuss an issue or aspect of the study. The researcher needs to guide the group to ensure that they stay on topic and that all voices are heard. Focus groups can be very challenging to conduct virtually, but it is possible. Focus groups also need to be kept to a small size (typically six to eight people), or they will be very hard to manage.

This chapter will discuss the use of interviews and focus groups to answer the research questions derived from Scenario II (Hoffman), in which public librarians are attempting to serve a new immigrant community, with mixed results:

(1) How do children and parents who come from Spanish-speaking backgrounds perceive libraries and literacy?

(2) What are the literacy concerns and issues that these families have about their young children, and how can the library address those concerns?

Interviews work very well when the researcher needs to gather a lot of information that is not readily answered by a questionnaire. Interviews allow the researcher to **probe** an answer, ask follow-up questions, and assess the respondent's demeanor. It is critical that the researcher establishes trust and rapport with the interviewee. Often this relationship is established by assuring the interviewee that his/her privacy will be protected through the use of pseudonyms and by changing or concealing identifying information.

One limitation of interviews is that they represent the point of view of a relatively small number of people. To counter this limitation, it is important to **triangulate** the data, meaning noting where multiple people say the same thing, or where observations or questionnaire data might validate the interviewees' perspective and vice versa. It is always important to frame the findings to make this limitation clear.

In Scenario II (Hoffman), we can imagine interviews with community stakeholders. When interviewing parents and children, the researcher hears from a few people that the new community members are uncomfortable at the library because someone told them to "go home." The researcher can share that information with the library director and board, without revealing it came from. Alternatively, interviews allow the researcher to follow up on important digressions. In the aforementioned scenario, imagine if an interview with parents reveals that their children like the technology in the library, but the parents do not know how to use computers. By asking follow-up questions, the researcher can try to establish what resources might help the parents make better use of the library. Alternatively, suppose the parents reveal that the Spanish language collection is weak, or that they really want specific kinds of resources (graphic novels or a stronger religion section, for example). In this case, the researcher can use follow-up questions to establish more clearly how the library can support their new community members.

Focus groups, on the other hand, are terrific for exploring ideas and hearing from a wide variety of people in a short period of time. In Scenario II (Hoffman), researchers could use focus groups of children and parents and ask the participants to find out what they know about the library. Those discussions may reveal that the parents are unaware of library programming or that they are concerned about their young children needing further exposure to English before starting kindergarten. As the parents talk, they may begin to describe their concerns and what their ideal program would look like. By allowing the parents to brainstorm, the researcher is gaining a tremendous amount of information in a short period of time.

Meyers, Fisher, and Meroux (2009) used a variety of data collection practices to determine how tweens (children aged 8–12) gathered everyday life information. The researchers put together a day-long event at the public library and combined small focus groups of three to five tweens, interviews, observations, and activities to answer their research questions. In the focus groups, the tweens were asked to imagine what a new tween neighbor might need to know about their community and they might send the new neighbor for information. Interviews followed the focus groups and offered tweens the opportunity to reflect on the focus group and activities and to share deeper or more personal thoughts on information seeking. The interviews were also used to ask the tweens about the strategies they use to keep track of information. The researchers then used their findings to make recommendations to librarians and other practitioners when working with tweens.

Though many people are comfortable with the concept of interviews and focus groups, there are, nonetheless, skills and techniques involved. As with most things, experience helps tremendously. Researchers using these techniques should practice using **reflective listening** techniques, asking clarifying questions, and redirecting conversations to ensure that the respondent stays on topic.

Interviewing and focus groups do not require many resources, though often providing snacks or pizza can help increase turnout. As with all research, it is critical to receive informed consent from your participants. This involves sharing an overview of the study, the risks and benefits of participating, and asking for the participant's consent. Recording equipment, often just a cell phone, is critical because it allows the researcher to focus on the respondents rather than the notes. When using recording equipment, it is very important to ask your participant(s) and to get his/her (their) assent on the recording. If you believe that recording may make the parents/child uncomfortable or untruthful about their opinions, feel free to ask an assistant to join and take notes. It will be difficult for an interviewer to take notes and conduct the interview at the same time. Finally, finding a quiet, nondistracting space in which to conduct the interview or focus group is important to protect your participants' privacy and maintain their focus.

Interviews and Focus Groups in Context

Research Questions That Emerged from the Scenario

In Chapter 5, Farmer uses the same scenario to demonstrate the use of action research to attend to questions about circulation in the Middle City Public Library (MCPL). When Karen Smith, the new MCPL Director connected with Jennifer Jones who is from the Middle City School District (MCSD), Jennifer indicated the importance of determining the ways that Spanish-speaking parents can be engaged in their children's literacy development. Though many questions can be extrapolated from Jennifer's aspirations, Karen and Jennifer's overarching question can be divided into two research questions well suited for using interviews and focus groups as data collection methods. The questions are as follows:

(1) How do children and parents who come from non-English-speaking backgrounds perceive libraries and literacy?
(2) What are the literacy concerns and issues that these families have about their young children, and how can the library address those concerns?

Justification for Using Interviews and Focus Groups

Using the right data-collection methods to answer research questions is crucial in any scholarly work as well as important for determining interventions and changes that will meet the needs of the community. There are many reasons why interviews and focus groups are best to examine the two research questions posed earlier. First, since Scenario II (Hoffman) mentions that the oral tradition is important to the community, interviews and focus groups (which are both data collection methods that are conducted orally) offer an opportunity to leverage the culture of the community to uncover perceptions about the library, literacy, and the needs of these non-English-speaking families. Jennifer and Karen can enlist the two Spanish-speaking frontline staff members to help them conduct the interviews and focus groups, who may also be well equipped to ask more targeted follow-ups based on what they know about the culture of these families.

Second, both these methods offer the opportunity for the interviewees/participants to determine the preferred paths to take the conversation during the interviews/focus groups. For example, immigrant parents may prefer to talk more about how they like or dislike the library based on their interactions with libraries in countries from which they have migrated. Other parents may be interested in pointing out the specific types of challenges that their children face in learning

English when English is their second language. Such flexibility garners descriptive insights that will offer Jennifer and Karen more in-depth perspectives on the continuum of relevant issues and concerns, and thereby be able to develop more responsive program and services.

Third, both methods also offer the interviewers the ability to bring the interviewee(s) back to a subject of interest to the interviewer if the interviewer needs a more in-depth description on a particular topic. This could be done via **prompting**, rephrasing the question, or asking for clarification.

One special characteristic of semi-structured interviews is that this method allows the capturing of candid and spontaneous responses in a casual atmosphere. This characteristic allows for the exploration of reflections, perceptions, and feelings. For focus group, the exchange of thoughts/perceptions, coupled with debates or agreement on ideas, allows richer conversations and allows participants to build or disagree with each other's thoughts as they speak. Probing and prompting from the moderator/facilitator can tease out various strands of the narrative to obtain a complete narrative.

Criteria for Determining/Recruiting Research Participants

Given what Karen and Jennifer want to accomplish, the research questions and experiences using these data collection methods, interviews should be conducted with 10–15 Spanish-speaking parents and children. The range is provided to allow Jennifer and Karen to decide how many interviews they would like to conduct based on staff availability and the amount of time that they have to conduct and analyze the interview data. Guest, Bunce, and Johnson (2006) analyzed 60 interviews and concluded that when topics and information shared become similar and the participants are relatively homogenous, **data saturation** occurs around the twelfth interview. For focus groups, two focus group sessions (one for children and another for the parents) can be conducted simultaneously to ensure parents and children are at the library at the same time, and children are not without childcare. Karen and Jennifer can conduct more than one focus group if there is staff time to allocate for this. For best interaction, it is recommended that the size of a focus group is between six and eight people.

Data Collection Steps

Interview and focus group data are collected using these steps:

Step 1: Developing an Interview and Focus Group Protocol

The research questions should guide the development of the interview and focus group **protocol**. The protocol is a guide that includes introductory remarks about the purpose of the interview/focus group, what will the information obtained be used for, and how will privacy and the confidentiality of the interviewee/participant be protected. Karen and Jennifer should brainstorm this content with the frontline staff and translate these protocols to Spanish. Interviews should be between 30 and 45 minutes (even shorter for children), and focus groups should be no longer than an hour. Ask permission to begin the interview/focus group, and also ask permission to record the interview/focus group (if it is to be recorded).

For example, the following is an introductory remark that Karen and her team could use:

> Thank you for coming in to participate in the interview/focus group today. The purpose of this session is for us to find out ways that the library can serve the reading and writing literacy needs that your children have. We will be using your responses to create and improve our services. Know that there are no wrong answers. Know that you can always refuse to answer these questions. We want to know about your experiences so we can help make it easier for your children to master these literacies. Information that you share with us today will only be shared with our team here at MCPL, and will not be shared with anyone else. When we share the information, we will not reveal your name, or anything that could link the information back to you. Do you have any questions before we begin? Do I have your permission to record the interview?

The next step is to create a protocol composed of the questions and prompts to stimulate conversations, ordered by priority and by topic. The questions can be open-ended and/or closed-ended. **Closed-ended questions** are answered by a simple yes or no response or one-word or short-phrase answers. For example, some closed-ended questions that Karen and Jennifer could ask the parents are the following:

(1) How often do you come to the library? Every day, once a week?
(2) What language do you speak at home?
(3) How many children do you have?
(4) What are the ages of your children?
(5) Do you have Internet access at home?
(6) How you rate the fluency of your child's English? Choose between very fluent and not fluent at all.

Open-ended questions require participants to engage in more thought, conversation, and prompting. For example, some open-ended questions that Karen and Jennifer could ask the parents are the following:

(1) What do you use the library for (if you used it before)?

(2) Can you explain why you rated your child's fluency in English as [insert the above response to the closed-ended question]?

(3) Do you have any concerns about your child's literacy development? Why? Why not?

(4) What help do you provide to your child in terms of learning to write and read in English?

(5) Do you have any thoughts about what the library can do to help you help your child with language acquisition?

(6) Do you have any thoughts about how the library can help your child directly?

A separate protocol would also be required for the child interviews and focus groups. Karen and her team will need to consider the children's ages when developing appropriate protocols. Permission from the parents must also be obtained before interviewing minors. The following are some sample open-ended questions that may be used in children's interview/focus group protocol:

(1) When you hear the word library, what is the first thing that comes to your mind?

(2) What type of help do you have in school that helps you to learn, write, and speak in English?

(3) Who do you ask help from when you have trouble with English?

(4) Have you ever participated in any of the library programming that we have offered? What about program X?

Step 2: Pilot Testing the Protocol

The purpose of **pilot-testing** interview or focus group protocol is to ascertain that participants will understand the questions that you are asking. Additionally, if any of these questions are likely to make the interviewee feel uncomfortable, that reaction will be also be evident in the pilot test. In this step, "test" the protocols with people who represent the various subgroups within the community that you are interested in interviewing. To pilot-test the interview/focus group protocol, Karen and her colleagues can invite one or two Spanish-speaking families in the community to provide feedback on their questions. These families should include different aged children and families that frequently come to the library as well as those who do not.

The pilot test ideally should be conducted the same way that you will conduct the interviews with the "real" participants. Record the start and end time to get an estimate of how long the interview questions will take to answer. The focus group questions can also be tested with these families, but time cannot be estimated as the actual focus group will involve a larger group. Take note when the pilot-test respondents ask for questions to be repeated, ask for further clarification of posed questions, or demonstrate hesitation to answer. These may be questions that need to be revised. After the pilot-test interview is over, engage the respondents in a discussion of the questions noted as potentially problematic. To consider cultural differences, ask the respondents if there were any questions that were not appropriate for their culture. Use all this feedback to revise and finalize the protocols.

Step 3: Recruiting Participants

In addition to the recruiting considerations introduced earlier in this chapter, in terms of recruiting Spanish-speaking parents and children for the interviews and focus groups, Karen and Jennifer should leverage the Spanish-speaking frontline staff members to recruit families that come to the library. Additionally, they must recruit Spanish-speaking family members who *do not* come to the library. This representation will ensure that these families' concerns and issues are incorporated into the design of any library programming and services, and these families will be encouraged to participate in the future. Create bilingual flyers and offer slots for interviews and focus groups at a variety of times, such as after-school, evenings, and over the weekend, to accommodate to participant's various schedules, and a variety of locations, such as the library, school, or community center. The MCSD and MCPL can partner with trusted partners, such as local community centers, the Boys and Girls Club, YMCA, or other social service agencies, to recruit families that do not frequent libraries. The focus groups can be held right before or after a popular program at the library or one of the partners' sites to encourage participation. Offering incentives such as children's programming while the parents' interviews are being conducted will also encourage participation.

Step 4: Conducting Interviews/Focus Groups

When it is time to conduct these interviews and focus groups, make sure that these interviews are done in quiet spaces in or outside of the library. The focus groups should be in a room that allows everyone to hear clearly and comfortably fit the number of people in the groups. Follow the interview and focus protocol and ask follow-up questions for clarification or more detail. Simply asking "tell me more about that" often provides deeper insights.

Remember to ask permission to record the interviews. If the interviewers are bringing in any note-takers, ask permission from the interviewees if it is acceptable for the note-taker to listen to the conversation. Always provide a way for interviewees to contact the interviewers after the sessions are over in the event that they have additional answers to provide.

Remaining Steps in Using Interview and Focus Group Data

Once data are collected, the next steps are to analyze your data, make some conclusions, and present your findings to stakeholders and often the participants themselves.

Step 5: Analyze Data

Once Karen and Jennifer have gathered data from a variety of sources and participants, they are ready to begin analyzing their data. Typically, researchers will read over transcripts of interviews and focus groups, examine notes from observations, review documents pertaining to the study, and engage with any other data sources they might have. As the researchers read, they consider their research questions, the things they have learned from other studies related to their research problem, and keep their minds open to new ideas.

As researchers examine the data, they will begin to note themes and patterns and ascribe a **code** to them. A code is a single word or a short phrase that describes the theme or pattern the researcher observes. As Jennifer and Karen uncover codes, they should note them in a list known as a **code book**. These days, coding is most often done on the computer using a software package such as Dedoose or NVivo. However, it is certainly possible to code without using software, by listing the codes on a piece of paper or an index card.

It is critical that Karen and Jennifer keep an open mind and consider their biases. Perhaps they already have an opinion of what the community's needs are. They will need to be mindful of to listening carefully despite their personal opinions. Additionally, Karen and Jennifer should take some time to code their data together. Each person codes the same data and compares their selections. When they have repeatedly come up a high percentage of the same codes, we can say they have achieved **inter-rater reliability.** Inter-rater reliability is an important measure of validity in qualitative research.

In qualitative research, **triangulation** of data is the best method for providing higher levels of confidence in findings. Yin (2014) wrote that triangulation can be by data source, method, researcher, theory, or data type. Miles, Huberman, and Saldaña (2014) described triangulation as a "way of life," noting "in effect, triangulation is a way to get to the findings in the first place—by seeing or hearing multiple *instances* of it from different *sources* by using different *methods* and by squaring the finding with others" (300). Karen and Jennifer will want to triangulate their findings to ensure that their findings have a high level of validity. At the conclusion of coding, Jennifer and Karen now reflect on what they found and how their findings connect to their research questions.

Step 6: Drawing Conclusions

It is vital that Karen and Jennifer explain their findings, draw conclusions as it relates to the research questions, and determine and discuss the concrete action items that result. They can even organize their actions and recommendations that must be taken based on the key library/school staff involved in serving this population, such as the MCPL, MCPS, frontend library staff, children's programming department, adult programming department, marketing department, funders, and community partners.

Step 7: Presenting Results

The findings, interpretations, recommendations, and conclusions, and how they relate to each research question, can be documented in the form of an **executive summary** (about two to four pages, intended for a quick overview of results) and a longer report. Augment the report with quotes and vignettes that illustrate the findings, recommendations, and conclusions. Quotes are powerful in conveying messages in your communities' voices. The executive summary and reports should be shared with all relevant parties, which may include library staff, library board/trustees, the city council, and other stakeholders.

Advantages and Disadvantages of Interviews and Focus Groups

Interviews and focus groups are wonderful techniques to probe your research question in a deeper manner than almost any other data collection technique. Through direct interaction researchers can follow up on interesting statements, ask for clarification when needed and develop a richer understanding of the findings. There are challenges to using these methods however. Some people are uncomfortable answering direct questions, especially if the topic is sensitive or if an answer would require revealing something personal or result in someone getting in trouble. In focus groups, sometimes a leader can emerge who dominates and steers the conversation in ways the researcher does not desire. Finally, both interviews and focus groups take substantial time on the part of the researcher and the participant. Finding a mutually agreeable time to complete the interview or focus group can be a barrier to participants.

These two techniques are often used for exploratory research, to follow on prior findings, and/or to uncover the "why" or "how" of a research question. However, interviews and focus groups are so foundational to qualitative research, and there are few situations in which they would not be helpful. Table 4.1 and Table 4.2 are separate summary charts for interviews and focus groups.

Table 4.1
Summary Table for Interviews

Overall purpose	*Interviews*: To gather information from individuals with insight, experience, or opinions about the research problem through direct interaction and with the ability to follow up for more detail as needed
Advantages	• Gaining deeper understanding of "how" and "why" questions • Allows the opportunity to follow up, seek clarification, and follow useful tangents
Disadvantages	• Requires establishing rapport and trust • Takes more time • Can be biased toward the perception of the interviewee
Steps in process	• Develop an interview "protocol." • Pilot test the protocol. • Recruit participants. • Conduct interviews. • Analyze data. • Draw conclusions. • Present results
Data collection methods	Guided conversations and questions with single participants
Data analysis methods	• Transcribing the interviews • Reading the transcripts for themes • Coding the transcripts according to the themes
Support technologies	• Recording devices • Data analysis software such as Dedoose or NVivo

Table 4.2
Summary Table for Focus Groups

Overall purpose	*Focus groups*: To gather information from small groups of people who have insight, experience, or opinions about the research problem through direct interaction with the researcher and each other, and with the ability to follow up for more detail as needed
Advantages	• Allows participants to build on each other's idea/thoughts
Disadvantages	• Some participants can dominate the discussion, resulting in nondominant participants thoughts being left out. • Facilitator/moderator must have experience to moderate discussion, to ensure goals of the session is met.

(continued)

Table 4.2
Summary Table for Focus Groups (Continued)

Steps in process	• Develop a focus group "protocol." • Pilot test the protocol. • Recruit participants. • Conduct focus groups. • Analyze data. • Draw conclusions. • Present results.
Data collection methods	Guided conversations and questions with small groups of participants
Data analysis methods	• Transcribing the focus group sessions • Reading the transcripts for themes • Coding the transcripts according to the themes
Support technologies	• Recording devices • Data analysis software such as Dedoose or NVivo

Glossary of Key Terms

Closed-ended questions: These are questions with a clear answer, such as Yes/No or concrete information (e.g., "What is your job title?").

Code(s): This is a single word or a short phrase that describes the theme or pattern the researcher observes.

Code book: The complete list of codes for a given study can be found in the code book.

Data saturation: This is the point at which the researcher sees the same themes emerging from multiple sources, interviews, and so on.

Executive summary: It is a short summation of a longer work designed to give a top-level overview of the study.

Focus group: It refers to a small group of people (typically six to eight) who meet together with a facilitator to share information, experiences, or opinions about the research question.

Inter-rater reliability: It refers to the process of multiple researchers comparing their codes for a given piece of data before coding the remainder to ensure that they share similar codes and definitions.

Open-ended questions: These are questions that require interpretation or longer responses and cannot easily be answered in a single phrase (e.g., "Tell me about a time when you had a successful literacy program in your library").

Pilot testing: It refers to a trial run of your interview, focus group, or other data collection tool, typically with a very small number of people.

Probing: It refers to following up on a statement in an interview or focus group to gather more information (e.g., "You mentioned that your circulation is down, but the picture book collection is frequently used in the library. Can you tell me more about that? Why do you think that is?").

Prompting: This is similar to probing, providing a redirect to keep your participant on subject (e.g., "We were talking about changes in circulation, but we did not get to your interpretation of why the numbers have changed. Can you tell me about that?").

Protocol: It refers to the text of introduction, questions, and statements that the researcher uses in an interview or focus group.

Reflective listening: It refers to carefully listening with the goal of understanding the participant's perspective and sharing back your interpretation to either obtain clarification or deepen the conversation (e.g., "I heard you say that many of the newer families appear reluctant to speak with staff, is that correct?").

Rich (thick) data: It refers to providing a level of detail about the situation, phenomenon, or observation such that patterns and relationships are clarified and can be considered in light of both the study in question and other situations.

Triangulate: It refers to comparing findings between sources and data collection strategies to determine whether the codes and findings are present in multiple places.

Triangulation: It is a data integration strategy that takes place at the interpretation phase of mixed methods research, after analyzing each data set, in which researchers display all relevant findings in one place and see if the findings agree, complement, diverge, or disagree.

Further Reading

Bassett, Raewyn, Brenda L. Beagan, Svetlana Ristovski-Slijepcevic, and Gwen E. Chapman. 2008. "Tough Teens: The Methodological Challenges of Interviewing Teenagers as Research Participants." *Journal of Adolescent Research* 23 (2): 119–31.

Dilley, Patrick. 2000. "Conducting Successful Interviews: Tips for Intrepid Research." *Theory into Practice* 39 (3): 131–37.

Heath, Sue, Rachel Brooks, Elizabeth Cleaver, and Eleanor Ireland. 2009. *Researching Young People's Lives.* Los Angeles, CA: SAGE.

Krueger, Richard A., and Mary Anne Casey. 2009. *Focus Groups: A Practical Guide for Applied Research.* 4th ed. Los Angeles, CA: SAGE.

MacMillan, Don, Susan McKee, and Shawna Sadler. 2007. "Getting Everyone on the Same Page: A Staff Focus Group Study for Library Web Site Redesign." *Reference Services Review* 35 (3): 425–33. doi:10.1108/00907320710774292.

Tammivaara, Julie, and D. Scott Enright. 1986. "On Eliciting Information: Dialogues with Child Informants." *Anthropology & Education Quarterly* 17 (4): 218–38.

Chapter 5

Action Research

Lesley Farmer, Professor
College of Education, California State University, Long Beach

Introduction to Action Research

Scenario II (Hoffman) illustrates a situation that can be investigated and addressed through action research, a methodology that allows researchers to operationalize one or more research methods (e.g., surveys or focus groups) to investigate a specific strategy or solution to an observed problem. Action research is a systematic, research-based approach to improving conditions in a specific setting. Its key distinguishing feature is "action," and the process entails actively studying one's own practice in order to improve it. Action research, though, is not just reflective practice; it begins with a careful examination of existing research studies that are focused on a well-identified problem. Factors contributing to the problem are carefully identified and aligned with appropriate research data collection and analysis methods that rely on relatable and valid assessment instruments.

Researchers typically use action research to achieve positive and practical social change. Lewin (1946), known as the coiner of the term action research, asserted that

> the research needed for social practice can best be characterized as research for social management or social engineering. It is a type of action-research, a comparative research on the conditions and effects of various forms of social action, and research leading to social action. (35)

Furthermore, this approach assumes that the researcher participates in the investigation as a credible stakeholder who can obtain insider information and who is likely to be helped through the findings and recommendations. At the risk of being self-serving, as long as the researcher is aware of, and documents, his or her relation to the problem and role in the research activities as well as follows all the data collection and analysis processes rigorously and in good faith, this research method can yield balanced, practical results.

The main limitation of action research is that it is not intended to be generalizable. Action research is tailored to specific variables that occur in a unique context. However, other researchers can build on action research, using other research methods to determine possible generalities or at least outcomes that may relate to similar settings or other conditions.

Scenario 2 (Hoffman) illustrates a common situation for librarians: noticing an area that needs improvement, trying to determine the underlying problem, and deciding how to solve it. The library director, Karen Smith, was interested in improving a specific library's service: the basic goal of action research. In the process of trying to figure out the underlying reasons for the low circulation of Spanish materials, Karen enlisted the help of the local school district's English language learner coordinator, Jennifer Jones, who faced a similar problem with an overlapping population: Spanish-speaking parents of the district's students. Karen and Jennifer worked together through the steps of action research to determine how best to address their problem.

Steps in the Action Research Process

Action research is conducted using the steps found in an iterative cycle of inquiry, as Figure 5.1 illustrates.

Figure 5.1
Iterative cycle of inquiry

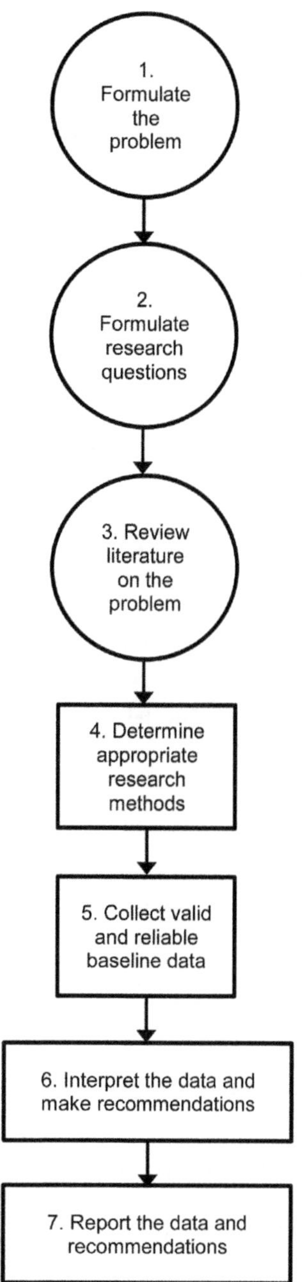

That is, as Figure 5.1 shows, one identifies a general issue, collects facts about the situation, uses the facts and an intended outcome to develop an action plan, implements and evaluates that plan, and reviews research results to modify the plan and possible add additional topics for investigation. Action research can stop at this point, but the full cycle of inquiry entails the following steps, as Figure 5.2 suggests.

When Karen and Jennifer set out to use action research to investigate their problem, they will follow six steps:

Step 1. Identify the Problem

This first step is critical and can be surprisingly difficult. Technically, Scenario II (Hoffman) involves two settings, thus two related action research projects; but for this discussion, the public library will serve as the focal point with the background question "How have *libraries* traditionally reflected the diversity of their communities through their programs and services, and how can they continue to do so today?" Because the scope of this question is vast and it may not shed light on the phenomenon currently occurring in the library, Karen wants to focus the problem central to her investigation on how increase the circulation of Spanish materials.

Figure 5.2

Extensions to iterative cycle of inquiry

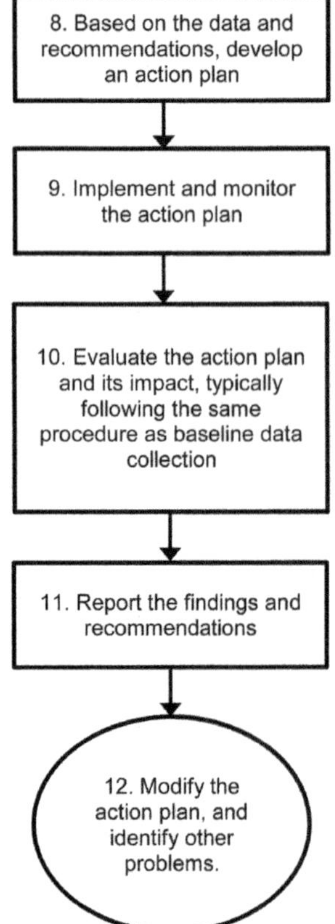

Step 2. Formulate Research Questions and Participants

To investigate ways to increase Spanish language circulation, Karen and Jennifer constructed two site-specific action research questions:

1. What factors impact the circulation of Spanish materials for MSEPL?
2. What actions can be taken to increase the circulation of Spanish materials for MSEPL?

Karen and Jennifer decided that their study will need to target Spanish-speaking library users. They considered including Spanish-speaking community members who did not use the library, but they determined that investigating the needs of this and other populations, such as learners of Spanish, was outside of the scope of their study. Their goal was to maximize access for the Spanish-speaking library users they had.

Library staff and community members were also identified as important participants. Library staff have direct contact with patrons, make collection development decisions, manage circulation, and design library programming. Karen and Jennifer agreed that their perspectives were important to include. Also, Karen and Jennifer wanted to include Spanish language community members because they were often influential in orienting citizens to and promoting the library's offerings.

Step 3. Review the Literature on the Problem

As with most kinds of research, the action researchers should locate studies that address the same problem in order to help identify possible contributing factors (i.e., variables), locate validated data instruments, and find out how other public librarians addressed the problem of low circulation of Spanish materials. Sources for Scenario II (Hoffman) may include the following:

- REFORMA: http://www.reforma.org
- SOL: Spanish in Our Libraries: http://www.sol-plus.net/plus/home.htm
- America Reads Spanish: http://www.americareadsspanish.org/
- WebJunction: https://www.webjunction.org/explore-topics/spanish.html
- Guidelines for Library Services to Spanish-Speaking Library Users http://www.ala.org/rusa/resources/guidelines/guidespanish
- Alire, Camila A. and Jacqueline Ayala. (2007). *Serving Latino Communities* (2nd ed.). New York: Neal-Schuman
- Avila, Salvador. (2012). *Serving Latino Teens.* Westport, CT: Libraries Unlimited
- Baumann, Susana G. (2010). *¡Hola, Amigos! A Plan for Latino Outreach.* Westport, CT: Libraries Unlimited
- Byrd, Susannah M. (2005). *¡Bienvenidos! ¡Welcome!: A Handy Resources Guide for Marketing Your Library to Latinos.* Chicago: American Library Association

These sources may include the findings of studies on similar topics, data collection instruments, and information about data analysis techniques.

Karen located relevant articles using appropriate databases such as Library Information Science & Technology Abstracts, ERIC, Chicano Database, Latino American Experience, and Hispanic American Periodicals Index.

In addition to reading published literature, Karen and Jennifer brainstormed possible reasons for low circulation. They considered the most current data they have on

- the nature of the collection (e.g., subject matter, reading level, format, and publication location since different types of Spanish are practiced in different Spanish-speaking countries);
- library staffing characteristics (e.g., Spanish fluency);
- means of access to the collection (e.g., physical location in the library, e-book access, language of the library catalog, and library portal content and language);
- public relations (e.g., communications channels/format, dissemination methods, content, frequency, language, and marketing); and
- community characteristics (e.g., demographics including country of origin, legal status, economic status, educational background, Spanish and English fluency and interest, personal interests and needs, prior experiences with libraries, library card holding status, and participation in planning).

As they review these sources, she should take notes as salient variables reoccur. After a while, patterns will emerge, and studies will start to reiterate the same underlying causes and effective solutions. These findings can be summarized and used to determine which data to collect and the process of data collection. Karen and Jennifer should consider other potential contributing factors, too, beyond what the literature and prior data suggest.

Step 4. Collect Data

With the literature review completed, Karen and Jennifer are ready to design their study. At this stage, they need to examine their research question and determine which kind of data would answer it.

Step 4a. Determine Appropriate Research Methods

Because Karen and Jennifer are interested in knowing not only those factors that encourage library patrons to use Spanish language materials but also how the library can increase its patrons' access, they consider whether their research questions would have quantitative answers, qualitative answers, or both. They decide that a mixed method approach of a survey with both closed- and open-ended questions and focus groups is best suited to identify the factors that influence patrons' use of Spanish materials and what actions the Spanish speakers feel would improve their access to the materials. Karen and Jennifer also determine that quantitative data like circulation data will help them to determine if the solutions they implement are indeed positively affecting the Spanish language materials' circulation.

Step 4b. Gather and Review Baseline Data

Karen and Jennifer pulled together existing baseline data, composed of prior patron surveys, focus group transcripts and reports relating to patron perspectives on new services, circulation statistics, table count logs (numbers and kinds of books and periodicals left on tables), and available public library data sets. They also gathered additional baseline data through staff interviews.

Karen was delighted to find that not only did she already have MSEPL's circulation records but also that she could further explore circulation patterns by material type (e.g., picture books, children's books, YA books, adult fiction, and nonfiction) and language. She also found that the library's regional consortia gave her access to statistics to benchmark MSEPL against comparable libraries serving similar populations.

Karen also pulled data about her staff's Spanish fluency, which she compared to comparable libraries' staffing patterns. Karen and Jennifer interviewed the staff who spoke Spanish to find out how they interacted with that population. During the course of these interviews, Karen and Jennifer learned that they had overlooked a key stakeholder—the public relations and community outreach staff! So, they interviewed these staff members and gathered copies of Spanish language advertisements and library publicity.

Jennifer gathered baseline data from the schools—enrollment demographics, school library circulation data, and school library catalog data.

As evidenced in the earlier section, data collection can be a complex, time-consuming process. It is important to gather a variety of data from their identified sources. In that way, the resultant findings can be triangulated to identify patterns across the respondents and resolve conflicting information.

Step 4c. Conduct Data Collection Procedures

Karen and Jennifer quickly realized that they would need a plan to conduct their data in which they each had defined responsibilities. Karen took the lead on updating the patron surveys to gather information about Spanish speaking library users' preferences and needs. To the extent possible, she based the survey questions on ones used in past library surveys. She also piloted the survey with a group of Spanish-speaking users that regularly met in the library's community room. Jennifer took the lead on developing interview and focus group protocols for library patrons and library staff. She and Karen conducted the interviews and focus groups together, with the help of library volunteers who acted as notetakers. Karen provided the library reference desk with new table log instruments.

Step 5. Interpret the Data and Implement Action Plan

Karen and Jennifer analyzed the data following procedures outlined in other chapters of this book. From their content analysis of the qualitative data, they were able to discern frequency patterns in the responses that detailed the reasons for borrowing behaviors, and led to recommendations about ways to change those behaviors. From their analysis of the circulation data and table logs, Karen and Jennifer were able to see which kinds of materials Spanish-speaking patrons took home and which they used in the library.

Step 5a. Report Initial Findings and Recommendations

The data findings, interpretation, and analysis were shared with the library staff, the library board or trustees, the city council, patrons, and the Spanish language community leaders. The executive summary, main findings, and recommendations were publicized on the library website, in the local media outlets and social media. The library website included a "suggestion box" email link for feedback and physical suggestion boxes were placed throughout the library.

Step 5b. Develop, Implement, and Monitor an Action Plan

The reason for data collection analysis, in combination with the literature review, is to make recommendations leading to an action plan. As with sharing of the findings and recommendations, the action plan should be created by the library staff and library governance board, with the input of major stakeholder decision-makers.

The action plan itself should include the goal, the objectives (i.e., strategies to achieve the goal), actions, persons responsible for overseeing the action, time frame, criteria for success, and instruments for measuring success. Karen supervised the action plan and communicated progress and benchmark successes with stakeholders and other interested parties.

While an action plan is informed by research, it does not constitute research itself. It is, in effect, an outcome of research. For instance, data collection and analysis may indicate that Hispanics are not checking out materials because they do not understand that this information is confidential and not shared with employers, government officials, or family members. A clear step the library staff can take, then, is to create a Spanish language poster or books that explain how to obtain a library card and patron privacy.

Karen monitored the action plan and worked with Jennifer to help staff overcome obstacles and make adjustments as needed (Kotter 1996).

5c. Evaluate the Action Plan

To measure the impact of the action plan, Karen and Jennifer employed the same sets of data collected by the same instruments in the same way. Since the goal is increased circulation of Spanish materials, circulation records served as the main measure, but these data were augmented by follow-up interviews and focus groups with library staff and Spanish-speaking library patrons.

Step 6. Report the Findings and Refine the Action Plan

Communicating the impact acknowledges the seriousness of the action plan and interest in serving the community. Typically, as with the original recommendation step, a small body of decision-makers would review the report. They might also be able to modify the action plan with little outside input if the changes are minimal. At this point, that same group may pose new queries about resources and services to the Hispanic population, such as increased programming, addition of Spanish-speaking library staff or at least volunteer translators, or other outreach efforts. These queries then lead to the next action research project.

In any case, Karen and her public relations team learned that they need to plan their publicity campaign systematically to broadcast to all the appropriate media outlets and stakeholders. The message should certainly highlight library program efforts and impact. If changes to the plan are needed and already determined, then that information can also be communicated. If community input is needed for a modified plan, then the message should underscore the value of community involvement and the direct action taken as a result of their voices.

Detailing the action research steps for Scenario II (Hoffman) illustrates the importance of collaborative participation and the complexity of a seemingly simple issue. It also shows how time-consuming and labor-intensive action research can be. The payoff is concrete action and results. While the underlying reasons for low circulation and the resultant action plan were not stipulated here, it can be easily imagined that one issue impacts another. For instance, if one reason that the community does not check out materials is because they are not aware of that collection, then changes in public relations are needed. The library staff may find that the community literacy is low and that they are more interested in getting health and social services information, so the library might prioritize that service over collection development. In that respect, the focus of the action research might need to change, depending on the data collected and analyzed, which is fine since the ultimate goal is improved library service for that population and the service area population as a whole. That is the beauty of action research.

Advantages and Disadvantages of Action Research

Action research is more of a **methodology**, that is, an epistemological stance, than a specific research method; action research can be undertaken using a wide variety of research methods. This pragmatic perspective frames the advantages and disadvantages of action research.

For instance, practicing librarians are likely to embrace action research because it is change-oriented, which can result in more effective professional practice and reinforces the idea of continuous improvement. As action research investigators, librarians do not have to distance themselves or recuse themselves from their settings but can leverage that insider status in order to gain information and insights that an outsider might not be able to obtain. Librarians also optimize their resultant action plans by considering the context of the research, namely, the population, stakeholders, environment, and situational properties. Librarians can be overt about their action research efforts with their community and colleagues, rather than trying to hide their investigation and, in the process, gain more group buy-in and sense of ownership. Particularly as the study is conducted as a collaborative project, not only might more data be garnered and accurately analyzed, but the process itself can strengthen professional ties. While this corollary result could "muddy" a more "pure" research study, for the purposes of action research, such changes in behavior would be considered a happy result that folds into the effort as a whole.

These same positive attributes may also be considered disadvantages. Because the investigator is an insider, that person's perspective is less objective, or at least disinterested, than an outsider's. The same motivation that could get community buy-in might also lead to hiding or "bending" pertinent information in order to reinforce existing values or evade unpleasant conclusions. Change, a philosophical bedrock of action research, can be threatening, even if it is beneficial. Indeed, action research can foster factions as well as collaborative bonds. Furthermore, because action research is couched in a specific context, it is hard to generalize the conclusions. The action plan might well be ineffective with a different population and setting.

While action research follows classic research design, it does not specify any particular research methodology. As in most kinds of research, the question leads to the type of method used, most likely a mixed method. The most relevant question is as follows: what information do I need to know, and how do I collect it? That kind of methodological flexibility enables the investigator to choose the most appropriate strategy, but it also means that such a choice relies on that investigator's prior knowledge of research methodology, which may be limited. Moreover, especially if done collaboratively, action research can be messy and time consuming.

The participatory nature of action research also touches on issues of control. As noted earlier, action research can engage many stakeholders, and the process as well as an action plan's effective implementation can empower the participants.

On the other hand, those same participants can also expropriate the investigation for their own purposes; the researcher at the least must share control and may lose it altogether.

As long as librarians realize the parameters and consequences of action research, they should seriously consider using this approach because it builds on reflective practice and make it more rigorous and systematic, which can result in more effective change.

Table 5.1
Summary Chart: Action Research

Overall purpose	To improve practice and conditions in a specific setting
Advantages	• Practical • Relevant • Actionable • Flexible • Inside view • Local buy-in • Empowering • Promotes change • Can be done individually or collaboratively • Supports continuous improvement
Disadvantages	• Not generalizable • Subjective • May be complex and time-consuming • May cause factions • Value driven • Control issues
Steps in process	• Formulate problem. • Gather data. • Analyze data. • Report results. • Plan action. • Evaluate action plan.
Data collection methods	Instruments for collecting baseline data (qualitative and quantitative)
Data analysis methods	Statistical tests that match the data (and instruments)
Support technologies	Match to the research step: for example, for data analysis, use content analysis tools (e.g., NVivo), video capture of processes, or statistical packages (e.g., SPSS). For reporting results, use data visualization tools (e.g., Tableau and infographic tools). For action plans, use planning tools (e.g., Gantt charts).

Glossary of Key Term

Methodology: It refers to the theoretical underpinning for understanding which method, set of methods, or best practices can be applied to a specific research endeavor. Research methods are used to enact research methodologies; "methodology" and "method" are not synonymous.

Further Reading

Coghlan, David, and Mary Brydon-Miller. eds. 2014. *The SAGE Encyclopedia of Action Research.* Thousand Oaks, CA: SAGE.

Cook, Douglas, and Lesley Farmer. eds. 2011. *Using Qualitative Methods in Action Research: How Librarians Can Get to the Why of Data.* Chicago, IL: American Library Association.

Johnson, Andrew P. 2011. *A Short Guide to Action Research.* 4th ed. New York: Pearson.

Sagor, Richard. 2010. *The Action Research Guidebook.* 2nd ed. Thousand Oaks, CA: Corwin Press.

Sykes, Judith A. 2013. *Conducting Action Research to Evaluate Your School Library.* Westport, CT: Libraries Unlimited.

Chapter 6

Historical Methodology

Suzanne Stauffer, Associate Professor
School of Library and Information Science, Louisiana State University

Introduction to Historical Methodology

Historical methodology is used to explore the history of a specific subject within a specific context, meaning during a particular time in a particular place and within a particular sociocultural setting. While Karen and Jennifer can and should read books and articles about how other libraries faced new and changing needs in the past, the solutions that worked for other libraries in other communities may or may not work for theirs. They need to understand the historical development of their community and its library in order to devise and implement the most effective strategies for them.

The first step in historical research, as in all research, is to decide what questions to answer and frame them properly. Good questions are operational, that is, they are explicit and precise and can be answered using historical data; they are open-ended and cannot be answered with "yes" or "no," which avoids bias, as the questions do not predict the answer and are not looking for information to support a predetermined conclusion; they are analytical asking "how," "what," and "why" and exploring interactions; and they are flexible and can be easily modified if necessary as new information is uncovered. The first question that Karen and Jennifer need to explore is how the community and library have changed over time in order to understand the social context in which the library exists today. What major demographic shifts has the community undergone in the past? What did the community look like when the library first opened? What services and materials did the library provide to that community? Who were the "movers and shakers" of the community at that time, and how did they influence the policies and services of the library? As the community changed over time, how did the library change with it? How did the influential groups in the community change? What changes took place in library policies, procedures, services, and collections in response to those changes? Which were successful and which were not? Were there marginalized or underserved groups historically, and if so, who were they? What has happened to them?

Once they have a clear picture of the events of the past, they can start to look more closely at the recent past. When and why were the current policies and procedures implemented? What goals and objectives were they designed to meet? What groups and individuals influenced their creation? Was there opposition, and if so, from whom? How was the library meeting the needs of the Hispanic community previously?

Research Participants

In addition to engaging with participants from previous eras through their writings and other materials, historians may collect oral history from older people who experienced the events that they are studying. In this case, Karen and Jennifer may choose to interview retired librarians, retired library board members and members of city government, and older, long-time members of the Hispanic community who can provide needed historical background and perspective.

Data Collection Methods

The data of history are, first and foremost, **primary documents**. These are created at or very near the time of the events and include manuscript materials such as autobiographies and memoirs, diaries, journals, oral histories, interviews, and personal correspondence, contemporary publications such as newspapers, magazines, newsletters, bulletins and yearbooks, and institutional and government documents such as official correspondence, annual reports, census records, memos, budgets, and maps. They may also include realia such as clothing, books, blueprints, toys, art objects, and photographs. These are found in local history collections, government archives, and library special collections and are increasingly digitized on the Internet.

Historians also make use of **secondary documents** or sources in order to provide the background and context for the subject they are studying. Secondary materials are created after the time that the events took place and are based on primary sources. They include the author's explications and judgments of the primary materials on which they are based, so that the values and judgments are from a different perspective than the primary sources. Typical secondary sources include biographies, local histories, and articles in historical journals, as well as full-length historical works. Textbooks and encyclopedias are considered tertiary sources in that they are usually based on secondary sources.

The historian must first verify that the documents are valid and reliable in the same way that a librarian will evaluate a website or reference book. Sources are evaluated for authenticity. That is, is the item what it claims to be? Does it physically appear to be what it claims to be? Is it created by a reliable source, such as a government agency? Is it located in or made available by a trusted source, such as a state archives? If it claims to be created by an individual, is there evidence for that? For example, is it part of a collection held at a recognized institution? Or, as we have all seen on *Antiques Roadshow*, does it have a barcode on the back of it or a "Made-in-China" sticker?

Historians also evaluate the credibility of a document, that is, the validity and reliability of the information contained in the source. They source the information by identifying the author, date of creation, and place of creation. They corroborate the information by comparing documents to each other to see if they provide the same information and lead to the same conclusions. They identify when and where the event took place and the context in which it took place.

Historians also evaluate their own ability to understand and analyze the information contained in the documents. They ask themselves whether they feel any uncertainty about the meaning of terms and phrases used in the source and also are careful not to fall into the trap of presentism, or thinking that the terms and phrases meant then what they mean now. They utilize secondary sources such as etymological dictionaries and phrase books to avoid these errors.

The historian can spend hours reading through the materials, copying or scanning relevant information. Digitized documents can often be searched electronically for specific names and events, but the researcher runs the risk of missing important information. Newspapers, in particular, are notorious for misspelling personal names, and using abbreviations or acronyms.

Oral histories are collected utilizing an oral history interview protocol. The purpose of an oral history is not to establish what happened when; that is established through the historical research already described. The purpose of oral history is to elicit the story that is not preserved in official documents and other records, to learn how individuals experienced the past. The interview protocol begins with standard demographic questions—name, age, years in the community, education, and so on—and then uses open-ended questions that guide the interview, but the subject being interviewed directs the interview. The historian must avoid bias and assumptions in designing the questions, avoiding leading questions that suggest a specific answer to the subject. A good initial question to ask an older member of the Hispanic community for this scenario would be, "Tell me what you remember about the public library when you were young." From there, the interviewer can ask probing questions based on the answer. If the subject has no memory of the public library, the interviewer might ask, "Tell me about your memories of the school library?" or "How did you get materials you needed for homework?" or "Where did you get books to read for pleasure?" or "What did you do for fun?"

Questions for retired librarians, board members, and other officials would be likewise open-ended but would focus on library policies and procedures and how they were created and implemented. "What do you remember about when and why [this particular policy] was implemented?" "What services do you remember offering to the Hispanic community?"

Data Analysis Methods

Analyzing historical data has much in common with analyzing literature. The historian looks for trends, for cause and effect, for interactions among individuals and groups, for repeating themes and events, and, especially, names. It is useful to begin with a chronology of events to be able to see the broad outlines of the landscape and then begin to fill in the details. Who was doing what when and where and what was the outcome? What happened after that and why?

Scholars and professional historians utilize an analytical framework that is based on the theoretical perspective they are employing to determine exactly how they will analyze the data. The specific method they use depends on this analytical framework. They may utilize a quantitative or phenomenological method, case study, grounded theory, oral history, mixed methods, discourse analysis, or historiography. Mixed methods or using two or more methods are the most common approaches. In our example, Karen and Jennifer are using case study, studying just their library, and oral history as well as some quantitative with the inclusion of demographic data and trends.

More than any other methodology, history is iterative. Once we have established trends and identified key players and events, we need to go back and look at our original data with new eyes. A comment in the minutes of a meeting, a line item in a budget, a letter between two individuals—each can take on new significance within the context that is being established. Oral history interviews can provide new perspectives and additional information and are especially revealing of the unofficial reaction to official decisions. They may answer the question of why a program or policy succeeded or failed.

Potential Reporting Venues

Historical research can be shared with others through newspapers, local history bulletins and newsletters, and state library association magazines. Oral histories are transcribed and deposited in repositories in local history societies, state or local archives, and in oral history collections at colleges and universities. The information that Karen and Jennifer collect should be summarized into a report that would be shared with relevant members of the library staff.

Why Use This Research Method?

Historical methodology (Table 6.1) has been described as creating a map of the past that reveals the landscape of history through time and space (Gaddis 2002). It is far more than a listing of names, dates, and events. It is an exploration of cause and effect. We use it to understand how we got from where we were to where we are and why the present is structured the way that it is, why certain groups are in power and enjoy privilege and why other groups are marginalized and underserved. We use it to show us where we went right and where we went wrong, to enumerate our successes and support them and our failures and rectify them. We identify influential individuals, organizations, policies, and events and explore how they interacted to create the results that we see today, for better and for worse. History can help us to avoid reinventing the wheel and prevent us from making the same mistakes over and over. It provides us with a deeper understanding of how personality and politics have shaped the policies, collections, and services that an institution offers today.

The disadvantage of historical research is that it is time-consuming and requires human expertise. Although technology has made access to primary documents easier, it cannot evaluate the documents or analyze the data. It requires interpretation of the data and cannot and does not pretend to provide statistically significant results. It cannot and does not pretend to provide absolute, final, conclusive answers to questions and have been accused being unreliable. Historians also may commit any number of historical fallacies, from fallacies of inquiry through fallacies of explanation to fallacies of argument (Fischer 1970). The fact that each generation of historians will reinterpret the data of history differently in light of its own perspective and its own understanding of the past is seen by those outside of history as a disadvantage and even weakness, while historians see it as evidence of the vitality of history.

Table 6.1
Summary Chart: Historical Methodology

Overall purpose	To understand why the present is structured the way it is
Advantages	Provides insight into human factors
Disadvantages	Interpretive rather than parametric
Steps in process	Iterative
Data collection methods	Locate and access primary documents
Data analysis methods	Interpretation
Support technologies	Websites that provide digitized documents and accurate historical information

Glossary of Key Terms

Primary documents: Primary materials are created at or very near the time of the events by eyewitnesses. They include official correspondence, annual reports, minutes of meetings, budgets, newspaper articles, diaries, journals, and personal letters.

Secondary documents: Secondary materials are created after the time that the events took place and are based on primary sources. They include the author's explications and judgments of the primary materials on which they are based, so that the values and judgments are from a different perspective than the primary sources.

Further Reading

Arnold, John. 2000. *History: A Very Short Introduction.* Oxford: Oxford University Press.

Fischer, David Hackett. 1970. *Historians' Fallacies: Toward a Logic of Historical Thought.* New York: Harper Perennial.

Gaddis, John Lewis. 2002. *The Landscape of History: How Historians Map the Past.* Oxford: Oxford University Press.

Howell, Martha, and Walter Prevenier. 2001. *From Reliable Sources: An Introduction to Historical Methods.* Ithaca, NY: Cornell University Press.

SCENARIO III

Teaching Research Skills

Angela Branyon, Postdoctoral Fellow
Darden College of Education, Old Dominion University

Herbert Smith teaches English at one of 12 high schools in a diverse, suburban public school district. The district has a high school drop-out rate of 2.45% compared to a national average dropout rate of 5%. The ethnic distribution is Asian—8.9%; African American—36.1%; Hispanic—7.6%; White—43.3%; and Other—4.2%. At Smith's high school, 74% of the students passed the English Readiness test, 72% passed the Math Readiness, and approximately 83% of the students at this school go on to either a community college or a four-year college or university.

Smith teaches an 11th-grade English class, which is the year that English classes concentrate on the process of researching and writing a thesis paper. Even though he breaks the assignment down into chunks, the project is dreaded because many students are not interested in researching an author or a literary topic. Smith wants to make this assignment more authentic and hopes to see the students more engaged in their topics and in their research. Each year, this county sponsors an All-County Reads program where every student in the high school and in the community read the same book culminating in the book's author spending the day talking with the students who have created the most original and interesting project. Smith sees this as a way to engage his students and have them work toward an authentic goal and thus become engaged in the research process. The book being read this year is by a nationally acclaimed author who hails from Smith's county where these schools are located. It is a murder mystery involving government espionage and conspiracies. Because all the students in the school will read this book, Smith approaches the history teacher, the science teacher, and the librarian to help him develop a research project that will actively engage the students; forge a desire to do critical research, which will delve deeply into an issue; and develop a real-world assessment to chart the students' progress.

Smith's yearly Goals for Growth, initiated by every teacher for evaluation purposes, include the integration of several content classes working collaboratively on a research project and presentation utilizing technology as a portion of the end product. Through his own experiences, Smith has learned that integration of content can demonstrate to students the unification of various subjects and experiences. This can allow students to see connections throughout their content classes, which may otherwise be missed. Through the use of parallel disciplines (English, history, science, and research), and with the school librarian and aforementioned teachers, Smith is hoping to involve his students in the creation of a research topic that will be of interest and engage them. Smith and his collaborative team decide to co-teach their 11th-grade students by using the novel as the impetus for a unit on the research process, including essential questions, critical thinking/reading skills, the use of experts, and incorporating technology from beginning to end of the process. In addition, they want to use this authentic scenario to stimulate students' curiosity and interest. Smith and his collaborative team anticipate that using a real-world problem (murder of the character in the novel) in conjunction with the new technological tools will motivate and engage students. The students will be adopting the roles of forensic scientists, detectives, and lawyers to research the murder of the character in the novel. Students will use the information in the novel to begin the investigation while improving their reading skills through comprehension strategies. The "forensic scientists group" will Skype with the local forensic pathologist who will guide them in researching the types of clues to look for when they "autopsy the body" and write their reports. The "student detectives" will Skype with the Chief of Detectives of the local Criminal Investigation Division who will demonstrate police procedures and how to "read for clues" by using logic and research. The "student lawyers" will Skype with the county's attorney general to research the law and to write their opening and closing arguments. The final chapters of the novel will be revealed only after the trial is completed to see if through the reading, writing, and research, students were able to unveil the actual murderer.

Smith has no documentation or prior experience concerning the success of this type of research project with a student body so encompassing, but he is eager to give it a try. He does, however, have anecdotal data that shows his students are much more involved when he uses real-life scenarios and games to teach content in his class. He is interested to see if adding student research will help the students become more engaged in the process. The collaborative team will work together to plan and co-teach the unit and assess student learning. While assessments indicate the students have done quite well in learning the technical skills necessary for the project's success, Smith has also observed that some of his students are asking better questions in class, indicating that they may be thinking more critically about the book and the project. They are also taking more books out of the library to read, and they are using technology to pursue research on topics of interest to them in and out of class and to contact the experts assigned to help with the project.

Smith does not have any empirical data to support his anecdotal data, nor does he know whether the students developed these skills and motivation for exploration due to the team's efforts.

Smith meets with his collaborative team to see if they have any formal data that might support his informal observations. None of the team has formal data. All are interested in doing some research on whether the students' research skills improved with the use of collaborative teaching, with the exploration of questions and topics that interest them, with the use of research led by with expert guidance, and with the use of technology. Although a more formal research effort will be needed to explore these ideas, all members of the team are excited to work together on it. Their first task was to determine an overarching research question as follows:

What instructional factors are most effective for improving research skills acquisition?

Chapter 7

Formative Learning Assessment

Joette Stefl-Mabry, Associate Professor of Information
School of Education, University at Albany, State University of New York

Introduction to Formative Assessment

A well-designed exam can provide accurate information about what students have achieved, but "it does not provide any information about learning *while* it is happening" (Frey 2014, 60). Although Scriven (1967) was the first to define formative evaluation as the evaluation of an ongoing and pliable educational program, Bloom (1969) shifted the term *formative* from evaluation to assessment. In the early 1960s, Bloom focused on individual differences, especially in students' school learning. The purpose of Bloom's taxonomy was to promote higher forms of thinking in learners. Bloom's framework provided educators specific vocabulary designed to advance student learning from lower levels of learner (rote memorization of facts) to analyzing and evaluating concepts, process, procedures, and principles (1956). Bloom identified three learning domains:

(1) The affective learning domain, which concentrated on the growth of feelings or emotional areas (attitudes/dispositions)
(2) The psychomotor learning domain, which focused on the development of manual or physical skills
(3) The cognitive learning domain, which targeted the growth and expansion of intellectual abilities (knowledge)

Educators rarely focus on learning objectives in the affective domain, and yet the affective domain is critical to the formative development of student success. It is vitally important that students feel comfortable asking questions, making mistakes, and asking for help, after all, the ability to ask good questions is far more important than the regurgitation of rote answers. Educators pay scant attention to the affective learning domain because many do not understand that self-regulation, confidence in working independently, and the ability to work collaboratively with peers all fall within the affective learning domain. Employers today are emphasizing the need for students to enter the workplace well prepared not only in the hard skills (knowledge and skills) but also in the soft skills or the ability to manage, interact, and get along with people (Ravindranath 2016). Another reason educators ignore the affective learning domain is because it is more challenging to design assessments that target the affective domain (Stefl-Mabry and Doane 2014). While it may be difficult to design affective assessments, it is not impossible, and with practice it becomes easier.

Formative assessment is the intentional effort to determine a student's status regarding his or her attainment of specific learning objectives. Unlike formative research, which is intended to improve designing instructional practice or process design, Popham (2014) provided a useful working definition of formative assessment: "Formative assessment is a planned process in which assessment-elicited evidence of students' status is used by teachers to adjust their ongoing instructional procedures or by students to adjust their current learning tactics" (290). Formative assessment is, as Popham (2014) stressed, a process and not a test; assessments, by their very nature, are not tests. Formative assessment involves a carefully designed iterative process integrated within instructional activities that makes visible a learner's level of attainment of specified learning objectives. Although educators may modify their teaching on the spot to improve **instruction** in response to students' puzzled looks or declarations of frustration such as "I can't do this," such in the moment changes are not formative assessments. While changes to improve instruction should be encouraged, such modifications are not formative assessments. Formative assessment is a process involving "serious upfront planning" (Popham 2014, 290).

Theoretical Background

Black and Wiliam (1998), two British researchers, published a seminal paper in which they reviewed nearly 10 years of empirical research on classroom assessment. Black and Wiliam's (1998) work provided the underlying empirical foundation of formative assessment and "show[ed] conclusively that formative assessment does improve learning" (61). Most importantly, Black and Wiliam (1998) concluded that if formative assessment is utilized by teachers, it is almost certain to work: they provided many examples of studies in which it was clear that formative assessment made a meaningful contribution to students' learning whether teachers made adjustments to their teaching instruction or whether students made adjustments to their own learning strategies. In confirmation, McMillan (2013) asserted that classroom assessment "is the most powerful type of measurement in education that influences student learning" (4).

For instruction to be successful in helping students achieve intended **learning goals** and **learning objectives**, teachers must assess their students *while learning* *is in progress* in order to gather information about students' developing understanding so that teachers can make adaptations to help students attain the learning objectives (Black and Wiliam 1998, 2003, 2009; McMillan 2013; Popham 2014). Assessment that occurs while instruction is in progress has been proven to have a positive effect on student learning (Furtak and Ruiz-Primo 2008).

Formative Assessment: The Importance of Planning and Precision

The ultimate goal of all formative assessment is to promote student learning (Wiggins 1998); however in some cases, assessments are developed that have little connection to the learning goal (Shavelson, Ruiz-Primo, and Wiley 2005). Effective formative assessments are informed by empirical evidence of cognition and learning, or what is referred to as *evidence-centered design* (Pellegrino 2014, 239). The formative assessment process begins by "defining as precisely as possible the *claims* that one wants to be able to make about student knowledge and the ways students are supposed to know and understand some particular aspect of a content domain" (Pellegrino 2014, 239–240). Pellegrino (2014) recommended being precise about the cognitive elements being studied, and to express those elements in using the verbs of cognition, such as compare, describe, analyze, compute, elaborate, explain, predict, or justify.

The next step in effective formative assessment design is to specify the forms of evidence that would provide support for those claims. This specification includes features that need to be present and how they are weighted in an evidentiary scheme—this entails identifying what matters most and what does not matter at all. According to Sadler (1989), three elements are required to successfully use assessment to promote learning:

1. A clear view of the learning goals derived from the curriculum
2. Information about the present state of the learner typically derived from preassessments
3. Action to close the gap taken through instruction

Each element informs the other. The appropriateness of the learning goals, the specificity of the learning objectives, the **validity** of the assessments in relationship to the learning objectives, the gathering and interpretation of assessment information or evidence of learning, and the relevance and quality of the instruction that ensures students will master the learning objectives are all critical determinants of the outcome.

Effective teaching must begin with a theory or model of cognition and learning in the domain. For most teachers, the goals for learning are established in the curriculum, which is usually mandated externally such as by state curriculum standards. But the externally mandated curriculum does NOT specify **learning outcomes** and objectives that are critical for assessment to be effective. As a result, educators and others responsible for designing curriculum, instruction, and assessment must fashion intermediate goals that can serve as an effective route to achieving the externally mandated goals. In order to do so effectively, educators must have an understanding of how students represent knowledge and develop competence in the domain.

Formative assessments must be grounded in cognitive theories about how students learn a particular subject matter to ensure that instruction centers on what is most important for the next stage of learning, given a learner's current state of understanding. "Research on cognition and learning suggest a broad range of competencies that should be assessed when measuring student achievement, many of which are essentially untapped by current assessments" (Pellegrino 2014, 243). Examples of such competencies include knowledge organization, problem representation, strategy use, metacognition, and participatory activities, such as formulating questions, constructing and evaluating arguments, and contributing to group problem solving. Such competencies and skills are important elements of contemporary theory and research on the acquisition of competence and expertise.

Context: Demographic Background of the District

In the text that follows, the *learning goals* and *learning objectives* that are the focus of the project presented in this scenario have been identified using italicized font. This will allow the reader to see the organic development of learning goals and learning objectives that inform the process of formative assessment.

The Scenario Problem

The major learning goal for Mr. Smith's 11th-grade high school students is to *"understand the research process and to be able to write a thesis paper."* Mr. Smith has broken down the assignment into manageable chunks, however *"students always dread doing the assignment."* Mr. Smith believes *"students are unenthusiastic"* about the project because *"they are not interested in researching,"* whether it be an author or a literary topic.

Mr. Smith values *"**authentic learning**"* and understands the *"importance of student engagement."* He would like *"to encourage students to demonstrate more commitment to their learning."* The districts' *All-County Reads Program* encouraging students to read the same book will be used as an impetus to bring together divergent content areas that are typically taught in isolation. He can use this murder mystery involving government espionage, embezzlement, and cybersecurity breach to create an interdisciplinary research project *"to demonstrate to students* *how the skills and knowledge of various disciplines are used to conduct research in solving real-life problems"* linking four disciplines: English, social studies, science, and information literacy.

Mr. Smith reached out to colleagues who represent different disciplinary areas. Three teachers in English, social studies, and science have agreed to collaborate, as has the school librarian. Everyone agrees that an interdisciplinary approach will benefit the students and help *"to improve the collaborative culture and school climate"* in the building. The group, the Interdisciplinary Consortium wants *"to design an authentic interdisciplinary research project that will incorporate practical and conceptual understandings from each of the four content areas."* They have decided to call themselves the *Interdisciplinary Consortium.*

Students will need *"to use the skills and knowledge from multiple disciplines"* to solve a series of student-generated research questions related to the murder of the character and the circumstances surrounding the homicide. Before the students begin their formal investigation of the crime, ***"they will research the various professions to familiarize themselves with the specific job responsibilities and the educational experience and training required."*** Thus, the project ***"will also provide students with an introduction to a variety of possible career paths."***

Using clues from the novel, students will *"will be able to connect, using various technologies"* actual members of the school community. Students will be able to tap into their specialty areas using well-designed questions and effective interview techniques. Thus, students *"will be encouraged to think and act like scientists"* throughout the project.

Mr. Smith envisions a student-generated thematic research project that will use the novel as the common thread to seamlessly weave the four disciplines: English, social studies, science, and information literacy together. Although the Interdisciplinary Consortium does not have prior experience in determining the success of such an ambitious project, they are willing to learn. The team will work together to plan and co-teach the unit and are committed to the systematic assessment of student learning. They would like to collect data to determine if an interdisciplinary research project improves students' attitudes, knowledge, and skills in each of the four content areas in addition to expanding students' research skills. The consortium's first task was to articulate an overarching research question and they decided upon: *"What instructional factors are most effective for improving research skills acquisition?"*

Using Formative Assessment to Determine Instructional Effectiveness

The consortium wishes to investigate instructional factors that improve research skill acquisition. To accomplish this, the group must first articulate learning goals for each segment of the project along with measurable and observable learning objectives. The most efficient way to do this is through the collaborative creation of a logic model. The primary purpose of the logic model is to articulate the underlying assumptions about how the expected outcomes of the learning program will be reached in the short, medium, and long term. The model provides a graphical representation of the logical relationships between the resources, activities, outputs, and outcomes of the interdisciplinary unit. The logic model provides the basis for a shared understanding of how the interdisciplinary instructional unit will progress. In addition, it facilitates the development of an evaluation framework, systematic data collection, and reporting (Clapham et al. 2017). A suggested template for the logic model is provided in Figure 7.1:

As indicated in the logic model in Figure 7.1, the consortium must identify unifying themes aligned to key ideas across the content areas. Before the team can begin identifying learning goals and objectives, they need to share a common vocabulary and understanding of educational assessment terminology. This is critical to the success of the project because the lack of an agreed-upon vocabulary and the "vagueness of the constitutive and operational definitions" of formative assessment contributes to the lack of understanding of what is actually being studied (Dunn and Mulvenon 2009, 2). Dunn and Mulvenon (2009) warned that without such understanding "empirical evidence supporting the impact of formative assessment on academic achievement will more than likely remain in short supply" (2).

Identifying the Learning Goals and Learning Objectives within the Scenario

For each of the learning goals, the consortium must create a list of learning objectives that are measurable and observable. Suggested learning objectives are provided in the following text. The group will need to do the same for other learning goals they deem valuable for students to attain within each of the disciplines: English, social studies, science, and information literacy. Learning objectives should reflect core capabilities, attitudes, skills, and knowledge that contribute to students' current and subsequent learning. It is important to note that only *after* the learning goals and objectives have been articulated should the consortium begin to plan instruction, for instruction is anything that is intended to help learners attain the learning objectives. Each learning objective provided in the following text is identified by its learning domain.

Figure 7.1
Suggested Logic Model for the Interdisciplinary Unit

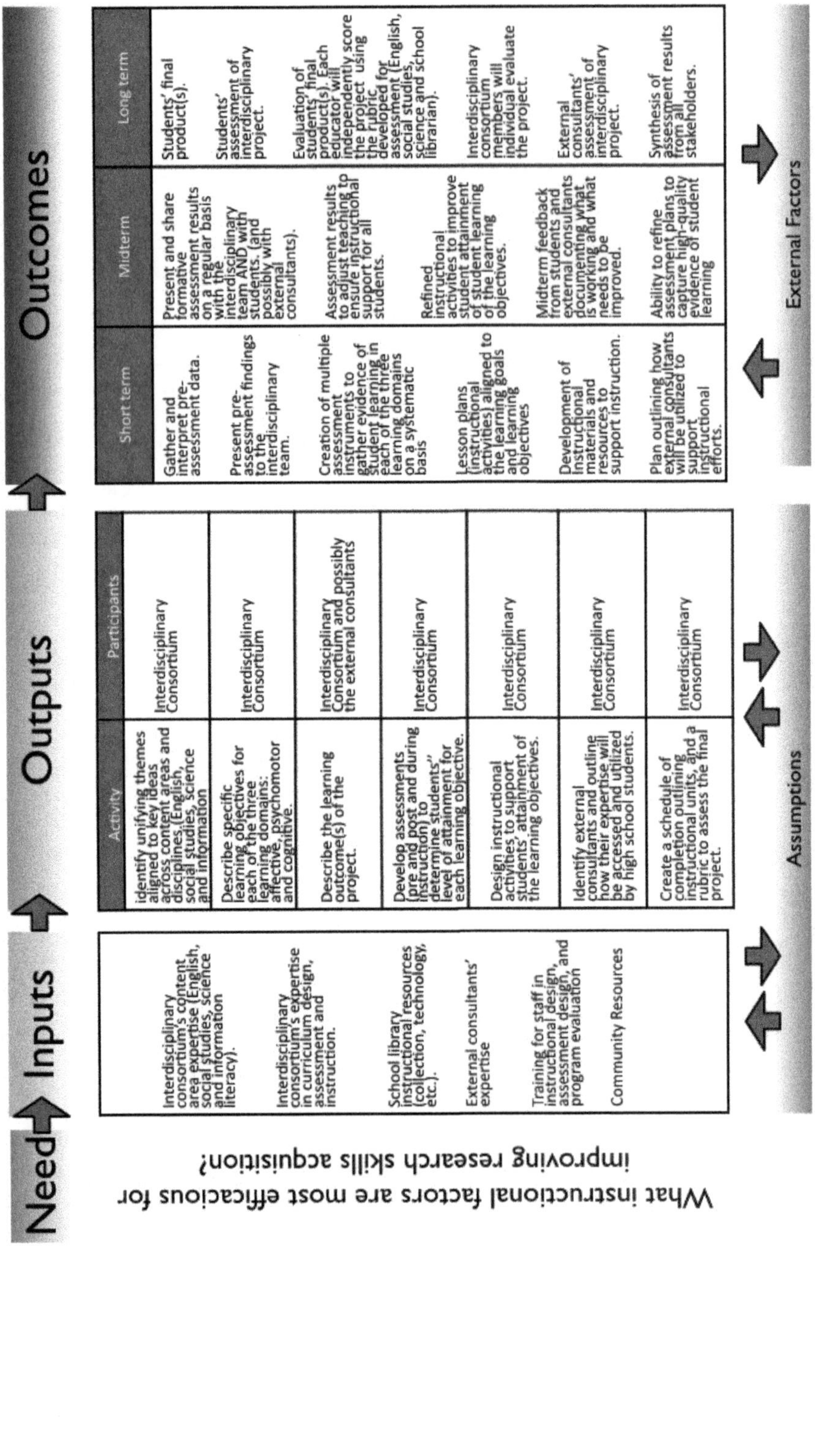

Learning Goals and Objectives of the Scenario

The following learning goals for students are accompanied by suggested learning objectives:

1. *Understand the process of researching and how to write a thesis paper*

   a. Learning objectives:

   (i) Students will select relevant information from a variety of primary and secondary sources related to the physical evidence found at the crime scene. [Cognitive and Psychomotor Learning Domains]
   (ii) Students will evaluate the reliability of eyewitness testimony and justify their positions. [Cognitive and Psychomotor Learning Domains]
   (iii) Students will prepare interview questions that are appropriate for each professional consultant. [Psychomotor and Cognitive Learning Domain]
   (iv) Students will synthesize the information gathered about the crime and provide substantiating evidence for why they believe the suspect is guilty. [Cognitive and Psychomotor Learning Domain]
   (v) Students will confidently present and defend their positions about how and why the murder occurred. [Affective Learning Domain]

2. *Demonstrate how the skills and knowledge of various disciplines are necessary in order to conduct research to solve real-life problems*

   a. Learning objectives:

   (i) Students will use mathematical modeling to predict the probability of guilt for one suspect over another. [Cognitive and Psychomotor Learning Domains]
   (ii) Students will formulate a model by creating and selecting statistical representations that describe relationships between the variables. [Cognitive and Psychomotor Learning Domains]
   (iii) Students will determine time of death by understanding tissue decomposition. [Cognitive and Psychomotor Learning Domains]
   (iv) Students will learn the history and importance of psychological profiling. [Cognitive Domain]
   (v) Students will understand racial disparities in the criminal justice system. [Cognitive Domain and Affective Learning Domains]

3. *Help to improve the collaborative culture (school climate) within the building*

   a. Learning objectives:

   (i) The consortium will conduct a survey on school climate within the building and analyze and interpret the results to determine if there are roadblocks to collaboration. [Affective, Cognitive, and Psychomotor Learning Domains]

(ii) The consortium will understand the process of group dynamics through the various roles and responsibilities each member of the consortium plays. [Affective, Cognitive, and Psychomotor Learning Domains]

(iii) The consortium will document evidence of student achievement and share the results with the students, colleagues, and district leaders. [Cognitive and Psychomotor Learning Domains]

Observed Behaviors within the Scenario

The observed behaviors are presented in the following text with assessments suggested to determine the students' level of mastery of the specified learning objectives. The consortium should engage in a blind assessment of students' work for each assessment. This will help to establish inter-rater reliability and determine the validity of the assessments. The purpose of assessments is to help students attain the learning objectives and to help educators improve their instruction. The onus of students' learning is on educators.

1. *Students always dread the project.* [Affective Learning Domain]

   a. Conduct a preassessment using Google Forms to determine students' preconceptions and misconceptions about the assignment. This can be used to establish a baseline assessment of students' information literacy skills (utilizing a Likert-type **scale**). Examine the various parts of the project and ask students how they feel about each specific part, that is, is it because they must work with a partner? Is it because they lack information seeking skills? Is it because they don't feel comfortable writing? Is it weaknesses in their reading ability? What exactly do the students dislike about the assignment? Use the information gathered from this assessment to inform the design of the project.

   b. Conduct a post-assessment, again using Google Forms, to determine students' attitudes toward the project (using the same questions as the preassessment). Compare how students felt at the beginning and end of the project.

2. *Students are unenthusiastic.* [Affective Learning Domain]

   a. Since this question is similar to question (1), the same pre- and postassessment questionnaire can be used. However, it is important to remember that assessments should be integrated seamlessly as part of instructional activities. Assessments should not interfere with instruction, nor take away from instructional time.

    b. Exit tickets may be used at the end of each class to determine students' level of satisfaction with the content and/or instructional method.

3. ***Students are not interested in researching.*** [Affective Learning Domain]

    a. Conduct a focus group to determine why the research process is dreaded by students. To ensure that this assessment is worthy of instructional time, present it as a "research project" in which students interview other students and report on what features of the research process their peers find problematic. Encouraging students to conduct "research" about their attitudes is a good way to validate students' feelings and demonstrate that their voices and feelings are important.

4. ***Student engagement in and commitment to learning are mixed.*** [Affective Learning Domain]

    a. The consortium will need to determine what student engagement looks like. For example, do engaged students ask more questions? Do engaged students work independently? Are engaged students less likely to be truant? Once the group decides upon the criteria used to determine students' level of engagement, they can then develop assessment measures to show evidence of engagement.

It is critical that the consortium keeps careful records of assessment results and shares the analysis with members on a regular basis. Assessment information provides important evidence about what works and what doesn't work regarding pedagogical and instructional techniques. It is vital that the consortium keeps track of the type of modifications they make to help students master the learning objectives. This will help the consortium answer the following question: What instructional factors are most efficacious for improving research skills acquisition?

Conclusion

How often should educators use formative assessment? Different educators (and educational researchers) will give different answers. Here is Popham's (2014) response:

> To be blunt, properly conceived formative assessment demands a heap of hard thinking on the teacher's part, not to mention the necessary collection of assessment evidence from students. Formative assessment has the clear potential to prove burdensome to teachers and, therefore, dissuade them from using it. But, as you'll soon see, formative assessment helps students learn. If it's not used, then students will be instructionally short-changed (295).

Teachers and librarians should be prepared when they walk into a classroom. Formative assessment (Table 7.1) provides the means to determine how well this is happening and to adjust instruction to help students learn. Formative assessment documents evidence of practice and provides evidence of what students are learning.

Table 7.1
Summary Chart: Formative Assessment

Overall purpose	• Documents evidence of practice where and when learning takes place in schools, classrooms, and libraries • Makes learning visible • Enables educators to systematically collect, analyze, interpret, and use assessment information to help students learn
Advantages	• Provides a chronological record of what, when, and how students learn • Allows educators to monitor students' learning and the effectiveness of instruction • Provides opportunities for educators to improve their instructional practice and while helping students learn
Disadvantages	• Requires preplanning and systematic reflective practice • Requires detailed record keeping • Requires an openness and willingness to modify pedagogical and instructional choices • Requires educators to methodically collect, analyze, interpret, and use assessment information
Steps in process	1. Identify learning goal. 2. Articulate specific learning objectives. 3. Design multiple assessments. 4. Ensure that assessments do not interfere with instructional practice. 5. Develop rubrics that clearly outline criteria used to determine quality of students' work. 6. Share rubrics with students. 7. Develop instructional activities to help students attain the learning objectives. 8. Collect assessment information. 9. Have colleagues use the same assessments and score independently. 10. Share assessment results with colleagues/students. 11. Use assessment information to inform, shape, and/or modify current or subsequent practice. 12. Reflect upon what worked, what and what did not, and what modifications were made to help students master the learning objectives. 13. Create an evaluation of the project to share with other educators in the district.

Table 7.1
Summary Chart: Formative Assessment (Continued)

Data collection methods	• Keep meticulous records of students' assessment results (see support technologies for useful tools). • Use Survey Monkey if appropriate. • Encourage colleagues to score the assignment using the same assessment instruments. • Design pre- and postassessments. • Design instructional activities to target learning objects.
Data analysis methods	Quantitative and qualitative
Support technologies	• Google forms: https://www.google.com/forms/about/ • Survey Monkey: https://www.surveymonkey.com/ • Poll Everywhere: https://www.polleverywhere.com/k12-student-response-system

Glossary of Key Terms

The following definitions are situated in the context of formative assessment; they may differ from the way the terms are used in other contexts. Many of the definitions are based upon the seminal work of Johnson (1967a, 1967b, 1976, 1977) and have been further refined by Doane and Stefl-Mabry (2014).

Instruction: An instruction is anything that is intended to help learners attain learning goals.

Learning goal: A learning goal is a capability to be developed through an educational program.

Learning objective: A learning objective refers to an intended state (what you hope students will learn).

Learning outcome: Learning outcome expresses a present or observed state (what students actually have learned and/or what attitudes, skills, and competencies (knowledge) the learner has actually attained.

Norming: Norming, also known as calibration, is "a process that brings a group of faculty raters together to decide how to assess student work in a consistent way" (Washington State University 2016, 3).

Scale: Scale refers to an ascending sequence of levels of attainment of a learning objective.

Validity: An assessment is valid if it accurately provides evidence of the extent to which a learning goal has been attained.

Further Reading

Black, Paul, and Dylan Wiliam. 2003. " 'In Praise of Educational Research': Formative Assessment." *British Educational Research Journal* 29 (5): 623–37. doi:10.1080/0141192032000133721.

Clapham, Kathleen, Claire Manning, Kathryn Williams, Ginger O'Brien, and Margaret Sutherland. 2017. "Using a Logic Model to Evaluate the Kids Together Early Education Inclusion Program for Children with Disabilities and Additional Needs." *Evaluation and Program Planning* 61: 96–105. doi:10.1016/j.evalprogplan.2016.12.004.

Johnson, Maurice. 1977. *Intentionality in Education: A Conceptual Model of Curricular and Instructional Planning and Evaluation.* Albany, NY: Center for Curriculum and Research Services.

McMillan, James H., ed. 2013. *SAGE Handbook of Research on Classroom Assessment.* Los Angeles, CA: SAGE.

Popham, W. James. 2014. *Classroom Assessment: What Teachers Need to Know.* 7th ed. Boston, MA: Pearson.

Stefl-Mabry, J. and Doane, W. E. J. 2014. "Teaching to Assess: Lessons Learned When Faculty and Preservice Educators Learn to Assess and Assess to Learn." Paper presented at the American Educational Research Association Annual Meeting, Philadelphia, PA. AERA Online Paper Repository.

Chapter 8

Participant Observation

Melissa Gross, Professor
School of Information, Florida State University

Introduction to Participant Observation

Participant observation research is a type of data collection in which the researcher is part of the environment under study and the subjects of the research know that they are being observed. Participant observation research is a natural extension of the process many teachers engage in when they observe what happens in their classroom. Observing a class is a skill that librarians and teachers use all the time to assess their own work as well as student understanding and progress. For many practitioners, this is an informal process of paying attention and noting what is working well and where the challenges are in achieving the desired learning outcomes with students. The participant observation method of data collection builds on these classroom skills by formalizing the process of observing, making the process even more deliberate and reflective.

Participant observation is a form of qualitative research that is used to gather information in authentic situations, such as the classroom or library and is motivated by a desire to understand the environment through the eyes of the people being observed. When researchers take on the role of participant observer, they are able to avoid the limitations of other types of research, such as experimental research, which often places subjects in artificial situations, and the constraints of survey research, which requires highly structured questions, often resulting in a superficial level of understanding.

Several things are considered when deciding to employ participant observation as a research method to assess teaching and learning. A researcher considering taking on the role of participant observer should deeply consider the drawbacks of studying a group that he or she is already integrated into (e.g., one's own classroom). Not only is it likely that the researcher will have an effect on the group being observed, but it is also very likely that the researcher will have difficulty remaining objective. The difficulty here stems from the likelihood that the researcher may have preformed opinions about specific individuals and/or the class as a group that will color the observations. These issues can be minimized by asking someone else to do the data collection. For example, researchers, professors or doctoral students, from a nearby college or university might be interested in helping out. Other colleagues in the school are another option for finding a more objective observer if needed. Another approach might be to enlist multiple observers and to work as a team. Having more than one person collecting and analyzing the data can provide a check on researcher bias as findings will need to be confirmed by others in the research group.

Special skills needed for this type of data collection are the qualities of being a good observer, which means being able to pay attention; accurately document the context, words, and behaviors witnessed; and being self-conscious about personal bias and the effect the participant observer is having on the research subjects and other people such as teachers, librarians, teacher aides, and administrators operating in the environment.

Another consideration is time. The researcher will need to set aside and then protect the time needed to conduct the research. The researcher will need to develop (and stick to) a plan for when observations will be made, set aside time for writing **field notes**, time to meet with other researchers if this is a team effort, and time to organize and analyze the data as the project rolls out. Participant observation can be carried out in the school context with relatively few costs beyond time. Paper, or a computer or tablet, can be used for keeping track of research plans and for recording quick notes and field notes collected as the research is conducted.

Just like other research methods, begin by developing a research question and then decide who, what, when, and how the observations will be used to address the research question. Next, consider the need for permission to proceed with the research plan. If the research objective is to improve teaching, formal permission may not be needed. However, to share what with others in presentations, writing, or any other type of public dissemination, get permission from parents and students. Check to see what the policy is at the institution or school district for documenting consent from parents and assent from students. Participation in research must be voluntary and students must be free to decline participation without feeling like their grades or their relationship with their teacher or their school will be jeopardized.

Participant Observation as a Research Method

Like other research methods, an observational study should start with an explicit statement of what the researcher wants to find out, that is, with a research question firmly in mind. Once the research question is clear, it is important to develop background knowledge that will help to inform the research design. Background knowledge includes developing a command of the research that has already been completed on the topic as well as understanding the context in which the research will take place. Luckily in the sample scenario, "Collaboration and Research Engagement," Mr. Smith already has a good understanding of student demographics and has acknowledged his own stake in the outcome of this research in terms of meeting his Goals for Growth that are part of his annual assessment.

Mr. Smith's research team developed the following research question: "What instructional factors are most efficacious for improving research skills acquisition?" While in many ways, this is a fine question, it is also very broad and expands the focus away from what they have already accomplished. A better question might be "How does a cross-disciplinary research assignment affect student engagement, critical thinking, and use of technology in the classroom?" This will allow the research team to focus on what is actually happening with students as they complete the collaborative assignment and clearly specifies those aspects of research skills acquisition in which the research team is particularly interested.

The next step is to make sure that all of the concepts identified in the research question have been defined. The concepts, or variables, in this research question that need to be defined are cross-disciplinary research assignment, student engagement, critical thinking, and technology use. The cross-disciplinary research assignment could be the murder mystery assignment already developed and piloted by the research group. Defining the other terms can happen through discussion within the team and may be aided by doing some research to see how others have defined these concepts. The research team will want to be clear about what student engagement, critical thinking, and technology use look like ahead of time, in order to be able to clearly identify these behaviors in their observations and to ensure that the observations of all members of the research team are measuring the same behaviors.

The next decisions to make are who will be observed, when and where the observations will take place, and how observations will be made. All of these questions must be answered before data collection can start. In the scenario for this section, Collaboration and Research Engagement, the population of interest is students in 11th-grade English, history, and science classes at the school where Herbert Smith teaches. So the "who" to be observed is the students.

As with other research, selecting participants is guided by understanding who has the information that the researcher needs in order to address the research question. Because Mr. Smith's research team is interested in student behavior related to an assignment, it makes sense for them to observe the students as they are oriented to the assignment and as they complete the work. In participant observation, the focus of the research is often on one particular site or a specific program, with the goal of developing a rich understanding of the context under study. A weakness of this approach is that it is not possible to predict what might happen in other classrooms based on this one participation observation study. Of course, this does not mean that what is learned may not be useful to other students in other classrooms. However, in order to know how transferrable the study's findings are, future additional investigations will be needed. It is possible to design a study using more than one school. Studying multiple locations at once is another way to determine whether the effects observed at Mr. Smith's school are also observed in other classrooms with other students.

Data Collection Procedures

Mr. Smith's research team is interested in student behaviors while they are completing the cross-disciplinary research assignment. The specific behaviors the participant researchers will be observing are those identified in the research question: student engagement, critical thinking, and use of technology in the classroom.

In performing the observations, it is important for the researchers to be self-aware about their own behaviors and to be as objective as they can be about what they are seeing. The researchers will want to be careful to notice their own biases and to be mindful that they are not influencing outcomes through their own behaviors. Because the observers are also participants in what is happening in the classroom or library, it will be difficult to take extensive notes while enrolled in these classes. Where they will be observed might be in one or more of the three classrooms and/ or the school library. This is a decision the research team will need to make based on how the assignment is to be carried out. The research team will also need to decide when the students will be observed and who will do the observing.

Fit between Method and the Research Question

The research question to be addressed is as follows: how does a cross-disciplinary research assignment affect student engagement, critical thinking, and use of technology in the classroom? Participant observation is a useful method in this case because the focus of the research is on student behavior within the context of the complexities of what goes on in the classroom or library environment. Participant observation allows the researcher to be honest about the fact that data are being collected and to remain engaged in the activities of the group. Further, it allows the researcher to form an opinion based on in-depth descriptions of actual activities as they are experienced in real time. Another strength of this approach is that it can be used to verify or help the researcher understand other related data that are collected in other ways. For example, what is learned from the participant observations can deepen understanding of students' performance on their final research papers.

Participant observation can also be performed using multiple observers. Having more than one observer can make the job of observing easier and also increase the validity and reliability of the resulting data, by comparing where the observations agree, clearing up inaccuracies in the data, and making it possible to talk through differences in perceptions of what happened during the observation period.

Criteria for Determining or Recruiting Research Participants

Mr. Smith's research team is interested in student behaviors while they are completing the cross-disciplinary research assignment. The specific behaviors the participant researchers will be observing are those identified in the research question: student engagement, critical thinking, and use of technology in the classroom.

In performing the observations, it is important for the researchers to be self-aware about their own behaviors and to be as objective as they can be about what they are seeing. The researchers will want to be careful to notice their own biases and to be mindful that they are not influencing outcomes through their own behaviors. Because the observers are also participants in what is happening in the classroom or library, it will be difficult to take extensive notes while observing. It will be possible to jot down quick notes about behaviors, things students say, and personal reactions and thoughts, but these notes will not be comprehensive.

As soon as possible after the observation period is over, the participant observer must sit down and write up field notes in order to ensure that as much of what happened as possible can be captured. Detail is important, so the closer to the actual observation that field notes can be written down, the more complete they will be. If too much time goes by, details will be fuzzy, and certain events may be forgotten. It is important for the researcher to capture what was observed as objectively as possible. The researcher will also want to capture his or her own thoughts, any personal bias he or she might have noticed, and new questions about student behaviors that come to mind. In writing field notes, many researchers differentiate between what was observed and personal reactions by enclosing research self-notes in brackets. It can also sometimes be helpful to draw a map of the room being observed, noting who was where in the room, as part of the field notes.

To stir memory, researchers can think about the specific students, who they interacted with, the setting, and how the setting may have affected certain behaviors, unplanned activities that happened, and body language. Also think about questions that were asked by students and how these questions were addressed, as well as other comments and reactions heard in the room. Set off what people said in quotation marks so that it is clear in the notes when someone is speaking. For Mr. Smith's research team, they may also want to keep a copy of the assignment with their notes to help think about how the assignment is related to behaviors.

It is also possible to video record during the observation period if the equipment is available, but give this some thought. The video will capture a lot of data and make a record that the research team can review and discuss. On the downside, it will be difficult to capture all activity in the video, and it will make the fact that an observation is being made very conspicuous. Knowing they are being video recorded may affect how the students behave, making the situation less authentic.

Data Analysis Methods

Notes and field notes are the data in a participant observation study. It is important to spend time reviewing and thinking about them from the very beginning of the study. Review notes between observations. In participant observation, like other qualitative methods, data analysis is a cyclical activity. What is learned from one observation should inform how the researcher approaches the next observation. When there is a research team, it is important for the team to review all the data and to discuss what the data mean and what is being learned that addresses the research question. In reading, rereading, and thinking about the data, it is important to differentiate always between the observation and the researcher's and teams' interpretation of the data. This is why putting thoughts and musings in brackets in field notes is important. Keep in mind what the research question is asking and mark up the notes to indicate which parts of the data relate to each question, new thoughts about what to observe next time, and themes or behaviors that repeat, as well as anything new or unique that comes out of the observations.

Data analysis can be done "by hand" as described earlier, or qualitative analysis software can be used to enter, categorize, and mark up the data. Some of the most popular programs of this type are NVivo, HyperRESEARCH, Dedoose, and ATLAS.ti. Note that these programs are aids to thinking about the data; they do not automatically analyze the data for the researcher. The work of thinking about the data is still the researcher's job.

Drawing Conclusions and Presenting Results

In qualitative analysis, the results of the study are presented mainly in narrative form. The researcher tells the story of the study as a way of explaining what happened, the logic that connects the observations to the interpretation and how the researcher, or in this case, Mr. Smith's research team, came to their conclusions about the relationship between the cross-disciplinary research assignment they developed and observations of student engagement, critical thinking, and use of technology in the classroom as the students worked through the assignment. One of the strengths of qualitative research is the ability to provide deep descriptions, and so descriptions and discussion should be detailed and follow a clear narrative line of thought. In the report, researchers use the data in their notes and field notes to help support and illuminate the points they make in describing what was learned. Text from the notes and field notes are typically placed in quotation marks in the report so that it is clear when the researcher is presenting data and when the data are being discussed. It is also possible to include maps, drawings, and so on as part of the report if such aids can help clarify the points that need to be made.

Why Use This Research Method?

As noted earlier, participant observation has many advantages for researchers who want to study actual behavior in authentic situations. Observation methods are perhaps the most valid way to study behavior. Other methods, such as survey and interviews that ask participants to describe their behavior, tend to have weak validity. This is not to say that participants want to be deceptive, but rather that people tend to be poor observers of their own behavior. When research data are collected in the context in which the behaviors of interest take place, this can result in insights about classroom behavior that other methods would not reveal. The data resulting from participant observations can be used for either descriptive or evaluative research purposes.

Participant observation research has at least two ethical advantages over other types of observation research. These stem from the fact that the researcher is able to reveal that research is going to take place to those who are going to be observed. While people often change their behavior when they know they are being observed, the participant observer can overcome this by building rapport with the group, so that they feel comfortable in the researcher's presence. In most cases, as the research progresses the situation is likely to begin to feel normal to participants and they will be less likely to behave abnormally. This may be especially true in classroom situations where students are used to and expect to be observed by teachers and librarians.

The second ethical advantage of participant observation is that subjects know they are being observed. This knowledge allows them the ability to make an informed choice about what behaviors, knowledge, attitudes, and so on. they want to display or keep hidden.

Perhaps the main difficulty of participant observation is the need for the researcher to maintain objectivity throughout the process of collecting, analyzing, and reporting the data. This is especially critical for librarians and teachers working with students they already know and have established relationships with. The nature of qualitative data is subjective and can be influenced by the personal attitudes and beliefs of the researcher. This is often referred to as researcher bias. A good qualitative researcher will work to be alert to their biases, to recognize and

Table 8.1
Summary Chart: Participant Observation

Overall purpose	To understand a phenomenon as it occurs in a specific environment
Advantages	• Authentic situation • Participants know they are part of a study and can choose what they want to reveal • Researcher can be candid about their role in the environment • Most direct way to measure behavior • Will reveal insights that methods cannot
Disadvantages	• Potential for personal bias to affect findings • Potential for reactive effects • May affect behavior of participants who are self-conscious about being observed
Steps in process	1. Develop research question and define variables. 2. Determine who or what will be observed. 3. Decide when observations will be made. 4. Perform observations. 5. Analyze data and draw conclusions.
Data collection methods	• Quick notes • Field notes • Video recording
Data analysis methods	Content analysis of notes, field notes, transcripts
Support technologies	• Can video record observations • Use pad or computer for note writing • Qualitative software such as NVivo, HyperRESEARCH, Dedoose, or ATLAS.ti

own them, and to do their best to keep them from affecting the data they collect and the inferences they draw from the data. See Table 8.1 for a summary of participant observation research methodology.

Glossary of Key Term

Field notes: These are notes taken by researchers during or after observations of the phenomenon being studied.

Further Reading

Fine, Gary Alan, and Kent L. Sandstrom. 1988. *Knowing Children: Participation Observation with Minors. Qualitative Research Methods Series, Volume 15.* Newbury Park, CA: Sage.

Hubbard, Ruth Shagoury, and Brenda Miller Power. 2003. *The Art of Classroom Inquiry: A Handbook for Teacher-Researchers.* Revised ed. Portsmouth: Heinemann.

Mills, Geoffrey E. 2013 *Action Research: A Guide for the Teacher Researcher.* 5th ed. Upper Saddle River, NJ: Pearson.

Pellegrini, Anthony D. 2013. *Observing Children in Their Natural Worlds: A Methodological Primer.* 3rd ed. New York: Psychology Press.

Schutt, Russell K. 2015. *Investigating the social world.* Thousand Oaks, CA: Sage.

Chapter 9

Assessing Learning with Rubrics

*Megan Oakleaf, Associate Professor and Director
of Instructional Design
School of Information Studies, Syracuse University*

Introduction to Rubrics

Rubrics are essential tools in the librarians' assessment toolbox. Rubrics describe the parts and levels of performance of a particular task, product, or service (Hafner and Hafner 2003). Rubrics are used to judge quality (Popham 2003) across a broad range of subjects (Moskal 2000). Rubrics can take the form of checklists, Likert scales, or **full model rubrics**. Full model rubrics are the most descriptive type of rubric. Formatted in a chart or table, full model rubrics include "criteria" or indicators of a performance down one column and levels of performance across the top row of a table (Callison 2000).

The first of two components that comprise a rubric is *criteria*. Criteria are the essential tasks or hallmarks that indicate a successful performance (Wiggins 1996). Performance descriptors are the second component of rubrics. Performance descriptors "spell out what is needed, with respect to each evaluative criterion . . . [for] a high rating versus a low rating" (Popham 2003).

In a checklist rubric, criteria are the focus, and only two performance descriptors exist: observed or not observed, as shown in Figure 9.1. Likert scale rubrics include criteria and performance level descriptors, usually represented by numbers, as depicted in Figure 9.2. Full model rubrics provide criteria; performance level descriptors, usually represented by words, as shown in Figure 9.3; and detailed performance descriptions in each intersecting cell of the rubric table, as seen in Figure 9.4.

Rubrics have two main categories: holistic and analytic. A **holistic rubric** "score[s] the overall process or product as a whole, without judging the component parts separately" (Nitko 1996). Holistic rubrics provide one score for a whole product or performance based on an overall impression. **Analytic rubrics** "divide . . . a product or performance into essential traits or dimensions so that they can be judged separately—one analyzes a product or performance for

Figure 9.1
Checklist Rubric

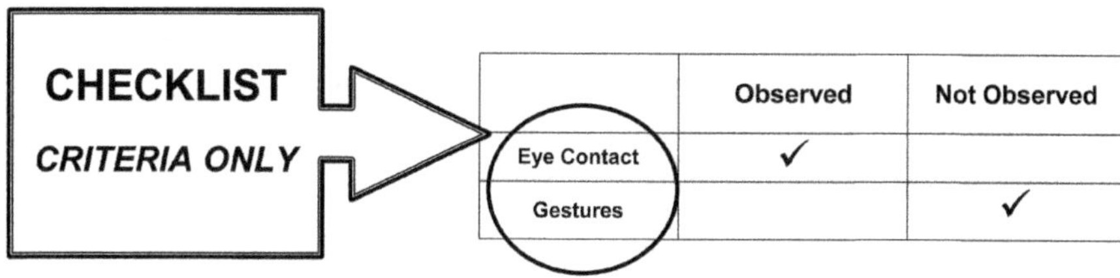

essential traits. A separate score is provided for each trait" (Arter and McTighe 2001). Individual scores can be summed to form a total score from an analytic rubric (Nitko 1996). By combining rich descriptions of learning with numerical scores, rubrics can serve as both quantitative and qualitative in nature. Examples of analytic information literacy rubrics can be found at Rubric Assessment of Information Literacy Skills (RAILS 2017b).

Analytic rubrics can be further divided into two subcategories: task/performance and developmental. Task/performance analytic rubrics assess the component parts of an artifact of learning; provide separate judgments of each component (criterion), as well as a summed total judgment; offer more detailed assessment data; give more specific feedback to learners' providers; and are better choices for evaluating complex artifacts of learning. Examples of analytic information literacy rubrics can be found at RAILS (2017c). Developmental analytic rubrics assess an artifact of learning as a whole, provide single, overall judgment of quality, are faster to use and less burdensome for large-scale assessments, and are usually sufficient for evaluating simple artifacts of learning (Depaul 2017). Developmental analytic rubrics are best for assessments used over multiple

Figure 9.2
Likert Rubric

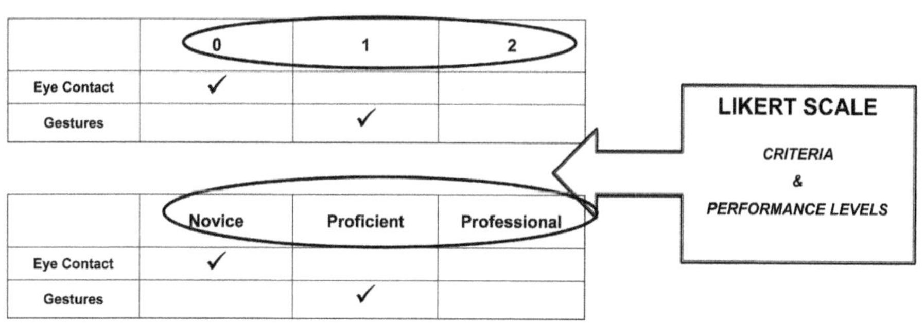

Figure 9.3
Example of Performance Level Descriptors

mastery, progressing, emerging, satisfactory, marginal, proficient,
high, middle, beginning, advanced,
novice, intermediate, sophisticated, competent, professional,
exemplary, needs work, adequate,
developing, accomplished, distinguished, introductory

assignments, time, programs, or groups. They are not primarily intended to assess an artifact, but rather to answer the question "To what extent are students developing a particular skill, ability, or value?" (Depaul 2017).

Description of the Research Method

The Research Question

In real life, it can be difficult to isolate and articulate a research question. Side issues, uncontrolled circumstances, and mismatches between what one wants to know and what one has the resources to know all can stymie librarians and educators seeking to define and investigate a clear research question. The scenario provided in this case is no exception.

In the provided scenario, Mr. Smith wants to determine whether a new instructional approach helps students become more engaged, and his colleagues "are interested in doing some research on whether the students' research skills improved with the use of collaborative teaching, with the exploration of questions and topics that interest them, with the use of research led with expert guidance, and with the use of technology." As a group of three teachers and a librarian, they determine that their research question is "What instructional factors are most efficacious for improving research skills acquisition?"

Figure 9.4
Full Model Rubric (Oakleaf 2009a)

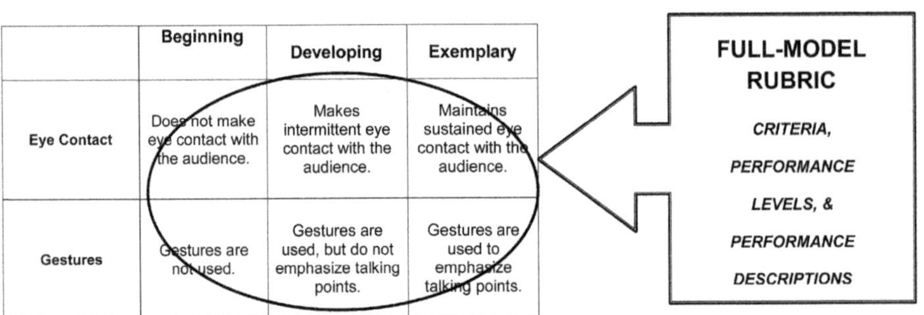

Unfortunately, their separate expressed desires for research and their initial research question do not match. The former seeks to determine (1) whether students are more engaged and (2) whether their different approach to teaching research skills improved student acquisition of those skills; the latter seeks to compare instructional factors. In theory, the former questions could be investigated. The latter cannot be, as the group has not set up a teaching situation in which different instructional factors can be compared. Rather they changed from one approach, assigning research papers focused on authors or literary topics, to a completely different and multilayered one—assigning "research" without precisely defined outcomes or a defined assignment output, focusing on a different topic, setting up a competitive atmosphere, collaborating across multiple subject areas and teachers, augmenting with undefined technology, incorporating outside experts, and adding role playing. By changing so many instructional approaches at once, they cannot isolate the efficacy of the individual instructional factors. Thus, their expressed research question must be abandoned until they can deploy the approaches in a more systematic way.

However, Mr. Smith and his team could potentially seek to investigate whether their instructional changes increased student engagement or improved student research skills, if they have artifacts collected from previous years and from the current approach that could be subjected to assessment and analysis. Thus, Mr. Smith could restate his research questions as follows: (1) Have the current changes to his instructional approach resulted in increased student engagement? (2) Have the current changes to his instructional approach resulted in improved research skills?

Fit between Method and Questions

Rubrics can be used to assess student learning if (1) the educators involved can clearly articulate what achievement of the learning outcomes "looks like" when enacted by students and (2) artifacts that demonstrate the achievement of outcomes are available. To use rubrics in this scenario, Mr. Smith and his team would need to articulate what student engagement looks like and what student research skills look like and then identify and gather artifacts of student work that demonstrate student performance of engagement and research skills.

For example, Mr. Smith and his team may decide that student engagement looks like

- eye contact,
- taking notes,
- actively listening and reacting,
- asking questions,
- responding to questions,

- participating and complying with requests, and
- interacting with other students. (Johnson 2012)

If Mr. Smith has access to artifacts that capture this behavior (or the lack thereof) from previous years and the current year, in which his changes have occurred, then he may be able to develop and deploy a rubric to assess those artifacts. Artifacts might include video of students listening to lectures, completed checklists of classroom observers, notes recorded by students, or captured student interactions.

Likewise, if Mr. Smith can define "research skills" clearly and in depth, using standard information literacy research or some other source, and has artifacts and research papers from the past and present, then the team could create and apply a rubric to assess the changes in skill levels. One complicating factor is that the scenario does not clearly state what the current artifact of student learning is, but one might assume that is an oversight in the scenario, rather than in reality.

Criteria for Determining Research Participants

Rubric assessment in among the more time-consuming approaches for investigating student learning. Consequently, it is important for educators to determine whether they need to assess all artifacts or only a sample. If students need to receive grades and the rubric is determined to be a grading tool, then all students in the population must be assessed. However, if educators are investigating the efficacy of an approach and not assigning grades using the rubric in question, then assessing only a sample of student artifacts is a much more practical and time-saving approach. If it is determined that only a sample of artifacts needs to be assessed, another decision is required: whether to use a random or **purposive sample**. Purposive samples can be constructed in a number of ways, and students may be included or excluded from the sample based on a predetermined set of characteristics, such as GPA, gender, ethnicity, at-risk status, and so on. Educators seeking a random sample may find that using a random number table simplifies the process of selecting artifacts to include or exclude from the set of artifacts to be assessed.

Data Collection Procedures

Conducting a rubric assessment of student learning is a multistep process. Educators must design the performance assessment that will generate the learning artifact for assessment, and they must decide whether to collect all artifacts that result from that assignment or limit themselves to a sample.

Educators must also create the rubric that they intend to use to assess the artifacts and collect their learning data. To start, educators should gather raw materials that will support creation of a rubric, including assignment sheets, relevant example artifacts, and so on. Then, they should commence rubric creation, following the four-part recommended rubric creation process (Stevens and Levi 2004). First, educators should reflect on the learning they would like to see demonstrated in the artifacts. They may ask themselves the following questions:

- What outcomes should students achieve?
- What does achievement of those outcomes look like?
- What do the best students do when demonstrating achievement of these outcomes?

Second, educators should list each of the ideas generated by their reflection activity. Stevens recommends brainstorming using Post-it® notes to record ideas from their reflections, one idea per post-it. This process can be completed independently or with a team. Third, ideas from the listing activity should be grouped into categories and labeled with a word or phrases; these words and phrases will become rubric criteria, usually entered down the left column of a rubric grid. Next, educators can determine the number of performance levels that will be included in the draft rubric. Typically, three to five levels are recommended. Once the columns for each level are created, a performance level description can be entered at the top of each. Finally, educators can use their post-it ideas to draft descriptions that will complete the intersecting cells of the rubric. Best practices suggest drafting the highest, most proficient level first, followed by the lowest level, and then wrapping up with the middle levels. Once an initial draft is composed, educators should share their draft with students and/or potential rubric raters and revise as needed.

If the learning artifacts that will be assessed have not already been gathered, that is the next stage of the process. Artifacts may be collected in print or via electronic means.

Next, educators should determine whether rubric scorers should be normed before rating student artifacts. The **norming** process follows a multistep process that is described elsewhere (Holmes and Oaklead 2013).

Once preparation is completed, scorers can view, analyze, and score each artifact, one at a time, using the rubric. Rubric scores may be entered via printed or electronic forms.

Data Analysis Methods

Once educators have assessed all artifacts in the sample or population, tallying basic results is straightforward. Typically, rubric assessment results are processed by summing the number of students whose learning performance falls into each cell of a rubric. This number can be shared in the raw as a total number of students exhibiting that level of performance for a given criterion. Alternatively, the raw number can be converted to a percent. Educators can report that X number or Y percent of students exhibited the performance as described in that cell of the rubric for each criterion. In some cases, rubrics may be anchored with numbers or points assigned to each cell. In that situation, educators can also report average scores for each criterion or sum criteria scores to express a "total" score on the rubric.

In some circumstances, rubrics may be used to make "high stakes" decisions. If major decisions are to be made based on the rubric assessment results, a statistically rigorous approach to investigating rubric scorer inter-rater reliability is appropriate (Oakleaf 2009b).

Presentation of Results

Once the analysis of a rubric assessment is completed, the presentation of those results is simple and intuitive. Educators can replicate the rubric and include the raw or percent scores of all students included in the analysis in each cell of the rubric. Easily understandable in both quantitative and qualitative terms, stakeholder audiences can quickly perceive how many or what percent of students have achieved each level of performance for each learning criterion. Furthermore, a well-written rubric lays out the continuum of expected learning performances, so audiences can also view the position of current students relative to desired learning goals.

Drawing Conclusions

At the end of a rubric assessment project, educators have a finite number of conclusions, such as the following:

- Students have achieved learning outcomes to a lesser, greater, or "as expected" extent. If students fall short, changes to instruction are merited. If students exceed expectations, educators might celebrate and then plan how they can communicate and extend the learning they've documented.
- The artifacts did or did not effectively or adequately capture performances of learning outcomes. If the artifacts did not elicit or encapsulate evidence of learning outcomes, the assignments and assessments that generated the artifacts should be evaluated and revised.
- The rubric did or did not effectively or adequately articulate performances of learning outcomes. If the rubric was ineffective or lacking, it should be evaluated and revised before another round of assessment commences.
- The raters did or did not effectively deploy the rubric. If multiple raters lacked consistency, they may need to be retrained, re-normed, or interviewed to surface the issues that diminished inter-rater reliability.

In the case of Mr. Smith, he and his team may find that their new teaching approach increased student engagement and/or improved student research skills—or that it did not. In most cases, rubric assessment becomes part of a continuous assessment cycle that seeks to improve instruction and assessment at each turn of the wheel (Oakleaf 2007, 2009a).

Why Use This Research Method

Rubrics offer a number of benefits to librarians seeking to engage in assessment. First, rubrics provide librarians the opportunity to discuss, determine, and communicate agreed-upon values (Callison 2000). Librarians who create rubrics in partnership with others must come to agreement with their collaborators upon the criteria by which student learning will be analyzed and evaluated. They must also come to consensus about what the different performance levels of each criterion "look like." Through the rubric development process, librarians engage in meaningful discussions that result in shared views of the learning outcomes under scrutiny. Once a rubric is created, it can be used to represent consensus views of librarians and their collaborators. They can also be employed to communicate shared values to others, including students, teachers, and other stakeholders (Stevens and Levi 2004). Finally, they help "combat . . . accusations that evaluators do not know what they are looking for" in a learning performance (Bresciani, Zelna, and Anderson 2004).

Rubrics offer a second important benefit: descriptive, yet easily digestible, descriptors (Bresciani, Zelna, and Anderson 2004). Because full model rubrics include descriptions of the key components of student learning at a number of performance levels, they provide detailed information for decision making. At the same time, rubric data is easily simplified. For example, one might report that a student performed at a "developing" level during 80% of observed performances. If more detail is required, the rubric definition of "developing" can be added to the percentage to make it more meaningful. In this way, rubric data can be reported in simple percentages or with details described in the rubric as the situation and audience require.

Rubrics offer librarians engaged in learning assessment a third significant benefit. Because rubrics analyze agreed-upon, detailed descriptions of library activities, they can prevent inaccuracy of scoring (Popham 2003), bias (Bresciani, Zelna, and Anderson 2004), and subjectivity (Moskal 2000). Since rubrics guide librarians to focus on essential criteria (Callison 2000), they can assess products and services more easily and objectively (Bernier 2004). Even in team or collaborative environments, rubric evaluations are "likely to be reasonably objective and consistent" (Bernier 2004) though there are documented barriers to these benefits. For example, rubric scorers who are unfamiliar with a learning outcomes-based approach to assessment, the content of a particular rubric, or the constraints and requirements of the artifacts of student learning serving as the basis of the rubric assessment may fail to provide valid and reliable scores, even when using a well-designed rubric (Oakleaf 2007).

Finally, rubrics provide the benefit of revealing the expectations of instructors and librarians. As a consequence, students benefit from greater "fairness" and can focus on achieving, rather than deciphering, learning goals. They also provide students with feedback about what they have already learned and what they have yet to learn. Thus, rubrics support student learning, self-evaluation, and metacognition.

The primary barrier to rubric assessment is the time required to develop and apply rubric to student artifacts (RAILS 2017). When rubrics are used by multiple scorers and the rubric results may have high stakes impacts, then rubric scorers must also participate in a norming process. This process adds to the time demands of a rubrics approach to assessment (Holmes and Oakleaf 2013).

Additional rubric barriers can be attributed to flaws in rubric design. Rubrics that are too long, too vague, or include jargon are problematic for both students and raters. Likewise, rubrics that lack either consistency or differentiation across performance levels are difficult for raters to use in a reliable fashion. When rubrics emphasize quantity such as how many times a behavior or skill is or is not demonstrated over how well a behavior or skill is demonstrated, educators miss an opportunity to place a student's learning on a continuum of development. Finally, overly negative or emotive wording in the lower levels of rubric performance descriptions can result in a punitive, rather than encouraging and supportive, experience for students (Oakleaf 2009c). A summary chart of this assessment method is presented in Table 9.1.

Table 9.1
Summary Chart: Rubrics

Overall purpose	To assess student learning outcomes Can also be adapted to assess other library services and resources
Advantages	• Agreed-upon learning goals • Detailed data, easily summed for reporting • Combat subjective, biased scoring • Reveal "hidden" teacher expectations • Support student learning, self-evaluation, and metacognition

Disadvantages	• Time
	• Common errors
	  ◦ Too long
	  ◦ Too "jargony"
	  ◦ Too vague
	  ◦ Inconsistent across performance levels (using parallel language helps)
	  ◦ Lack of differentiation across performance levels
	  ◦ Too much emphasis on quantity (how many times) over quality (how well)
	  ◦ Too negative at lower levels

Steps in process	• Gather raw materials that will support creation of a rubric.
	• Follow the three-part recommended rubric creation process.
	  ◦ Reflect
	  ◦ List
	  ◦ Group
	• Share draft rubric with students and/or potential rubric raters and revise as needed.

Table 9.1
Summary Chart: Rubrics (Continued)

Data collection methods	For analysis: • Gather learning artifacts. • Determine whether to assess all artifacts or only a sample. If a sample is selected, decide whether to use a random or purposive sample. Random samples may involve the use of a random number table. • Determine whether rubric scorers must be normed before rating student artifacts. The norming process follows a multistep process. • Score one artifact at a time, using the rubric. Rubric scores may be entered on printed forms or automated means may be employed.
Data analysis methods	For reporting: • Sum the number of students whose learning performance falls into each cell of a rubric to report as a total number or convert to a percent. Then report that X number or Y percent of students exhibited a performance as described in that cell of the rubric. • A statistically rigorous approach to investigating rubric scorer inter-rater reliability may be useful on occasion.
Support technologies	N/A

Glossary of Key Terms

Analytic rubric: Analytic rubrics "divide … a product or performance into essential traits or dimensions so that they can be judged separately—one analyzes a product or performance for essential traits. A separate score is provided for each trait" (Arter and McTighe 2001). Analytic rubrics can be further divided into two subcategories: task/performance and developmental.

Assessment (the product or outcome): information on the extent to which intended learning outcomes have been attained.

Assessment (the process & instrument): the means by which information on the extent of attainment of learning goal is obtained.

Core capability: A capability that contributes to concurrent and subsequent learning and/or has powerful application to the world outside of the learning environment.

Curriculum: A structured set of learning goals.

Educational evaluation: the use of information to improve (increase the value of) an educational program.

Educational program: any intentional effort directed to the attainment of one or more learning goals.

Formative assessment: Assessment is a process carried out to form or inform an educational program for currently participating learners.

Full model rubric: Full model rubrics are the most descriptive type of rubric. Formatted in a chart of table, full model rubrics include "criteria" or indicators of a performance down one column and levels of performance across the tope row of a table (Callison 2000).

Grading and grades: Aggregating disparate source of information e.g., assessments, tests, attendance, student behavior into an overall value referred to as a grade, e.g., midterm grade, course grade.

Holistic rubric: Holistic rubrics provide one score for a whole product or performance based on an overall impression.

Instructional worthiness: educators need to constant ask themselves: "Is this an activity worthy of instructional time?" If the answer is no, then valuable time should not be spent on the activity. Instructional time is wasted and learners experience frustration when they are asked to perform tasks that have little connection to what is being taught and has little value beyond the completion of the task.

Norming: Norming, also known as calibration, is "a process that brings a group of faculty raters together to decide how to assess student work in a consistent way" (Washington State University 2016).

Purposive sample: A purposive sample is a "non-probability sample that is selected based on characteristics of a population and the objective of the study" (Crossman 2017).

Rubric: A scheme for characterizing the levels of attainment of a learning objective.

Testing and tests: Aggregating the results of assessments of disparate learning objectives into an overall score.

Further Reading

Belanger, Jackie, Ning Zou, Jenny Rushing Mills, Claire Holmes and Megan Oakleaf. 2015. "Project RAILS: Lessons Learned about Rubric Assessment of Information Literacy Skills." *Portal: Libraries and the Academy* 15 (4): 623.

Holmes, Claire, and Megan Oakleaf. 2013. "The Official Rules for Norming Rubrics Successfully." *Journal of Academic Librarianship* 39 (6): 599.

Oakleaf, Megan. 2007. "Using Rubrics to Collect Evidence for Decision-Making: What do Librarians Need to Learn?" *Evidence Based Library and Information Practice* 2 (3): 27–42.

Rubric Assessment of Information Literacy Skills (RAILS). 2017. "About Us." *Railsontrack.info*. Accessed June 29, 2017. http://railsontrack.info/about.aspx.

Stevens, Dannelle D., and Antonia J. Levi. 2004. *Introduction to Rubrics: An Assessment Tool to Save Grading Time, Convey Effective Feedback and Promote Student Learning*. Sterling, VA: Stylus Publishing, LLC.

SCENARIO IV

Games as Learning Tools

Heidi Neltner, Instructional Technology Specialist/
Certified School Librarian
Fort Thomas, KY Independent Schools

Robertson Elementary is a high-performing K–5th grade school in a middle-class community that is very invested in education. The school comprises approximately 385 students, with 18 classroom teachers, and 7 "special" area teachers including the librarian, Jennifer Blevins. 12% of students qualify for free or reduced lunch and the minority population only makes up about 6% of the population, with another 6% qualifying for an Individualized Educational Program (IEP).

Despite a heavy community involvement, over the past few years, Robertson Elementary has seen a slight decline in math scores, which has prompted some discussion about the validity of standards and instructional practice. Along with that decline, Jennifer Blevins has noted a rise in parent and teacher concerns about students and screen time, especially screen time related to gaming. Many students in the school appear to be avid fans of a game that has just released an "educational" version, and Blevins is wondering if there is a way to hook kids into math and problem solving in general by capitalizing on the popularity of gaming.

To support math instruction, the Parent Teacher Organization (PTO) has offered a grant of $1,000 to purchase materials that could be used by all students. Over the past few years, Blevins has seen many articles about "gamification" and "game-based learning" and believes that encouraging students to engage in problem solving through something like gamification or game-based learning might generate many meaningful learning opportunities for students at her school. Blevins is particularly interested in using the PTO money to buy the educational version of the game so many of her students are playing obsessively, or a subscription to another game-based math program that students might find appealing.

Many teachers at Blevins's school have expressed frustration over technology, and bandwidth is often a problem when it comes to quickly accessing Internet site. Blevins is a bit worried about what kind of information she will be able to share with teachers to give some of the reluctant teachers more incentive to try game-based learning strategies with math, and she is not sure if there is enough research out there that will support the time it might take to implement such learning strategies. However, there has been an initiative in her district, and it is a school goal to encourage a more encompassing integration of technology, so Blevins feels fairly confident an approach like this would be supported by her administration.

In the last week, a classroom teacher working on a master's degree project approached Blevins and asked her to brainstorm some ideas with her about current trends in education and ways those trends could be used to benefit or potentially harm instructional practices. This gamification and game-based learning seem like a trend that could be a good one to explore more with the teacher, and it could be an excellent gateway into a collaborative relationship.

In considering spending the PTO money, Blevins knows she has a lot of information to gather. She needs to know if gamification and game-based learning are the same or two different things, and she needs to know what research there is in support of using these trends to inspire learning. She also needs to conduct some sort of survey to find out which of her faculty members would be interested in learning the programs and using them with her class. It would also help her to know if she has any teachers who are already familiar with gaming formats that would be good for students to use to reinforce math or problem-solving skills. Finally, Blevins wants to make sure that her school has the technology and infrastructure to successfully support such an initiative.

Blevins knows that if she pursues this, she will have to become a school resource for the use of the technology and programs and that she herself will need to look for and create resources that will support her staff in integrating any new programs she finds to purchase, but she believes this is a challenge that could just benefit the entire school community when it comes to inspiring the students at her school to learn in new ways. Her overarching research question is as follows:

Are games effective learning tools?

Chapter 10

Formative Research

Minkyoung Kim, Instructional Consultant
Texas Tech University
Charles Reigeluth, Professor Emeritus
School of Education, Indiana University

Introduction to the Formative Research Method

Formative research is a type of case study research to advance knowledge about means to accomplish a goal by either developing a new, grounded, **design theory** or improving an existing one. It tries to identify better means—such as instructional methods, technologies, practices, or processes—for accomplishing given goals within given situations. Therefore, formative research is useful when researchers want to develop or improve such means using an iterative process of implementing and improving interventions in collaboration with practitioners. It mostly uses qualitative methods as it explores strengths, weaknesses, and possible improvements in means within context, but sometimes it uses mixed methods. Like different routes on an automobile trip, most means such as instructional methods will eventually accomplish their goal, so validity is not the major research objective. Rather, the objective is to find the best of the known methods to accomplish their goal in a variety of situations; that is, do you need to get there fast, or do you prefer to take the scenic route. Thus, formative research addresses usefulness (preferability) more than truthfulness (validity), though construct validity is still of great importance.

Requirements

Formative research is drawn from case study research and formative evaluation methodologies. Hence, the first requirement is one or more real-world cases to study, along with expertise in case study methods. The second requirement is expertise in formative evaluation, which includes observation, interview, and document analysis skills, to answer three main questions: "What worked well?" "What needs to be improved?" "What improvements might be made?"

Therefore, it requires expertise in qualitative methods, including data collection and analysis. Some quantitative methods are also typically useful. A third requirement is the understanding that the best means for accomplishing any given goals are context-specific, and therefore it is important to identify the ways in which the means should differ for different classes of situations, to the extent possible. This is done primarily by investigating cases that are as different as possible from each other.

Why Use It?

Formative research has many advantages. First, it investigates within a real-world environment, complete with all its systemic interdependencies and interactions among methods and situational variables, so it helps build an understanding of them. Second, it goes beyond description—and even summative evaluation—to include formative evaluation, so it finds specific ways to improve the design theory or methods for that case(s), as well as providing rich description of the case(s) to aid use of the design theory in both practice and further research. Researchers and practitioners can all benefit from more detailed guidance for applying the design theory to diverse situations. Last, it can give an absolute sense of levels of performance on outcomes of interest. In sum, formative research is ideal for identifying ways to improve current instructional theories, models, practices, and technologies, and also for developing new ones.

Limitations

A limitation of formative research is lack of generalizability of the findings from a single case. Of course, this limitation applies to all kinds of research studies, including experimental studies. However, this problem can be addressed by replicating the study in different situations and identifying situational variables that call for different methods. Moreover, formative research does not compare the effectiveness of two different methods, as its main concern focuses on *im*proving methods rather than proving them.

Description of Formative Research

In this section, we describe formative research as it would be applied in the scenario for this section. However, since formative research is for situations in which the goal is to build or improve a design theory, the scenario needs to be modified a bit for formative research to be appropriate. Hence, we offer the following minor changes:

> Jennifer Blevins has noticed a rise in time students spend on digital gaming, and one teacher in the school already had some success last year using an

adaptable adventure game that teaches math and problem solving, so the school has decided to promote its use among the rest of its teachers. In the last week, another classroom teacher working on a Master's degree project approached Blevins and asked her to brainstorm some ideas with her about ways that technology could be used to benefit instructional practices. Blevins sees this as a great opportunity to further explore how they might be able to improve on the way her pioneering teacher used the game last year, so that she could better support her staff in its use, because she believes this is a challenge that could benefit the entire school community by inspiring the students at her school to be more engaged in their learning. But Blevins has very limited knowledge on how her teachers can implement and use this and other educational games in an effective way. Therefore, Blevins' overarching research question is moved from "Are games effective learning tools?" to "What guidance can we offer teachers for the use of educational games in Robertson Elementary School?"

Research Questions

Fortunately, Blevins has one pioneering teacher who already successfully used an adaptable adventure game last year. This case provides a great opportunity to conduct formative research to develop guidance for other teachers. Moreover, she has another teacher working on a master's degree project about ways that technology could be used to benefit instructional practices. This provides another opportunity to conduct formative research to improve the guidance for teachers. The specific research questions for both cases are the following:

- What worked well for the use of this educational game?
- What needs to be improved?
- What possible improvements could be made?

Research Design

Specifics of the research method vary depending on the kind of formative research study. In this scenario, formative research can be used *post facto* by retrospectively studying the first teacher's case to develop a new design theory, and it can be used *in vivo* by the second teacher to study the case as it unfolds. In addition, such studies can be classified as using **designed case** or naturalistic case, depending on whether the situation under investigation is manipulated in any way by the researcher. A *designed case* is one that was created using the existing theory or method under investigation, while a *naturalistic case* is one that was not specifically designed according to the theory or method of interest, but serves the same goals and situations as that theory.

Table 10.1
Types of Formative Research

	For an existing theory	For a new theory
(*In vivo*) **designed case**	Designed case for an existing theory (second case) – creating a case using an existing design theory – investigation **during** the case – manipulation of the case	Designed case for a new theory – creating a case to help you generate the design theory – investigation **during** the case – manipulation of the case
In vivo **naturalistic case**	*In vivo* naturalistic case for an existing theory – selecting a case within the scope of an existing design theory – investigation **during** the case – **no** manipulation of the case	*In vivo* naturalistic case for a new theory – selecting a case to help you generate the design theory – investigation **during** the case – **no** manipulation of the case
Post facto **naturalistic case**	*Post facto* naturalistic case for an existing theory – selecting a case within the scope of an existing design theory – investigation **after** the case – **no** manipulation of the case	*Post facto* naturalistic case for a new theory (first case) – selecting a case to help you generate the design theory – investigation **after** the case – **no** manipulation of the case

In this scenario, Blevins wants to develop guidance for the use of an educational game through the first teacher's case, and that case was not based on an existing design theory. Therefore, it is a naturalistic case, and it is *post facto* because the case occurred prior to her initiating the study. However, the case with the second teacher will be conducted this year using the guidance or design theory from the first teacher's *post facto* study, so it is a designed case that uses an existing theory and is conducted *in vivo*. Table 10.1 shows the six variations of the formative research method.

Data Collection Methods

This section provides the specifics for conducting formative research using the modified scenario to help the reader understand both naturalistic and designed cases, both *in vivo* and *post facto*, and for both a new theory and an existing theory.

The ***post facto* naturalistic case** was selected based on the goals and situations for which the new theory is intended. The second step is to collect three major kinds of data: (1) descriptive, (2) evaluative, and (3) formative. The descriptive data give detailed information on "what happened" so that researchers and practitioners can replicate the case in the future. The evaluative data identify the strengths and weaknesses of what was done to identify what should not be changed and what should be improved. The formative data focus on "how it could have been done better" to identify how each weakness might be improved.

These three kinds of data can be collected through three main methods: observations, interviews, and documents. *Observations* can only be done in *in vivo* naturalistic and designed cases, unless video tapes were made of the earlier case as it unfolded. Observations focus on descriptive and evaluative data. For *in vivo* naturalistic cases for an existing theory, they help the researchers to see what elements of the theory were present or missing in the case, and what elements in the case were missing in the theory. To increase the reliability of the data, it is recommended to conduct observations with more than one researcher, as observations are typically subjective.

Interviews allow the researchers to probe the reactions and thinking of the participants, to describe what happened, to identify strengths and weaknesses in what was done, and to explore improvements for the case. They can be done during or after the implementation of the case (*in vivo* or *post facto*). Conducting interviews during the case can help to avoid the memory loss problem, but it might cause intrusiveness. Interviews can be with individuals or focus groups, and they can use open-ended or directed questions.

Documents on methods, outcomes (particularly measures of outcomes), and **situational factors (or situationality)** can help researchers to make judgments about descriptive, evaluative, and even formative data. They are particularly useful for triangulation.

In this scenario for the first case, observations are not possible, because the case has already ended. Interviews of the pioneering teacher will be done to describe (1) what he and his students did with the game last year, (2) his thoughts about the strengths and weaknesses of those actions, and (3) his thoughts about possible improvements in what he and his students did. The document review will look at the game itself, any records produced from students playing the game, measures of student learning, and teacher records or lesson plans about the use of the game.

For the second case, the designed case for an existing theory, the teacher/researcher will observe herself and her students as she uses the design theory from the first teacher's study as guidance. The observations, mostly in the form of field notes, will be used to describe what happened, possibly identify some strengths and weaknesses in what happened, and even record the teacher's own hunches as to how it could have been done better. The teacher/researcher will also interview a purposeful sample of students to get their perspectives on the descriptive (what was actually done), evaluative (strengths and weaknesses of what was done), and formative (how it could have been done better). Finally, the teacher will administer measures of student outcomes, through tests, surveys, and other means, and review the game itself, to add to or confirm the descriptive, evaluative, and formative data.

For the second case, the teacher/researcher can revise the methods as the data are collected and analyzed, so that the improvements or revised methods can also be studied. A single case can have many iterations of data collection and revision, resulting in more substantive and reliable revisions.

Data collection for any case can take place on many levels, from the macro to the micro. For both these cases, the macro level includes such comprehensive or broad issues as criteria for selecting or redesigning the game to add features the game should have, whether the students work in teams or alone on the game, how self-directed the students are in learning from the game, how much guidance and feedback the teacher should provide, and how much reflection and self-evaluation the students should engage in. The macro level also studies the interactions among these broad features of the case. The micro level incudes such narrow issues as the form that the guidance should take each time it is offered, the form the feedback should take each time it is offered, and the nature of prompts to guide each incident of reflection and self-evaluation. The narrower the level, the more iterations of data collection and revision are possible, but data should typically be collected on all levels.

Data Analysis Methods

Data analysis involves data reduction, data display, and conclusion drawing. *Data reduction* is selecting, simplifying, abstracting, and transforming the raw data. The analytical procedure focuses on categorizing the data by the types of observations or the types of answers to questions during interviews.

Qualitative data from each case can be analyzed using the constant comparative method or thematic analysis. For the *constant comparative method*, collected data are broken down into discrete parts and each part is coded into a category, comparing each part with other previously coded parts, open coding. Then, the categories are integrated to make connections among them, axial coding. Finally, the core categories are identified, selected, and systematically related to other categories: selective coding. The comparative method can be used to analyze situational factors for the formative data.

Thematic analysis is a recursive process that begins during initial data collection and continues after data collection is completed. Categories are created in a systematic manner from a combination of *a priori* guiding questions and emergent themes. Data analysis involves regular and reflective review of the database, refining and generating the themes, with interpretation continuing throughout the entire research process, from data collection to the write-up phase. It can be used to analyze descriptive data, evaluative data of strengths and weaknesses, and formative data of potential improvements.

Three types of data to be analyzed include descriptive, evaluative, and formative. *Descriptive data* are typically analyzed as (a) a chronological description of what happened, (b) thematic analysis of principles that appear to underlie what happened, and (c) comparative analysis to identify situational factors that influenced differences in what happened. *Evaluative data* are typically analyzed using thematic analysis of strengths and weaknesses. *Formative data* are usually analyzed with a thematic analysis of potential improvements and a comparative analysis for situational factors.

Data Display

Although the ways of presenting results can vary depending on the number of cases and the number of research questions, results should be presented for descriptive, evaluative, and formative findings, complete with variations in the guidelines based on situational factors.

First, *descriptive findings* about what happened should be described in a detailed manner or rich description. Descriptive findings can be presented either chronologically or thematically, or both. They usually begin with a chronological description of the case, which ranges from the macro perspective about the whole series of events to the micro perspective about shorter series of events often repeated throughout the whole series. Then they describe both descriptive and design principles that appear to underlie or have guided the experience, drawn from thematic analysis. When presenting descriptive findings, it is important to describe situational factors such as the students, content, and contexts that might account for differences in what was done. It is always advisable to summarize with tables or graphics at the end of this section.

Evaluative findings describe strengths and weaknesses from evaluative data. Strengths describe what worked well, and weaknesses indicate what did not work well. *Formative findings* offer suggestions of possible improvements from formative data. It is advisable to use a table to show the alignment of the suggestions for each evaluative factor, as shown in Table 10.2.

Table 10.2

Example of Presenting Formative Findings

Strengths (What worked well)	Weaknesses (What did not work well)	Suggested improvements
• Assessment for learning • Flexible structure • Cognitive scaffolding	• Insufficient instruction	• Provide more practice opportunities • Increase group activities

Drawing Conclusion

Conclusions can vary depending on the kind of study. If the study is to create a new design theory, the conclusions should offer a tentative new theory, whereas if it is to improve an existing design theory, it should offer tentative revisions for the theory.

For *creating a new theory*, the purpose of the first study with the pioneering teacher is to develop a new theory for the use of an educational game through a *post facto* naturalistic case study. Therefore, in the conclusions, you should offer a tentative design theory based on your findings. As it is just one case, it is not possible to generalize your theory to the full range of situations for which the theory is intended, so there will likely be holes and other inadequacies in the theory. You should try to identify and describe any such inadequacies, and those should be tested in additional studies to improve the theory. Also, you should offer a research agenda that identifies the nature of formative studies (e.g., situational factors) you think would help most to further develop the theory.

For offering tentative *revisions for an existing theory*, you should use your findings to revise and elaborate the existing design theory. Your suggestions will not become trustworthy until they have been more thoroughly replicated and qualified based on situational factors. Additional formative research studies will provide the needed replication in diverse situations.

The ultimate conclusion should be a tentative complete set of revised guidelines, design theory for practitioners to use and researchers to further develop, along with limitations and recommendations for future research.

Methodological Issues

Qualitative research has been criticized for lacking rigor, validity, and reliability by proponents of the quantitative approach. The criticism for case studies is often related to lack of rigor in the methods. However, these concerns can be addressed by paying close attention to three methodological issues: (1) construct validity, (2) trustworthiness of data collection and analysis procedures, and (3) transferability/generalizability to the theory.

Construct validity focuses on establishing correct operational measures for the concepts being studied. In this scenario, the main constructs are the methods for the use of the educational game, the situations that influence the use of methods, and the indicators of strengths and weaknesses that are the criteria for outcomes. To assure construct validity, an expert should be involved in developing a list of criteria based on the operational definition, and the criteria should be reviewed by another expert.

The *trustworthiness* of data collection and analysis procedures is influenced by two major factors: thoroughness and credibility. *Thoroughness* of the data can be enhanced through several techniques, including advance preparation of participants, gradually decreasing obtrusiveness, and iteration until saturation. Students are often hesitant to criticize their instruction. Therefore, it is important to prepare the participants to be critical. Establishing rapport with the participants will tend to make them more open to sharing their reactions. It is natural to start with fairly obtrusive probes in the early rounds of data collection. However, they should gradually become less obtrusive to confirm the earlier findings and improve external validity. Also, to be thorough, it is advisable to continue the iterations of probes until you have reached saturation.

Credibility of the data can also be enhanced through a variety of techniques, including triangulation and member checking. First, triangulation entails gathering data from multiple sources such as observation, individual or group interviews, and document review. Furthermore, triangulation of investigators can also be utilized, which occurs when several researchers work together to evaluate the case(s), to reduce personal bias and get some sense of the credibility of the findings. Because of the uniqueness of each individual, researchers have a diversity of approaches and perspectives. Second, member checking entails requesting participants to review the interpretations and asking them to correct inaccurate interpretations. Member checking should be done with each participant as soon as possible after the information is recorded.

Transferability/generalizability to the theory refers to the degree to which the results of the research can be transferred or applied to other situations. To enhance transferability, the researcher must provide a thick description of phenomena to help readers make a judgment about applicability to their situation. Also, situational factors should be recognized by looking for different results in different iterations, and purposely varying elements of the situation in the iterations of data collection to see if the results differ.

Benefits of Formative Research

This research method is for researchers who want to improve the quality of teaching and training by improving instructional design theory and the learning sciences. To build and improve knowledge about instruction and learning, researchers have to understand both "what is" (descriptive knowledge/theory) and "how to do" (design theory/guidance). To improve the means for accomplishing goals, the primary research concern is usefulness (preferability) rather than truthfulness (validity) and requires research to improve rather than research to prove. Few research methods have been developed to serve this purpose. Design-based research (DBR) is a notable exception, and formative research is a specific kind of DBR that offers more detailed guidance about how to do it than is available for DBR in general.

Strengths of formative research include its ability to provide a description of case(s) that helps you to understand the methods in a given situation and thereby

Table 10.3
Summary Chart: Formative Research

Overall purpose	To advance knowledge about means to accomplish a goal by either developing a new, grounded, design theory or improving an existing one
Advantages	• Investigates in a real-world environment • Helps build an understanding of systemic interdependencies among methods and situational variables • Finds specific ways to improve the design theory • Provides rich description of the case(s) • Can give an absolute sense of levels of performance on outcomes of interest
Disadvantages	• Lack of generalizability without replication • Does not compare the effectiveness of two different methods
Steps in process	For an existing theory 1. Select a design theory. 2. Design an instance of the theory. 3. Collect and analyze descriptive and formative data on the case. 4. Revise the instance. 5. Repeat the data collection and revision cycle. 6. Offer tentative revisions for the theory. For a new theory 1. Create a case to help you generate the design theory. 2. Collect and analyze descriptive and formative data on the case. 3. Fully develop a tentative theory.
Data collection methods	• Observation • Interview • Document review
Data analysis methods	• Constant comparative method • Thematic analysis

to replicate in similar situations (Table 10.3). Also, it gives you formative information on specific ways to improve the methods (design theory) for that case(s). Furthermore, concerns about rigor can easily be addressed through attention to the three methodological issues mentioned earlier. And formative research enables continued improvement of educational design theories over many iterations across diverse situations.

Glossary of Key Terms

Design theory: A design theory offers means to accomplish a goal or set of goals in different situations.

Designed case: It refers to a case that was created or managed using a design theory.

***In vivo* naturalistic case:** It refers to a case that was not designed or managed using a design theory, and that is being studied while it happens.

***Post facto* naturalistic case:** It refers to a case that was not designed or managed using a design theory, and that is being studied only after it happened.

Situational factors (or situationality): Situational factors influence the outcomes of one or more methods and therefore the preferability of the method(s).

Further Reading

Reigeluth, Charles M., and Theodore W. Frick. 1999. "Formative Research: A Methodology for Creating and Improving Design Theories." In *Instructional-Design Theories and Models, Volume II: A New Paradigm of Instructional Theory*, edited by Charles M. Reigeluth, 633–51. Mahwah, NJ: Lawrence Erlbaum.

Reigeluth, Charles M., and Yun-Jo An. 2009. "Theory Building." In *Instructional-Design Theories and Models, Volume III: Building a Common Knowledge Base*, edited by Charles M. Reigeluth and Alison A. Carr-Chellman. New York: Routledge.

Lincoln, Yvonna S., and Egon G. Guba. 1985. *Naturalistic Inquiry*. Beverly Hills, CA: Sage Publications.

Merriam, Sharan B. 1988. *Case Study Research in Education: A Qualitative Approach*. San Francisco, CA: Jossey-Bass.

Yin, Robert K. 2014. *Case Study Research: Design and Methods*. 5th ed. Los Angeles, CA: SAGE.

Chapter 11

Correlational Research

Nelson Maylone, Professor
College of Education, Eastern Michigan University

Introduction to Correlational Research

Our librarian Ms. Blevins has informally researched the topics of "game-based learning" and "gamification" and wonders if use of the educational version of a popular video game might contribute to a rise in math test scores at Robertson Elementary School. She is also potentially faced with the challenge of convincing parents and other staff members that such gaming is beneficial for students. Ms. Blevins feels that teaming with a classroom teacher who is working on her master's degree might result in the production of solid evidence that games are indeed effective learning tools. Her chief research question is "Are [electronic] games effective learning tools?" And this chapter attempts to answer an even more specific question: *Would **correlational research** be helpful in this scenario?*

Sociologically speaking, correlational research—a quantitative method—compares two or more variables from one group and attempts to establish a relationship between the two variables (or among more than two.) Such research looks for a similarity or connection between the variables (sometimes called covariation), unlike descriptive research (or *univariate analysis*), which considers one variable at a time, resulting in simple statements regarding what *is,* according to reliable data. Here is a simple example of descriptive research: a college student might peruse a state-supplied table that gives the average housing price for all of that state's school districts for a given year, and the student might note that half of the districts' average housing prices are above $86,000. That "conclusion" is essentially inarguable, given the presumed high **reliability** of the data source. One can understand why this is sometimes called entry-level research.

Arriving at conclusions via correlational research may take more work: two or more variables from the same group are checked statistically to see if they are somehow related. One could, for example, determine the correlation between a group of students' scores on the SAT and the students' heights. The specific research question might be "Do tall students tend to score higher on the SAT than do short students?" (Note that although the meanings of the terms "tall" and "short" may seem obvious, they would need to be assigned numerical definitions when doing the research.) In any case, the answer to the question is likely to be *no*; the research would probably show little or no connection between those two variables. But who knows for sure in absence of the research?

While the choice of variables when doing correlational research is wide open, the researcher generally starts with a reasonable hunch regarding the potential connection between or among variables. It is hard to imagine the benefit of undertaking a correlational research study to determine the relationship between a population's ice-cream consumption and that population's number of second cousins!

Done properly, correlational research can take considerable time and possibly money; it depends upon the accessibility of the needed data and the potential need to verify all the data before using it. The relevance of this to Ms. Blevins's situation will be noted shortly. If the data (numerical lists of the variables) are readily available ("archived"), the researcher may have an easier time of it. Going back to the student SAT scores versus student heights example, it may be that the SAT scores are readily available in the school counseling office (assuming district policy allows such access.) Ascertaining the true height of every student is more problematic (do "trained measurers" find everyone's height, or can the researcher rely on self-reported student heights?), but this could conceivably be done. Note that the larger the population, the more confidence the researcher can claim regarding result reliability.

Frequently, however, data needed for correlational research are not at all handy, or may be unreliable. If a researcher wishes to establish the relationship between keyboard typing speed of a school's 10th graders and their average daily time spent on social media, at least two serious roadblocks arise:

1. Establishing a single student's keyboard speed is easy enough, but how does one determine speeds for, say, 300 students? Given today's pressures on teachers to stick to and fully cover local curricula, it is unlikely that sufficient instructional time could be sacrificed to determine the keyboard speeds of hundreds of students.
2. How does a researcher determine students' average daily social media time? Physically or virtually monitoring all of them for a sufficient number of days is out of the question, so surveying is in order. But to what extent will student survey responses be reliable? Might some students exaggerate or minimize reports of their social media time, for any of number of reasons?

So, any potential correlational research must consider whether or not the study is do-able, whether there is a strong likelihood that the results will be worth the work and cost and that they will be reliable enough to be useful. Additionally, correlational research contains an inherent weakness: the establishment of causality (a *relationship* between or among variables) does not establish *causality* (one variable *causing* another.) This does not mean, however, that causality cannot exist; it may. For example, the daily high temperature in Columbus, Ohio, obviously has a strong correlation with daily household hours of air conditioner use in that city. This does not absolutely *prove* that high temperatures cause increased use of air conditioning, but it is a reasonable assumption. So, while correlational research primarily deals with the cold manipulation of numerical values, common sense must be brought to bear both when deciding upon a research question and when considering results.

Sometimes, a researcher may find a strong statistical correlation between or among variables, but the connection may be puzzling. For example, a finding may be that as ice-cream consumption (variable A) rises in Omaha, Nebraska, so does the murder rate there (variable B); there is a strong (or *large*) correlation between the two. (More on the statistics of correlation later.) It might seem that, if one eats ice cream in Omaha, one is compelled to commit murder! In fact, variable A is *not* causing variable B … there is a hidden variable at work here: temperature. Hot weather prompts people to eat more ice cream; heat also—for various reasons—pushes some individuals to commit criminal acts, including murder. To reiterate, two variables can be strongly related or correlated, but one is not necessarily the cause of the other.

As implied before, if one decides to go forward with a correlational study, the researcher generally begins with a *research question*. The question should be tightly written to address only the issue at hand. Here are two examples of research questions:

1. Does consumption of sugary sodas by seven-year-olds correlate with their average number of sleep hours?
2. Does the installation of raised highway lane bumps have a relationship with a decrease in accidents caused by vehicles inadvertently leaving their lanes?

Once a solid research question has been settled upon, a research **hypothesis** needs to be established. A hypothesis is an early or possible explanation for some phenomena related to two or more variables. It can also be seen as a best ("educated") guess as to what the results of the study might be; specifically, if any significant correlation will be found via the study. The hypothesis has the researcher—appropriately—taking a stand before that is actually justified. Here are some examples of correlational research hypotheses:

1. The more light to which potato plants are exposed, the larger the resulting potatoes.

2. The heavier the vehicle, the less likely that collisions in which the vehicle is traveling at a speed greater than 30 mph will result in one or more fatalities.
3. At the ABC factory, the longer time workers are given for lunch, the higher is factory productivity.

Sometimes, a researcher puts forward a *null* hypothesis. In that case, the researcher decides to assume that no significant correlation will be found between or among the variables under consideration. An example of a null hypothesis is "There is no relationship between the number of 'chapter books' children read in 3rd grade and their achievement on a standardized mathematics test at the end of their 3rd grade in school." Use of a null hypothesis does not necessarily indicate that the researcher truly believes that no correlation will be discovered between or among the variables; it is simply a sort of safe approach to the research; it can conceivably help assure objectivity on the part of the researcher. Naturally, the researcher may find that there is indeed a correlation (relationship) between variables. In that case, we say that the null hypothesis has been *rejected.*

The strength of any correlation, or more properly the **correlational coefficient** (once the numbers have been "run"), is given as a value from −1.0 to +1.0. Both −1.0 and +1.0 are indicative of perfect positive and perfect negative correlations between variables, and a correlational coefficient of 0.0 tells us that there is no relationship whatsoever between the variables. A positive coefficient tells us that both variables go in the *same direction.* For example, when highway speed limits are higher, there tend to be more accidents. Similarly, a negative coefficient tells us that the variables under consideration go in *opposite* directions. When the acid content of rain in an area goes up, plants tend to grow less high . . . and example of negative correlation. So, a finding of a correlational coefficient of, say, +0.87 for two variables must be considered strong. (Note that definitions of strong, moderate, weak, etc., may vary according to disciplines. What may be labeled a strong correlation in the social sciences may be seen as only moderate in a hard science; say, chemistry.) Tables 11.1 and 11.2 should help to illustrate the concept of correlational coefficients.

Consider the values of variables A and B in this table . . . it does not matter here from whence the data came. Note that a one-to-one correspondence between the values on each side of the chart is implied. That is, 0 "goes with" the opposing 0, 1 "goes with" the opposing 1, 2 "goes with" the opposing 4, and so on, as shown in Table 11.1.

The correlational coefficient in this case is +1. Why? Because *every variable A value perfectly and consistently predicts the value of its corresponding variable B* value. We can even state the relationship in words in this case: all values in the second column are mathematical squares of their corresponding values in the first column. (Or, if one prefers, all values in the first column are the positive square roots of their corresponding values in the second column . . . same thing!)

Table 11.1
Values for Variables A and B: Perfect Correlation

Variable A	Variable B
0	0
1	1
2	4
3	9
4	16
5	25

Now, consider the sets of data in Table 11.2.

A sharp eye will catch that the values of variable B are *nearly* the squares of their corresponding values in the first column; they are just a little off in each instance (and they are not off by exactly the same or by predictable amounts) The variables are not *perfectly* related, but they seem to be fairly *strongly* related. Indeed, if one were to compute the correlational coefficient statistically (more on the issue of computation shortly), one would get something like +0.91, which is close to +1.0—certainly worthy of being labeled "strong."

Finally, look at Table 11.3.

There appears to be no connection between the sets of data, no way of even coming close to predicting a variable B value from knowledge of its corresponding variable A value. Would one be surprised if a variable A value of 61 corresponded to a variable B value of 1,000,245? Probably not, in that there appears to be no rhyme nor reason to the correspondence. Upon asking an appropriate computer statistics program to give the specific correlational coefficient, these data would surely give something near 0.0. (Curiously, in spite of no apparent connection between the values of the variables, the coefficient would not likely be *exactly* 0.0; a coefficient of something like +0.003 might be expected. This is because sets of data—especially those taken from "real life"—rarely produce correlational coefficients of *precisely* zero.)

Table 11.2
Values for Variables A and B: Strong Correlation

Variable A	Variable B
0	0.3
1	1.4
2	5
3	9.001
4	17.6
5	24.99

Table 11.3
Values for Variables A and B: No Correlation

Variable A	Variable B
−14	80
3500	−1
6.444	22
3.14159	−0.2
100	−50,009
−0.00027	24.9

Correlational Research versus Experimental Research

At this point, one should contrast correlational research with another type. In correlational research, there is no attempt to manipulate variables' values. Just grab them (or develop them), taking care to check that the data are from reliable sources and are useable in our study (which may be easier said than done!). This is not the case in **experimental research**. There, the researcher purposely manipulates one or more variables to see how the manipulation impacts other variables: "Will doing *this* result in *that*, and to what extent?" The name of this type of research comes from the fact that the researcher is literally performing an experiment.

As one might imagine, there are numerous restrictions on experimental research as opposed to correlational research. In the case of correlational research, one can simply subject available data to statistical analysis. With experimental research, one must generally *do something* to members of a population—at least in the case of research on humans—with the intent of discovering the effect of the treatment on the subjects. (Archived data rarely are adequate for experimental research, although this is conceivable. Such research can be called *quasi-experimental.*)

Here is an example of experimental research: a group of volunteers take a particular nutritional supplement daily for six months to see if the supplement has any effect on subjects' weight. Of course, there are many considerations to be made when settling upon such a study's methodology. How can subject compliance be assured to a reasonable degree? Might it be that volunteers for such a study are already considering a weight loss program, making it difficult to determine if the supplement is responsible for the results? Is there any chance that the supplement is harmful, calling into question the ethics of the study? *Note that, in spite of the difficulties inherent in conducting* experimental research, it may end up proving better information than does correlational research: *it can firmly establish causal relationships between variables.* ("When one does *x* to *y*, a predictable change occurs.")

How are correlational coefficients (referred to as *r*, from the Greek letter *rho*) computed? Generally, via a measure called the *Pearson product-moment coefficient* (or, sometimes, simply *the Pearson.*) Although there are a number of limits on what types of variables should be used when computing the Pearson coefficient, only one is perhaps in need of mention here: the two variables under consideration should be *linear.* That is, when the variable pairs are plotted on a coordinate plane—forming a *scatterplot*—the points should lie roughly along a straight line (called *the line of best fit.*) The more line-like the group of points, the closer the correlational coefficient will be to +1 or −1. The cloudier the group of points, the further from +1 or −1 will be the coefficient. If the points are not at all linear, use of the Pearson is inappropriate. (One should not confuse the Pearson correlational coefficient with the *slope* of the line of best fit.) To help make clear linearity, consider Figures 11.1 and 11.2.

Figure 11.1
Strong Correlation Scatterplot

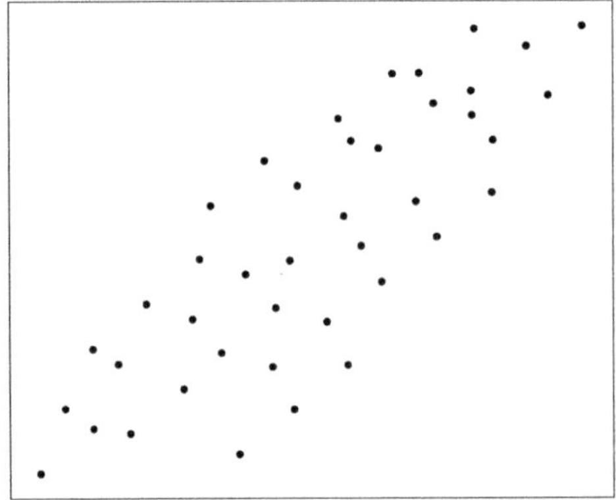

Figure 11.2
Weak Correlation Scatterplot

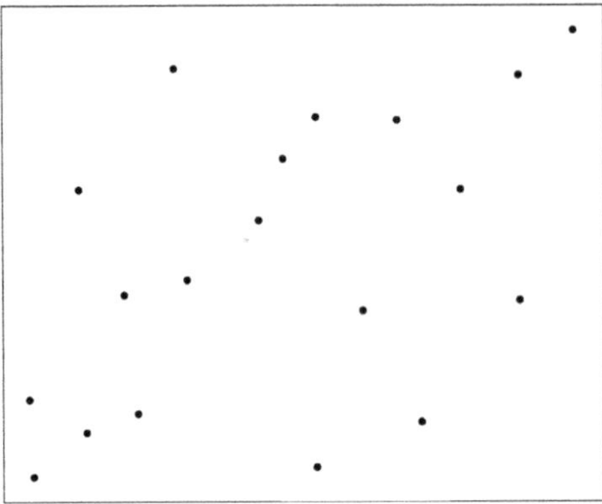

Note that in Figure 11.1, the plotted points more or less form a straight line, suggesting that use of the Pearson is justified for the data. In Figure 11.2, the scatterplot points are nonlinear, or "cloudy"; use of the Pearson is inappropriate. There exist other statistical measures for use in cases of nonlinearity.

One should be thankful for modern computer-based statistics programs; the formula allowing one to compute the Pearson correlational coefficient may appear intimidating. A higher-than-average knowledge of mathematics is required to compute by hand. The formula is nonetheless given here for reference:

$$\rho X, Y = \frac{cov(X,Y)}{\sigma_X, \sigma_Y}$$

where *cov* is the covariance and σ_X is the standard deviation of σ_Y.

It is much simpler to first ensure the accuracy and usability of one's data, insert the variables' values into two columns on a spreadsheet, and let the computer do the rest! (Note that one may examine ways in which *more* than two variables simultaneously combine to predict an independent variable; this statistical technique is referred to as multiple regression. Ms. Blevins and her student research partner need not consider this more complex undertaking.)

Correlational Research and Our Scenario

With that more-than-sufficient correlational research background under our belts, let us now return to Ms. Blevins's questions; the implied question of whether correlational research is an appropriate approach for her and her student partner, and the explicit question of whether games are effective learning tools. The straight answer to the first question is, no, correlational research cannot be recommended to Ms. Blevins in this case.

Having said that, Ms. Blevins's thoughts and general questions are exactly those that she and others at her school should be considering before making the proposed technology investment. However, it is unlikely that she would be able to conduct any useful correlational research that would tell her if the specific game under consideration (or *any* costly, similar computer-based game) would be an effective learning tool. It would be conceivable, had the educational version of the game been used by thousands of students over several years, that a carefully designed—and expensive—research study could find a strong or even moderately strong correlation between student use of that particular game and "student learning." (Although hanging over that scenario is the fact that—remember?—correlation does not equal causality.)

Even if funds were available to conduct such a correlational study, numerous problems present themselves. As a start, the researchers would have to define "student learning," and that is enormously tricky. Does "student learning" mean a greater-than-one-year-jump in students' standardized math test scores? Would excellent gains in scores need to continue for several years before the school could declare success and reasonably attribute this to use of the game? Does "student learning" refer to a specified bump in student Grade Point Average (GPAs)? Would the researchers be happy if increased student learning were simply verified by teacher anecdote? Furthermore, given modern privacy policies, the researchers would likely have access only to publicly available, non-disaggregated test results, and those data would not include individual student scores. It is unlikely that any school or school district would allow further access to student test data. And Ms. Blevins obviously cannot conduct her own study unless the games are already in use in her school! Even then, the low number of students involved (along with other confounding factors) would make her conclusions suspect. (If the number of data points used in correlational research is too low, the results are unreliable.)

Even if the game were being used by many students somewhere for some extended period of time, there are the other attendant issues: Did teachers and students use the game properly? Were there other improvements to teacher effectiveness that might have contributed to higher student test scores? Was the study experimental? If so, it would have required exposing *some* students to the "treatment" (use of the game over time), and withholding that treatment from other students. If it was suspected in advance that the game was indeed worthwhile, how could the researchers avoid parental charges of "using our children as guinea pigs"? And what about student transiency . . . that would be nearly impossible to factor in. And if the study were sponsored by the game manufacturer—a huge conflict of interest—the conclusions would be suspect.

So. . .

. . .Ms. Blevins would not likely be able to conduct a useful/reliable correlational study on her own,

. . .it is unlikely (although not impossible) that there would already exist a reliable study that looked for a connection between use of a *version* of that game and "student learning." Ms. Blevins would not be the researcher in that case anyway, and

. . .the educational version of the game is new, so there can exist no such study!

Now it may be that once all of this had been pointed out to Ms. Blevins and her student, she would be willing to settle for solid preexisting research that *generally* supported the use of such games for increasing student learning . . . that would be helpful for her to know. (Of course, in that case, she would simply be conducting a *literature review* . . . she would be doing no actual correlational research on her own.) A study or studies that included math test scores as one of the variables would be a gem of a find, with results sufficiently relevant to support a case for use of a game in her school. So while this chapter has attempted to make clear why Ms. Blevins and her research partner would not be able conduct any true correlational research, the results of which might support the use of the educational game in question, all is not lost for Ms. Librarian. Consider the following:

1. She and her student partner could certainly develop and conduct a helpful survey to determine if Roberson School faculty members are interested in learning about gaming programs in general and perhaps using them with their students. This is not correlational research, but it *is* research. Ms. Blevins would have to ask herself some important questions before proceeding, including these:

   Am I confident that my research partner and I can develop a sufficiently valid survey?
   Might there exist an 'off-the-shelf', pre-validated survey that would serve our purpose? Could we modify such a survey to more specifically fit our needs? Would the survey be strictly quantitative, or would faculty members have the opportunity to provide qualitative comments? And would we know how to properly decode or simply summarize the comments?

2. Ms. Blevins has indicated that she wishes to know if any of her colleagues are already familiar with games or gaming formats that might be helpful to students as teachers attempt to raise Robertson mathematic scores. Ascertaining this would require the use of a survey, but there would be little need to worry about survey **validity** developing, conducting, and analyzing results of this survey would likely be well within her current skill set.

3. Ms. Blevins naturally wants to have a better understanding of the school's technology infrastructure. Her best approach? Simply requesting a meeting with the district's technology director—assuming the district has one—or perhaps just the building principal. Naturally, such an information-gathering meeting should come early, before Ms. Blevins and her research partner move too far ahead. If they find out that the school does not currently contain sufficient technology infrastructure to support the sort of educational gaming that they have in mind, it is possible that their proposal could act as a catalyst for needed technology improvements in both the school and the district. Or, if they are told that the current technology infrastructure cannot support the game in question, and that infrastructure improvements are not forthcoming, at least Ms. Blevins and her student research partner will have that important information.

To summarize in attempting to determine if the game under consideration might act to improve Robertson Elementary School math test scores, Ms. Blevins and her student need not consider correlational research. However, there exist other approaches to exploring the problem of declining scores, such as experimental and quasi-experimental designs. Correlational research methodology is summarized in Table 11.4.

Table 11.4
Summary Chart: Correlational Research

Overall purpose	To establish the relationship between or among two or more variables.
Advantages	Establishment of correlations may inform courses of action. May be easier to conduct than experimental research. Researcher may be able to draw on existing ("archival") data.
Disadvantages	Establishment of correlation can never guarantee causation. Quality of results is dependent upon quality of data utilized, and this may be difficult to ascertain.
Steps in process	1. Decide upon a research question for which correlational research is applicable. 2. Specify the variables to be studied. 3. Collect the data (multiple values or "scores" for each variable). 4. Compute the correlational coefficient. This can be done by hand, but the process may be tedious and subject to error. A statistical computer program offers a better approach. 5. Decide upon the significance of the correlation coefficient to the research question.
Data collection methods	The researcher may gather data via well-conceived and well-constructed surveys, questionnaires, etc., or, may "grab" existing data from reliable sources, such as government documents.
Data analysis methods	The sets of data must be subjected to ("run through") an appropriate statistic program that will compare the data to determine the strength of any relationship.
Support technologies	Most spreadsheet programs include the ability to compute basic correlational coefficients. IBM's SPSS software package—along with many others—offers more comprehensive data analysis. An Internet search will reveal numerous existing surveys and questionnaires, which may be of help to the researcher.

Glossary of Key Terms

Correlational research: It is a research approach that attempts to establish a relationship between or among variables. Correlational research can never establish causation (see "Experimental research"), but it can suggest it.

Correlational coefficient: It is a value between −1.0 and +1.0, generated by use of an appropriate statistical program, and indicative of the strength of a correlation. A correlational coefficient of 0.0 indicates no relation between the variables under consideration. Correlational coefficients near −1.0 or +1.0 are considered strong. Coefficients may also be weak, moderate, or perfect. The most common version of a correlational coefficient is the Pearson product-moment correlation.

Experimental research: It is a research approach in which one variable (the "independent variable") is isolated and manipulated to observe any effect on a second variable (the "dependent variable.") In experimental research, an attempt is made to control the environment so that consideration of other variables can be eliminated. Experimental research attempts to establish *cause and effect* ("causation") and stands in contrast to correlational research.

Hypothesis: It is a suggested explanation for phenomena based on limited or incomplete evidence. A *null* hypothesis is one that assumes there will be no significant relationship between two variables.

Qualitative research: In contrast to quantitative research, **qualitative research** attempts to reach conclusions based on the examination of nonnumerical data or evidence. The data used may be "freshly" collected by the researcher, or may be preexisting ("archived") data.

Reliability: Reliability is the trustworthiness of the results of an assessment, the degree to which results are stable, consistent, and replicable.

Validity: It refers to how well a test, survey, or other measurement tool measures that which it purports to measure.

Further Reading

Mertler, Craig A., and C. M. Charles. 2010. *Introduction to Research.* 7th ed. Columbus, OH: Allyn and Bacon.

Creswell, John. 2013. *Research Design: Qualitative, Quantitative, and Mixed Methods Approaches.* 4th ed. Thousand Oaks, CA: SAGE.

Jackson, Sherri L. 2015. *Research Methods and Statistics: A Critical Thinking Approach.* 5th ed. Boston, MA: Cengage Learning.

Thompson, Bruce, Karen E. Diamond, Robin McWilliam, Patricia Snyder, and Scott W. Snyder. 2005. "Evaluating the Quality of Evidence from Correlational Research for Evidence-Based Practice." *Exceptional Children* 71 (2): 181–94. doi:10.1177/001440290507100204.

SCENARIO V

Impact of Collaboration and Scheduling on Learning

Bree L. Ruzzi, Doctoral Candidate
School of Education, Old Dominion University

Zoe Daniels has been the school librarian at Red Pond Elementary School for five years. Red Pond is a medium-sized PK–5 elementary school in a southeastern state. Red Pond has approximately 42 teachers: 30 classroom teachers, 5 special education teachers, and 7 specialist teachers, including Zoe. The population of Red Pond is highly military and thus somewhat transient, mostly middle class. Student population is 650 students with approximately 60% white, 25 % black, 7% Asian, 4% Hispanic, 1% Native American, and 3% Not reported/Other. Exceptional student needs include 11% of student body having Individual Education Plans, 3% are English language learners, a preschool program for special needs children ages 2–5, and speech services are available for identified children ages 2–12. Additional specialist resources include weekly art lessons, weekly music lessons, and daily physical education classes. In addition, Red Pond has a gifted teacher who plans and teaches with all classes, a computer specialist who collaborates and teaches with each grade level, and a Reading Resource teacher who plans with each class to assist with reading lessons.

During Zoe's interview for the librarian position at Red Pond, Zoe advocated for flexible scheduling of the library. The library schedule had previously been on a fixed schedule; however, Zoe provided valuable national research and statistics in support of flexible scheduling. This included, but was not limited to, evidence of increased book circulation in flexible library schedules, where students can visit the library as needed, not solely during the weekly scheduled class time. She supported this research by providing examples of how scheduling classes in a flexible manner often results in longer and more meaningful lessons, thus promoting student immersion in literacy and research skills as guided by the curriculum and teacher needs, versus the fixed one-slot-per-class-per-week model. The principal of the school, Mrs. Beemer, agreed to change the library schedule to a flexible schedule on a provisional basis.

Zoe also advocated to be included in grade-level collaboration to effectively plan with teachers for library instruction and to provide materials for lessons and units. These changes initially caused pushback from some of the faculty. Many of the teachers were resistant to losing their dedicated weekly library resource time, as well as sharing valuable grade-level collaboration time with the school librarian. In the initial stages, some teachers refused to sign up for class times and/or insisted Zoe not need to attend planning sessions. While acceptance was slow, in the end persistence paid off. The change and growth was not easy or quick, but the vast majority of the teachers eventually recognized and expressed appreciation for the in-depth lesson planning, the assistance with students learning difficult concepts and skills, and the general *camaraderie* that is often produced through regular collaborative sessions. Mrs. Beemer was also very pleased with the growth and metamorphosis of the library program and became, herself, an advocate of flexible scheduling. Within three years, all but three classroom teachers in the school were fully participating in the collaborative units and meetings.

Zoe carried on happily for the next two years constructing and refining lessons around student and classroom needs. She was sure to incorporate state and local standards in all lesson plans to show how she supported the curricula, the teacher needs, and the student needs. She kept communication logs to show when and where collaboration with teachers took place, as well as any interactions with parents and students. She solicited input from faculty, staff, parents, and students when ordering library materials, to both better support the curricula and provide materials based on patron interest. Zoe felt successful in the instruction, collaboration, and relationships within the school community that she was forging. Unbeknownst to her, change was in the air.

During Zoe's sixth year at Red Pond, principals were moved within the school system and a new principal was assigned to Red Pond. Zoe was confident in her success with the library program, having the majority of teacher support as well as lesson plans that clearly supported learning goals and state standards. She was also confident that the national research and statistics she previously cited would be enough to show the importance of flexible scheduling in the school library program. However, Zoe was mistaken. The new principal, Ms. Night, has different views and expectations of the school library program than the previous principal. Not only is Ms. Night not an advocate of flexible scheduling, she also wants to transfer the allocated library funds to the Reading Resource program to purchase guided reading book sets. In addition, she is not interested in national research or statistics, but asks Zoe to provide site-driven proof of the library program's success. As Zoe prepares for her meeting, she identifies the one essential question she needs to answer:

How have librarian-teacher collaboration and flexible scheduling impacted student achievement at Red Pond?

Chapter 12

Through the Lens of Evidence-Based Practice

Ross J. Todd, Professor
School of Communications and Information Rutgers,
the State University of New Jersey

The Core Beliefs Underpinning Evidence-Based Practice

The Red Pond Elementary School's current situation not just questions local school-based practices, but more directly, it targets some of the core values of school libraries and the professional role of school librarians. Certainly, the long-standing rhetoric of school libraries and their place in schools' learning agenda centers on providing the best opportunities for children to learn and achieve in a rich information and technological environment, and providing the scaffolds for the ongoing development of intellectual agency, social and cultural agency, and personal agency: the embodiment of learning for life. Over a number of decades now, this learning agenda has positioned school libraries as essential for addressing curriculum standards, and essential for addressing the complexities of learning in information and technological environments.

Even more deeply than that, the very nature of school librarianship is being questioned by the school principal, with assumed knowledge about school library practice, and how core practices of school librarianship are enacted in a school setting. In her early years at the school, the school librarian has clearly been empowered to establish practices that represent the goals and intents of the profession. With early resistance, there has been persistence, and over time, a dynamic and valued professional practice has been established where learning is nurtured through the collaborative effort of all.

And this connects us to the concept of evidence-based practice. School librarianship, as an applied science and profession, derives its practice mandate from a diverse body of theoretical and empirical knowledge. Active engagement with this body of knowledge and evidence derived through scholarship not only provides the building blocks for practice, but it also enables the profession to continuously transform and improve. Leading this transformation is the professional expertise of school librarians, certified through a program of university graduate education, who possess expertise, insights, and skills based on theoretical and empirical knowledge, as well as accumulated wisdom derived through reflective practice that they weave into daily routines, decision making, and strategic planning. They continuously develop their knowledge and skills through professional development and ongoing engagement with a constantly emerging body of research-based knowledge and its application to practice. Thus, the professional role of school librarians is founded on a strong evidence base, welding together research, experience, and insights. At its essence, the practice of school librarianship is one of transformation—from theory to action. One of the key mechanisms underpinning the professional practice is the student-centered transformation of information to knowledge, and the development of attitudes, values, and beliefs enabled through carefully designed instructional interventions and reading literacy programs. These programs guide and engage students in their inquiry learning and reading development, enable them to build new understandings of curriculum content, and develop personal viewpoints and perspectives. The school librarian at Red Pond Elementary has been exemplary in building this practice, one that has engaged so many in the school to implement a shared, collaborative, and systematic approach to fostering student achievement.

All of this implies that the value and impact of the school library practices can be measured. The transformations as learning outcomes, as well as personal, social, and cultural growth can be documented, measured, and disseminated. Evidence of this transformation and the development of intellectual, social, and cultural agency are often not fully understood, nor seen, nor acknowledged by many stakeholders, including some school leaders. Evidence-based practice plays a key role in developing and disseminating evidence of the impact and value of school libraries. Perhaps this is the missing link in the transformation of the school's practice in relation to the school library; while the infrastructure is in place in terms of collaborations and flexible scheduling, the availability of evidence of the impact of the successful transformation is not necessarily there.

Now, the new school principal is asking the school librarian to provide site-driven proof of the library program's success and especially seems to target **instructional collaborations** with teachers and how these are scheduled in the library program. Is this an unreasonable demand? Not at all. Two things are at play here: accountability and local evidence. While the principal appears to have a lack of robust knowledge about key tenants of professional school library practice, as shown in lack of understanding of the role and value of flexible scheduling and a team-based instructional process, the principal is asking the school librarian to account for her professional actions and their outcomes. Professional school library responsibility is an accountable responsibility. In leadership roles, accountability is the acknowledgment and assumption of responsibility for actions, products, decisions, and policies including the administration, governance, and implementation within the scope of the role or employment position and encompassing the obligation to report, explain, and be answerable for resulting consequences. An essential component of sustainable development of the school library profession is accountability. The principal is asking for accountability through an evidential warrant for professional practice. She is asking to show value and impact through evidence, and specifically, local, individual school-derived evidence. She is right on the mark.

What Is Evidence-Based Practice in the Context of School Libraries?

Evidence-based school librarianship is an approach to professional practice in school libraries that systematically engages **research-derived evidence** found in the corpus of scholarship of the field and its allied disciplines, school librarian-observed evidence, and local user-reported evidence. This engagement with evidence is fundamental to iterative processes of decision making, development, and continuous improvement to achieve the school's mission and goals, which fundamentally center on student achievement, quality learning, and quality teaching. At the heart of evidence-based practice in school librarianship is the student's information-to-knowledge experience enabled through school library initiatives.

First, evidence-based school librarianship is founded on the conscientious interpretation and integration of research-derived evidence to shape and direct professional practice. The school librarian at Red Pond Elementary is well aware of the central importance of this scholarly evidence and has engaged with this and disseminated it to build her case for the implementation of a flexible schedule and for the team-based instructional program. While this was a slow and at times resistant process, she demonstrated engagement with this literature, analyzed it, and presented it to shape her argument. Second, at the same time, the day-by-day practice meshes professional wisdom, reflective experience, and understanding of user needs with the judicious use of research-derived evidence to make judgments and decisions about how to deliver the instructional and service roles of the school library, such as reading and literacy programs, to meet the goals of the school. Third, an integral component of evidence-based school librarianship is the systematic collection, integration, and dissemination of evidence of the tangible impacts and outcomes of school library practices in terms of organizational goals and objectives: student achievement and the development of deep knowledge, deep understanding, and competencies and skills for thinking, living, and working. Thus, evidence-based practice of school librarianship demonstrates the value-added role of an individual school library to the life and work of a school, outcomes that center on learning, literacy, and living and the development of students personally, socially, culturally, and globally.

This holistic approach to evidence-based practice in the context of school libraries welds three dimensions of evidence: **Evidence for Practice**, **Evidence in Practice**, and **Evidence of Practice**:

- Evidence for Practice focuses primarily on examining and using best available formal empirical research and methods to form practices and inform current actions, and to identify best practices that have been tested and validated through empirical research. This is posited as the *informational dimension* of school library practice.
- Evidence in Practice focuses on reflective practitioners integrating available research evidence with deep knowledge and understanding derived from professional experience, as well as implementing measures to engage with local evidence to identify learning dilemmas, learning needs, and achievement gaps to make decisions about the continuous improvement of the school library practices to bring on optimal outcomes and actively contribute to school mission and goals. This is posited as the *transformational dimension* of school library practice.
- Evidence of Practice, as the measured outcomes and impacts of practice, is derived from systematically measured, primarily user-based, data. It focuses on the real results of what school librarians do, rather than on what school librarians do. It focuses on the development of local measures to identify outcomes and impacts, going beyond process and activities as outputs. It establishes what has changed for learners as a result of inputs, interventions, activities, processes, and charting the nature and extent and quality of effect. This is the *formational dimension* of school library practice (Todd 2009).

These three dimensions are summarized in Table 12.1.

These dimensions or phases are not posited as linear and static; rather, they are presented as a dynamic, iterative, and integrative process of welding evidence from multiple sources in a cycle of continuous transformation of data, information, knowledge, and wisdom to inform practice, to generate practice, and to demonstrate outcomes of practice. They become a framework for thinking about decisions and actions. They become a framework for planning and implementing advocacy initiatives, instructional and service initiatives, and for developing approaches to creating sustainable school libraries. And indeed, they are at the center of the principal's request for local evidence (Todd 2009).

Evidence-based practice is an approach to best practice. It asks school librarians in their local contexts to take action. It asks school librarians to engage in local initiatives that go beyond mere evidence-informed practice and information-based

Table 12.1
Dimensions of Evidence for Research and Practice

Evidence FOR Practice	**FOUNDATION** **Informational** Existing formal research provides the essential building blocks for professional practice: questions, samples, methods, analysis, and claims.
Evidence IN Practice Applications/ actions	**PROCESS** **Transformational** Locally produced evidence; data instruments are developed to capture data generated by practice. These are meshed with research-based evidence to provide a dynamic decision-making environment and process: librarian-observed evidence.
Evidence OF Practice Results—impacts and outcomes; evidence of closing of gaps	**OUTCOMES** **Formational** User-reported evidence. Learner changes as a result of inputs, interventions, activities, processes, and charting the nature, extent, and quality of effect.

evidence, to a central focus on knowledge based-evidence. The school principal's request for local proof is important. Why does she not think that the research evidence, the Evidence for Practice, is enough? As a new principal, responsible and accountable for all the school's intellectual investment and financial investment, she needs to know what is happening on the ground.

This focus on the "local" was brought home to me with the Parliament of the Commonwealth of Australia's Inquiry titled "School Libraries and Teacher Librarians in 21st Century Australia" that took place in 2011. This extensive inquiry led by a team of 12 politicians gathered input through 387 written submissions and 12 hearings across Australia and acknowledged the central importance of the role of school libraries and school librarians. The parliamentary committee recognized the evidence available in national and international research that demonstrates the significant contribution to learning outcomes in a fully resourced school library, when staffed by a fully qualified and active teacher librarian, can make. The committee also brought attention to the central importance of local evidence, which was missing from the many hearings. The report concluded: "We recommend that the profession as, a whole, needs to develop the capacity to articulate needs from research-based evidence and local evidence collected in the school" (Parliament of the Commonwealth of Australia 2011, 118). More than ever, we are reminded of the central focus of evidence-based practice: your own evidence of your practice, and the urgent need for each school librarian to build a compelling and diverse portfolio of local evidence deeply linked to the learning agenda of the school.

The Methods of Evidence-Based Practice: Multiple Types of Evidence

Evidence-based practice for school libraries focuses on tangible, observed, and reported data that are derived from systematic and replicable measures of learning outcomes. Evidence-based practice of itself is not a method. It is a practice that systematically makes use of a range of methods to gather data for essential purposes. In doing so, it moves beyond informal and casual observations, personal experiences, advocacy, testimonials, intuitions, gut reactions, and anecdotal evidence as basis of claims. Such approaches may facilitate the interpretation of data, but do not form the basis of verification, nor the basis of evidence-based practice. Evidence-based practice has no one prescribed method. One of the criticisms of an evidence-based practice approach by practitioners is the perception that it requires school librarians to be expert researchers, trained in a range of quantitative and qualitative methods. This certainly helps, but is not a requirement. What it does require is for school librarians to know the fundamentals of information literacy: how to identify needs (or questions); how to locate and access information; how to gather, analyze, and synthesize this information; and how to apply this information.

As with any data-driven methods, it is the central question, and not the methods that drive the approach to evidence. The school librarian at Red Pond Elementary School is challenged by the school principal to ask some key questions about the impact of her practice. Some of these questions might be the following:

- How does the school library help students learn at Red Pond Elementary School?
- In what ways do students who have been taught information literacy competencies through instructional interventions, in collaboration with teaching partners, perform better academically than students who do not have such instruction?
- How do the students at Red Pond Elementary School develop reading and literacy capabilities through MY school library reading programs?

And, given the request for local evidence by the school principal,

- How do I disseminate the impact of the school library and demonstrate its educational, social, and cultural good?

These questions place emphasis on outcomes and shift the focus from the medium to the message; from articulating what school librarians do in their day-to-day work, to articulating what students become. By placing emphasis on systematically gathered evidence, it moves school library advocacy from a "tell me" framework to a "show me" framework. Accordingly, evidence-based practice first and foremost validates that quality learning outcomes can be achieved through the school library; second, and through this, it validates the important role of the school librarian as an instructional partner in the school, and a key team member in achieving the school's mission and goals.

So, what are some of the data collection procedures? When trying to choose a particular method, there are several key processes to engage in. First, review the published research on the specific question you want to answer. This is important for a number of reasons because individual research studies, as Evidence for Practice, usually provide some key pointers to data collection. They often provide specifics in terms of what groups of students were chosen and how they were chosen. Sometimes these studies can be large and encompass large groups of students and/or teachers, so it is important to look at how the participants were chosen and see if this can fit within a local context, for example, all the students, all the teachers, or a subset of each; a grade level; and a specific subject area. The formal published research provides some guiding principles to help the school librarian make decisions about what to do.

Evidence for Practice is such an essential component of evidence-based practice for another reason. Accessing this research on a challenged area of practice, such as school libraries and student achievement, shows the methods and tools used to gather data. These provide a framework for the development and adoption of methods and tools in the workplace. Even if data collection instruments are simplified, being based on existing research they provide a key way to link back local findings to the wider research on the topic. A key point to be made here is that when developing evidence-based practices, the search for data collection instruments does not have to mean reinventing the wheel; they often exist already.

One of the advantages of having built a culture of collaboration in the school is that the whole data collection and analysis can be a collaborative effort. The librarian at Red Pond Elementary School would be wise to engage her teachers, who have been on the collaborative journey already, to be part of this data gathering process. One of the stumbling blocks to evidence-based practice is having the time, and the processes in place to do this, so making it a collaborative team effort distributes the workload. Even when open-ended interview or survey questions are posed, a team approach to coding and data analysis will overcome some of the time issues.

In terms of school libraries and student achievement, there is a considerable body of published research in school librarianship that can inform the school's approach. A ready guide for the school librarian is Scholastic's "School Libraries Work" (2016), a powerful synthesis of the body of research, which links to the actual research studies, their methods, and findings. This provides directions for the approaches to be taken at the school. This might take several forms: a school-wide survey of how the school library helps students learn (a macro approach) or gather data on an individual collaborative instructional unit, or even at the output level—such as an assessment task or product developed by the student that demonstrates their learning (a micro approach).

Gathering data from students and how that evidence will be reported poses some additional challenges, particularly in terms of ethics. It is very important that the school librarian understands and complies with any procedures that are in place in the schools and in the district regarding collecting data from students. Again, the Evidence-for-Practice framework is invaluable here. When the large research project (Todd and Kuhlthau 2005) on how students learn through Ohio School Libraries in 2003–2005 was developed, a survey instrument was created that could easily be replicated either at a state, or local school or individual class-room level. In this study, data were collected from 39 effective school libraries across Ohio; the participants included 13,123 students in grades 3–12 and 879 faculty. The focus question of the study was "How do school libraries help students with their learning in and away from school?" Two survey instruments were created: Impacts on Learning Survey (Students) and Perceptions of Learning Impacts (Faculty). "Helps" were measured using a likert scale for 48 statements of learning outcomes to provide a quantitative measure, and a **Critical Incident** response to capture the voices of students to provide a qualitative measure. The 48 statements were grouped in terms of 7 sets of "help":

1. how helpful the school library is with getting information you need;
2. how helpful the school library is with using the information to complete your school work Information Literacy skills);
3. how helpful the school library is with your school work in general (knowledge building, knowledge outcomes);
4. how helpful the school library is with using computers in the library, at school, and at home;
5. how helpful the school library is to you with your general reading interests;
6. how helpful the school library is to you when you are not at school (independent learning); and
7. general school aspects—academic achievement.

The Critical Incident response asked one question: "Now, remember one time when the school library really helped you. Write about the help that you got, and what you were able to do because of it." The purpose of this was to validate—"witness"—quantitative data; to elucidate "helps" not identified in 48 statements; and to provide the "voice" of the students. The researchers captured 10,316 valid statements. This is an immense set of data. In terms of evidence-based practice, the instrument is readily available in the published literature. It is an example of an evidence-based practice survey that could be tailored to a specific grade level, or even to a class level to understand how school libraries help students learn. Gathering background data from the students such as the cultural diversity in Red Pond Elementary can enable the librarian to see if the diverse nature of the school population impacts the results. The whole instrument does not need to be used. It can be easily simplified to a particular group of statements. It can be short or long depending on time. The Critical Incident can be used alone; this question gathers both inputs (what help did you get) and outputs (what you were able to do because of it). In other words, it connects the actions of the library to student-centered outcomes.

One of the most effective processes is to collect data within the boundaries of a collaborative instructional unit. An example of an evidence-based practice approach that integrates Evidence for Practice, Evidence in Practice, and Evidence of Practice is the collaborative instructional framework developed by Kuhlthau known as Guided Inquiry. This framework has emerged out of a 30-year research agenda and based on an empirical model known as the Information Search Process (ISP) developed in the 1980s and refined in the 1990s.

This theory of information seeking and use has been significantly elaborated and developed as an instructional framework, known as Guided Inquiry, where teams of educators including librarians, classroom teachers, specialist educators such a reading and literacy coaches engage in the design and implementation of a constructive journey of resource-based inquiry. Guided Inquiry articulates a design process that centers on seven phases: Open, Immerse, Explore, Identify, Gather, Create and Share, and Evaluate (Kuhlthau, Maniotes, and Caspari 2012). Embodied in this design are rich opportunities for students to engage with and develop information literacy capabilities and critical and reflective thinking on their journey of discovery and inquiry. Students can, while developing deep knowledge and understanding of curriculum content, develop personal, social, and cultural agency.

Why is this referenced as an approach to evidence-based practice? One of the tools that has been developed and publically available to provide evidence of students of students' learning though an inquiry process is the *Student Learning through Inquiry Measure* (SLIM). Accompanying the instruments to collect data from the students is *SLIM Handbook*, the *SLIM Reflection Instruments and Scoring Guidelines*, and a *SLIM Scoring Sheet*. These are available through the Center for International Scholarship in School Libraries (CISSL) at Rutgers University. This is a data collection tool that the school librarian could integrate into the collaborative inquiry units. It collects categorical and open-ended data at two or three points in the inquiry unit, enabling the instructional team to chart the growth of learning, and to work diagnostically as the learning takes place.

All of the aforementioned approaches require considerable planning, time, and effort. However, gathering evidence can also be very simple. At the end of a collaborative instructional unit, the use of a thoughtfully designed or chosen assessment rubric can provide a cumulative picture of the learning that has taken place, as long as there is analysis of the responses and developing some claims based on the data. Also, at the end of an instructional unit where there has been focus on an information literacy capability, a simple feedback strategy might be used, to gather impact of learning. Digital tools such as sticky note tools enable this feedback and reflection to be captured quickly. The essential key again is the accumulation of the evidence and taking the time to analyze it and develop some statements (claims) about what the evidence shows. If the school librarian has time, she could bring a team of teachers together to analyze school-based test score data, specifically focusing on library-centered practices: for example, matches between scores and high-use library groups, matches between scores and grades involved in reading enrichment programs, improvement in critical thinking on test score measures after inquiry-based interventions, and the like.

A sustained practice over time might be to develop an inventory or portfolio of the instructional collaborations involving the school librarian and make this part of a larger portfolio of evidence. This should document the number of collaborations, instructional focus of collaborations (list curriculum standards and school library standards), focus of instructional interventions, subject/grade levels, teacher and librarian observations of student engagement, teacher and librarian summary of outcomes, and careful summaries of assessment data and other data collected. If the school principal wants specific evidence of the nature and extent of teacher collaborations with the school librarian, a more sophisticated approach again will draw on the Evidence-for-Practice scholarship.

Of note is Montiel-Overall, who has done a considerable body of research in this area for a number of years. The research papers present a number of methods and tools that can be adapted for a local school to identify, for example, the level of involvement in instructional collaborations. Montiel-Overall's work is teacher focused, and the studies have used teachers as participants. Getting the evidence from teachers is critical. For example, Montiel-Overall's Teacher Taxonomy of Resource-Based Teaching and Learning, and the corresponding *Taxonomies of the School Library Media Specialist* (Loertscher 2000), which identifies levels of participation in collaborations, can be a useful tool for creating and describing the levels of collaboration that the school library is involved in. This can also identify the value of flexible scheduling.

Monteil-Overall's research makes use of qualitative methods such as focus groups and interviews. While these are time consuming, they enable the school librarian to probe into the level of collaboration and why, the barriers and enablers that teachers face with collaborations, and the perceived benefits and outcomes (Montiel-Overall 2015).

Another example of the published scholarship on instructional collaborations is the New Jersey School library study: *One Common Goal: Student Learning. Report of Findings and Recommendations of the New Jersey School Library Survey Phase 2* (available at http://cissl.rutgers.edu/images/stories/docs/njasl_phase%20_2_final.pdf). The goal of this phase of research was to examine the dynamics of a selected sample of effective school libraries to establish the key inputs, both library and school-wide inputs, that enabled the school libraries to thrive and contribute richly to the learning agendas of the schools.

In this study, participating schools were chosen because their teaching faculty were engaged in a substantive number of team-based instructional collaborations with the school librarian, as identified in data provided in Phase 1 of NJ study. Here is an example of Evidence for Practice that the school librarian can draw on to build evidence of her own collaborative practices. In each of the schools that formed the sample, schools were asked to establish a focus group that comprised of the school principal, several classroom teachers from different curriculum content areas who were involved in instructional collaborations with the school librarian, curriculum supervisors/curriculum head, and any specialist teachers such as reading/literacy teachers, special needs teachers, and the like. A qualitative method, focus groups, was used to collect the data. This is time consuming, but far less time consuming than using individual interviews.

The researchers took a narrative approach, capturing the "story" of the dynamics, outcomes and impacts of instructional collaborations, and produced a rich body of data expressed in participants own words and context, in a time-efficient and nonintrusive manner as possible. This is another example of a teacher-centered study. One of the criticisms of focus groups is that they have limited generalizability to a population. In the case of Red Pond Elementary School, this is not the goal. The principal wants evidence of the local, not the general. Of course, open-ended questions are more difficult to interpret because they are not fitted into a set of fixed categories, and the time-consuming aspect centers on making sense of the diverse interpretations and constructing the narrative story. However, the published research typically also provides a framework for this interpretive work. This is the interaction of Evidence for Practice and Evidence of Practice. More often than not, the specific research study will identify the categories used to code the findings, or group the findings around a set of meaningful headings. There is no need to reinvent the wheel, so to speak. Decisions about questions, methods, sample, data collection instruments, approaching to coding and analyzing data, and ways of presenting findings are modeled, and reduce the complexity of decision making and the time-intensive work in a busy school library. And they provide a larger scholarly framework for positioning the findings in the local school with a wider body of research.

While the school principal may only be interested in local evidence, the school librarian must never miss an opportunity to link any presentation of local findings with the wider research arena. Work informatively, and educationally, in this respect.

One of the important skills of research, and indeed evidence-based practice, is to make statements about what the evidence tells. This is the outcome of analysis and synthesis of the data collected. It is the claims that can be made on the basis of evidence. Depending on the evidence-based practice approaches used, some of the claims that the school librarian might make can be along these lines: Students in classes that have collaborative library instruction borrow 23% more books than those students who do not have such instruction; As a result of instructional interventions focusing on evaluating websites, the grade 5 students inquiry projects showed improved ability to identify good to websites, with only 5 students out of 42 showing evidence of incorrectly chosen websites. This is the crystallization of the vast body of evidence; it is the sense-making of the collected evidence and must not be overlooked as part of evidence-based practice.

Conclusion

Evidence-based practice (Table 12.2) is an approach to professional practice that integrates Evidence FOR Practice, Evidence IN Practice, and Evidence OF Practice (informational, transformational, and formational). It engages with a diverse range of methods to systematically gather evidence of the value, outcomes, and impacts of practice. While this approach is described within this chapter in the context of school libraries as in its related scenario, it is equally at home in other types of libraries such as public, academic and other fields such as medicine and social work.

The school librarian at Red Pond Elementary School had much to gain by approaching her professional practice through and evidence-based practice lens. She is already engaging with some steps in the process, for example, she is utilizing the body of scholarly literature to build her practice and her arguments about practice, and showing deep commitment to these in the wake of opposition. Now she is called on to build her evidence base. The scholarship will help her make decisions about the what, who, and how of the needed evidence. Much already exists, not just in terms of research, but in terms of developed applications for professional practice, and it is a matter of critically assessing these, transforming them (the Evidence-In-Practice dimension) and applying them to the local context. She is well ahead in the evidence journey.

Table 12.2
Summary Chart: Evidence-Based Practice

Overall purpose	• An approach to documenting, measuring, and disseminating the evidence of value and impact of a professional practice.
Advantages	• Plays a key role in accountability for developing and disseminating evidence of the impact and value of libraries. • Is fundamental to iterative processes of decision making, development, and continuous improvement required to achieve an institution's mission and goals. • Meshes professional wisdom, reflective experience, and understanding of user needs with the judicious use of research-derived evidence to make judgments and decisions. • Well suited to a collaborative research effort where shared expertise can work to outcomes in a timely way; builds a community of advocacy based on evidence.
Disadvantages	• Requires systematic gathering of data preferably over time, using a range of data collection methods and tools. • May be seen as time consuming; requires early planning, commitment, and situating it in the programs and schedules of the school or library. • Requires access to a rich body of current research literature that provides the foundation: evidence for practice; also requires understanding what the published scholarship actually says.
Steps in process	• Iterative. • Requires early and careful planning to integrate into practice. • Effort and time are required for analysis—identifying key patterns to inform decision making; effort required to craft and disseminate the narrative of outcomes and impacts. • Importance of all working with a timeline and establishing work-arounds when school or library programs are interrupted.
Data collection methods	• Varied. • Use of several different methods (triangulation) contributes to a more compelling narrative.
Data analysis methods	• Varied • Team approach to coding of qualitative data reduces overall load of work and builds consistency of coding and pattern identification.
Support technologies	• Use of online survey software can support tabulation and generation of descriptive statistics; contribute to categorization of open-ended data. • Use of visualization, storytelling, and infographics tools can create compelling ways to disseminate outcomes and impacts.

Glossary of Key Terms

Critical Incident: "To be critical, an incident must occur in a situation where the purpose or intent of the act seems fairly clear to the [participant] and where its consequences are sufficiently definite to leave little doubt concerning its effects" (Flanagan 19327). (See also Chapter 16.)

Evidence for Practice: It refers to evidence that examines and uses the best available formal empirical research and methods to form practices and inform current actions, and to identify best practices that have been tested and validated through empirical research.

Evidence in Practice: It refers to evidence that focuses on integrating available research evidence with deep knowledge and understanding derived from professional experience, as well as implementing measures to engage with local evidence to identify learning dilemmas, learning needs, and achievement gaps to make decisions for continuous improvement.

Evidence of Practice: It refers to evidence derived from systematically measured, primarily user-based, data.

Instructional collaborations: Where a team of educators work together and share expertise to plan, design, implement and assess an instructional unit to meet curriculum standards and school goals

Research-derived evidence: evidence found in the corpus of scholarship of the field and its allied disciplines, school librarian-observed evidence and local user-reported evidence, that is interpreted and integrated in order to shape and direct professional practice.

Further Reading

Knowledge Quest. January/February 2015. (entire issue). http://knowledgequest
.aasl.org/examine-evidence-based-practices-role-school-librarianship-janfeb
-2015-issue/.

Kuhlthau, Carol C., Leslie Maniotes, and Ann Caspari. 2012. *Guided Inquiry Design: A Framework for Inquiry in Your School.* Santa Barbara, CA: Libraries Unlimited.

Montiel-Overall, Patricia. 2015. "Toward a Theory of Collaboration for Teachers and Librarians." *School Library Media Research, 8.* Accessed June 29, 2017. http://www.ala.org/aasl/sites/ala.org.aasl/files/content/aaslpubsandjournals/slr/
vol8/SLMR_Theoryofollaboration_V8.pdf.

Scholastic. 2016. *School Libraries Work: A Compendium of Research Supporting the Effectiveness of School Libraries.* New York, NY: Scholastic. Accessed June 29, 2017. http://www.scholastic.com/SLW2016/.

Todd, Ross J. and Carol Kuhlthau. 2005. "Student Learning through Ohio School Libraries, Part 1: How Effective School Libraries Help Students." *School Libraries Worldwide 11* (1): 89–110.

Todd, Ross J. 2009. "School Librarianship and Evidence-Based Practice: Perspectives, Progress, and Problems." *Evidence Based Library and Information Practice* 4 (2–3): 78–96.

Chapter 13

Causal Research

Shana Pribesh, Associate Professor
Darden College of Education, Old Dominion University
Kristen Gregory, Doctoral Candidate
Darden College of Education, Old Dominion University

Introduction to Causal Research

Researchers often want to isolate exact reasons why things happen in the social world; however, this is tricky business, to say the least. Librarians are often asked questions, such as Do library collections organized by genre *cause* students to take out more STEM books? Do e-books *cause* students to read more closely? Do the actions of librarians *cause* a change in student achievement? To answer such questions of *cause*, we need evidence that is collected in a manner that we can undoubtedly link causes to effects. Linking causes and effects is a really challenging task because there are many things that can complicate the relationship between causes and effects. For example, how do we know if organizing a library by genre influences students' circulation habits if the uptick in circulation of STEM books could have been caused by other reasons such as a teacher mandate (e.g., a mandate for students to take out an STEM book) or proximity to the science fair date? Identifying these other possible influences is necessary in order to better understand the cause-and-effect relationship. This chapter presents ways that librarians can use research design and statistical methods to make causal inferences.

Conditions for Causal Inference

The first step to simplifying this tricky business of causal research is to better understand the five conditions that are necessary in order to make causal inferences (a fancy way of saying "link causes to effects"). We will look at each of these conditions using the example of genre-organized libraries (cause) and circulation rates (effect).

The first condition is called *Causal Relativity*. This simply means that at least two groups are needed to compare: an **experimental group** who experiences the **treatment** and a **control group** who does not. For example, the experimental group would experience genre-organized libraries, while the control group would not. Thus, we can compare the circulation data of the two groups in order to determine whether or not genre-organization has an impact.

The second condition is *Causal Manipulation*, or treatment. In order to determine cause, we must have an experimental group that undergoes a treatment. A treatment is any change or condition that of interest. In this case, our treatment is the condition of having a genre-organized library. Multiple experimental groups make it even more interesting according to how much of a treatment each group receives, think "dosage" in medical terms. A researcher could organize the library for one experimental group by general genres, and then organize the library for the second experimental group by subgenres. Remember, the control group will not experience this treatment, so their library would not be organized by genre at all. Do not feel bad for the control group. In social experiments, the control group gets the status quo—what they would have gotten anyway. This approach is not withholding anything from them but rather trying to determine if the treatment has an impact.

The third condition is *Temporal Ordering*, or a fancy way of saying that the cause comes before the effect. One might be thinking "Of course the cause has to precede the effect!" Well, it can be complicated in the real world because it can be tough to tell when events actually happen. Causes and effects can occur simultaneously, or the cause and effect can have a circular effect on one another. For example, librarians may notice that there is an increase of nonfiction circulation rates and thus pull all nonfiction books for easier access (notice here that our effect has occurred before our cause). The bottom line is that in order to conclude a causal **inference,** the cause *must* occur before the effect.

The fourth condition also seems self-evident: *Covariance*. Simply put, covariance means that when the cause changes the effect also changes. There is no cause-and-effect relationship if the two are not related. Thus, in our example, if we implement the treatment of a genre-organized library, we must also see some change in circulation in order for there to be a relationship. As one changes, so does the other. No change, no causal relationship.

The fifth and final condition, *Eliminate Alternate Explanations*, is the focus of our decisions related to research design and, to some degree, statistics. In order to make a causal inference, isolate what is causing the change (effect). If our research design is tight, we can be confident that a change in circulation is the result of our treatment of a genre-organized library. However, **confounding variables**, other pesky influences on circulation, can sneak in such as impending science fair date, teacher mandate, and others. To eliminate those alternate explanations, choose from a tool kit of statistical methods.

Research Designs for Causal Inference

The most rigorous research design for linking cause to effect is the *True Experimental Design*. The True Experimental Design, also known as a randomized control trial (RCT), has four qualities. The sample being studied has to be representative of the larger population one wants to make inferences about. Achieve this by taking a random sample from the population (i.e., take a random sample of fourth graders to make inferences about all fourth graders). Second, one needs experimental and control groups to compare. Third, randomly assigning students to each group will help to result in similar groups by evenly spreading out the sample's quirks across the two groups. Last, measure where the subjects are before the treatment or pretest and after posttest. In Scenario V (Ruzzi), the two groups should be the same on the pretest, or taking out the same number of books but will be different on the posttest. The genre-organized library's students take out more books than the non-genre-organized library.

Sounds easy, right? Several issues can compromise a true experimental research design. First, it is challenging to get a representative sample of a population in school settings because student populations are usually defined by parental choice and/or socioeconomic status. To randomly assign children can be untenable, since the researcher cannot tell people where to live or even which classes their children have to attend. Confounding variables are aplenty in a school setting. Sometimes the experimental and control groups interact with one another during the school day, leaving one uncertain that the treatment was only given to the experimental group. Finally, the pretest and posttest measures are often not reliable and valid. Thankfully, there are many research designs that try to mimic a True Experimental Design when one or more of these qualities are compromised.

Matching Designs attempt to manually compensate when one cannot randomly assign subjects to an experimental or control group. Oftentimes a researcher has an experimental group but will need to manufacture a control group. For example, if a school has a genre-organized library, it is not likely that the librarian will create a second non-genre-organized library for the control group and then randomly assign the students to each library. To find a comparison group, find a similar school, preferably in the same school division to hold constant the effects of school division policies. Identify a school that looks similar across many **variables** that might influence the effect (circulation data): size, structure, student population, teacher population, reading levels, poverty levels, grade distribution, librarian staffing, and schedule. Matching on several characteristics results in a control group that is similar to the treatment group without using **random assignment**.

When a researcher is not successful in securing a control group even through matching, use a *Time Series Design* to create a comparison within one group over time. Use these types of designs when we have small populations for which it would be difficult to find matches. While there are several ways to construct a time series research design, the one most appropriate for Scenario V (Ruzzi) is to let each student serve as his/her own control and experimental group. In our example, measure the circulation data across several quarters or years to establish a baseline (control). Then, once the library was reorganized by genre, measure the circulation data across several quarters or years to determine the effect of the treatment (experimental). To control for other things going on in the school or curriculum (remember those confounding variables?), alternate baseline and treatment measures for the various students.

Finally, use statistics to make up for the flaws in research design. While statistical tools are no match for great research design, they can help to better approximate cause and effect. Using statistical tools such as regression discontinuity and propensity score analyses to build simulated control groups that on paper match the experimental groups.

Thus far, the presented research approaches have involved quantitative data collection that just means that we look at numerical data instead of collecting individual spoken or written perspectives. This in no way is meant to devalue the importance of qualitative research. Qualitative research designs can help parse out cause-and-effect relationships and are an important consideration for complementary or follow-up studies that investigate how the treatment affected students and circulation data, as well as the perceptions of the students, teachers, and librarians about why one treatment worked and another did not. Strict quantitative causal research designs do not yield these rich perspectives.

And, it might go without saying, always pay special attention to protecting human subjects. Obtain permission from parents and the students themselves as well as the school and school division before conducting research that concerns human subjects. See Tables 13.1 and 13.2 for summaries of two types of research designs.

Table 13.1
Summary Chart 1: Matched Sample Design

Overall purpose	Fake random assignment
Advantages	• Control group that is similar to treatment group • Very strong quasi-experimental design that minimizes internal threats to validity
Disadvantages	Could be hidden differences in groups
Steps in process	For each subject in the treatment group, match with someone in control group that is the same on important characteristics such as pretest.
Data collection methods	Extant data
Data analysis methods	T-test (if two balanced groups)
Support technologies	Statistical analysis software (e.g., SPSS)

Table 13.2
Summary Chart 2: Time Series Design

Overall purpose	To provide a control group that is similar to the treatment group
Advantages	No one is "denied" the treatment.
Disadvantages	Groups that go before (i.e., fifth grade in 2016) could be inherently different from those that follow (i.e., fifth graders in 2017).
Steps in process	Subjects in earlier time period are assigned to control group (0), those currently participating are treatment group (1).
Data collection methods	Extant data
Data analysis methods	T-test (if two balanced groups)
Support technologies (if applicable)	Statistical analysis software (e.g., SPSS)

The Case of Collaboration and Flexible Scheduling at Red Pond Elementary School

It is important to be able to justify teaching practices and instructional decisions, for both the decision-maker and the administration. As was the case at Red Pond Elementary School, administration often changes and we cannot rely on leadership knowing what we are doing in our classrooms simply through their observations or experiences. When Ms. Night arrived as principal at Red Pond, she expectedly asked for faculty to justify the instructional decisions they had made. The great thing is that Ms. Night asked specifically for site-based justification. Time for a research project!

Specifically, Ms. Night asked Ms. Daniels to examine two separate interventions. The first involves fixed versus flexible scheduling. Although we know a fair amount scheduling, that work has been based on correlational research designs and cannot rigorously rule out alternate explanations. Here was Zoe Daniel's chance to fill that gap. The second intervention concerned grade level collaboration between teachers and the school librarian, an intervention that took two years to get up and running.

We can take this information and fine-tune our research question to ask "To what extent have librarian-teacher collaboration and flexible scheduling impacted student achievement at Red Pond?" We are looking at three variables in this study: librarian-teacher collaboration, flexible/fixed scheduling, and student achievement. The first two variables are considered **independent variables** (our potential causes), and the last variable is considered the **dependent variable** (our potential effect). This may seem like a tricky research question because it asks the librarian to investigate two interventions at the same time, but the two can be examined separately with solid research design. The other considerations that are common to all our programs involve time and money. Although Ms. Night did not specify a timeline or budget for Ms. Daniels to complete her study, we can assume that the timeline is immediate and the budget is nonexistent.

To design a research study, remember the five conditions necessary to make causal inferences. A research study must have experimental and control groups (causal relativity), a treatment (causal manipulation), a cause before the effect (temporal ordering), changes in both the cause and effect (covariance), and no confounding variables (eliminate alternate explanations). Additionally, the research design should be as close to a true experimental design as possible by meeting as many of its conditions as possible (random sampling, experimental and control groups, similar groups, and pretest and posttest measurements). Let us break our research question into two to design our study.

The first treatment, fixed versus flexible scheduling, is perhaps the easiest to examine. The first research question was "To what extent has flexible scheduling impacted student achievement?" While Red Pond can act as the experimental group because they received the treatment of flexible scheduling, we will need a control group in order to satisfy causal relativity. One option to accomplish this is to treat the school as an individual subject and conduct a time series analysis with multiple outcome variables. For the control group, Zoe could gather data from the school for six years prior to the implementation of flexible schedules on grade level circulation rates, grade level reading scores, teacher turnover, and other pertinent variables. She can then compare those to the six years of data after flexible schedules were implemented for the experimental group. A second, and stronger, option is for Zoe to find a school or schools in the division that had similar characteristics to Red Pond Elementary and has a fixed schedule to act as the control group. This school(s) should match Red Pond on grade level circulation rates, grade level reading scores, teacher turnover, and other variables perhaps such as proportion-free and reduced-price lunch eligibility. Zoe could then conduct a time series analysis using both schools. This is powerful because we might see that the outcome variables do not change for the six years before flexible scheduling was implemented but changes for one school after flexible scheduling was implemented, while the fixed schedule schools' data remain static. Having several years' worth of data pre and post the intervention assures us that the intervention impact was not from some other intervention such as a change in curriculum or vice-principal (thus eliminating alternate explanations). Conducting an experiment with existing data is advantageous as it does not involve expensive and time-consuming data collection. The matched designs help us approximate random assignment, and, thus, in this study we have met all of the conditions for causal inferences and three of the four qualities of the true experimental design.

Our second research question is "To what extent has flexible scheduling impacted student achievement?" This intervention is a tougher nut to crack because in addition to Ms. Daniels collaborating with teachers, there is also a reading resource, gifted, and computer technologist who collaborated with teachers in the same time period. However, isolating the collaborative value of one over the others can be done. Three teachers declined Zoe's invitation to collaborate. These teachers' classes can become the control group where students received the status quo, collaboration with the three other teachers but not with the school librarian. Our experimental group will consist of all the other students in the school whose teachers collaborated. Ms. Daniels should match similar students from each group in that they look alike at the beginning of the year in terms of grade, reading score, poverty level, and gender. Thus, we create a treatment group that starts off the year at the same level as the control group, as confirmed by pretest measures. Student achievement within the two groups may diverge as the year progresses and the experimental group receives the treatment their teacher collaborates with the librarian. Posttest measures would identify how much of an impact the treatment had on student achievement. To strengthen this study, Zoe should look at several years' worth of data in this manner so that Ms. Night can be assured the results are not from an anomaly. Again, this study uses historic data, thus there is no additional data collection or prolonged timeline.

Both of these studies involve some cooperation with personnel that control student records. As Ms. Night asked for these studies, one hopes that she will be helpful in asking central office for de-identified student records to be used both for group creation and student achievement data. Zoe Daniels could probably create the two groups for the first study on fixed versus flexible schedules by using her contacts at fixed-schedule schools. As with any research study, **Institutional Review Board (IRB)** approval and permission from school personnel, parents, and students must be attained prior to the start of the study. The bottom line is that the data are there; we just have to ask nicely.

The other thing that both of these studies utilize is some basic statistics. In order to compare groups (flexible to fixed schedule; collaboration to noncollaboration), Zoe should use t-tests. T-tests compare the means of two groups of similar size to determine if they are statistically different. These statistics can be calculated by hand (the horror!), Excel, or fancier statistical programs such as SPSS. If statistics are scary, they can also be calculated by a collaborating math teacher. Do not let a lack of familiarity with statistics stymie an investigation!

With a little bit of historical reflection and data analysis, Zoe Daniels could become one of the premier library researchers who uses causal research designs to provide evidence on which the leadership team will make decisions. Well done Red Pond Elementary!

Glossary of Key Terms

Confounding variables: These are variables that have not been controlled by the researcher and thus negatively impact the internal validity of the experiment.

Control group: It refers to the group of participants who do not experience the treatment.

Dependent variable: Dependent variable, also called outcome variable, is influenced by independent variable.

Experimental group: It refers to the group of participants who experience the treatment; also called treatment group.

Independent variables: These are variables that are manipulated in an experiment in order to determine possible change in the dependent variables, also called predictor variables.

Inference: It refers to a data-driven conclusion that links causes to effects.

Institutional Review Board (IRB): This is a committee that reviews, approves, and monitors research involving human subjects in order to ensure that research is conducted ethically and participants' rights are protected.

Random assignment: It refers to the process of assigning participants to different groups (control group or experimental group) using a random procedure.

Random sample: It refers to a batch of participants randomly selected from the larger population to be included in the study; each participant has an equal chance of being selected.

Treatment: It refers to a change or condition that is under investigation, also called manipulation or intervention.

Variables: Variables are factors that can "vary" from one participant or context to another; researchers can measure, manipulate, and control for variables.

Further Reading

"Evidence Based Medicine: PICO." Accessed June 29, 2017. http://research guides.uic.edu/c.php?g=252338&p=1683349.

Schneider, Barbara, Martin Carnoy, Jeremy Kilpatrick, William H. Schmidt, and Richard J. Shavelson. 2007. *Estimating Causal Effects: Using Experimental and Observational Designs.* AERA. Accessed June 29, 2017. http://www.aera.net/Portals/38/docs/Causal%20Effects.pdf.

Shadish, William R., Thomas D. Cook, and Donald T. Campbell. 2002. *Experimental and Quasi-Experimental Designs for Generalized Causal Inference.* 2nd ed. New York: Houghton Mifflin.

"Social Research Methods Knowledge Base." Accessed June 29, 2017. http://www.socialresearchmethods.net/kb/desexper.php.

Straus, Sharon E., Paul Glasziou, W. Scott Richardson, and R. Brian Haynes. 2010. *Evidence-Based Medicine: How to Practice and Teach EBM.* New York: Churchill Livingston.

SCENARIO VI

Co-Teaching, Student Learning, and Faculty Collaboration

Mirah J. Dow, Professor and Director, Ph.D. Program
School of Library and Information Management,
Emporia State University

Central State University, with 186 bachelor's and master's programs, is a state-funded university with approximately 6,214 enrolled students including 9% international students from 55 countries. The university has 242 full-time faculty. The average undergraduate class size is 24 students. The university began in 1863 to prepare teachers. A program to educate librarians began in 1900. Today, the Teachers College and the School of Library and Information Science are considered university flagships.

Dr. Ward is a professor of physical sciences at Central State University with expertise in the areas of physical sciences, elementary science education, research, and evaluation. He has leadership roles at the university and statewide in organization and implementation of grades 4–12 science and engineering fairs. Dr. Ward has been awarded grant funding for innovative teaching by the State Space Grant Consortium and the National Science Teachers Association. Five years ago, he received a national education grant to attend professional development on the topic of co-teaching that he has since used to inform his design of assignments and instruction of future elementary education science teachers.

At Central State, Dr. Neary is a professor of library and information science who is educated and experienced as a teacher and school librarian. Dr. Neary has directed the university's school library licensure program and currently directs the university's only Doctor of Philosophy program. In addition to teaching reference and user services, Dr. Neary teaches master and doctoral students quantitative, qualitative, and mixed methods concepts and methods. She has experience as an instructional partner with teachers at the middle school, high school, and college levels. Her recent professional development includes participation at the State

Center for Science and Mathematics Education in a series of workshops titled *Classrooms as Discovery Creations.*

Dr. Ward and Dr. Neary's most recent co-teaching has been in the context of teaching Dr. Ward's introductory level course, Our Physical World, with enrolled future elementary education teachers of physical sciences wherein students learn the scientific method. Dr. Ward's course is delivered in face-to-face instruction during class sessions that meet two times each week for an hour and two times each week for two hours, a total of six hours/week during a 16-week semester.

Their co-taught unit covers 12 weeks of the semester and addresses the overarching goal of learning in the physical sciences to help students see that there are mechanisms of cause and effect in natural systems that can be understood through a common set of physical and biological principles. Ultimately, the two professors want the future elementary education teachers to learn to identify authentic topics and problems from real-life situations. They also want teachers to design studies to appropriately address the topic/problem rather than to continue in the established trend of elementary science teachers and their grades 4–12 students typically using the Internet to find an already designed study that has been used many times with no identified, realistic rationale using research-based evidence.

When co-teaching, both professors deliver a series of face-to-face, interactive discussions with students about the eight steps in a quantitative experiment using a two-part research process model developed by Dr. Neary. Then, students are given detailed assignment instructions for the unit in three parts to design and complete a control variable experiment. Dr. Neary provides a resource guide for this unit available on the university's website. Major emphasis in the assignment is on selection of a topic and identification of a problem; accessing and selecting appropriate sources of authority on the topic and evaluating information and evidence found in selected sources on the basis of accuracy, validity, importance, and context; making connections from science to real-word questions; developing a range of questions to frame the search for new understandings; and appropriately identifying experimental study variables. In addition to learning substantive content knowledge and the scientific process, Dr. Ward's students observe co-teaching at its best.

Dr. Ward and Dr. Nary collected scores on two groups of undergraduate students with 28 students in each group. In addition to Dr. Ward's scores from semesters when no co-teaching took place, the professors now have students' scores on all three parts of the co-taught, regularly assigned unit to design and complete a control variable experiment. The professors want to design a study to determine what advantages undergraduate college students realize as a result of experiencing co-teaching by two professors, one a science teacher and the other a librarian, and to determine and describe the instructional elements of their co-taught physical sciences unit that includes four student learning outcomes: (1) students will accurately identify variables from examples provided by the professor; (2) students will accurately write a problem statement and identify variables; (3) students will accurately write a problem statement and conduct a control variable experiment; and (4) when given a scientific problem statement under test conditions, students will accurately identify independent, dependent, and control variables.

The professors agree that their new theory, the *intensity theory of co-teaching*, can be used to explain what happens when two educators work together to build maximum intellectual strength in themselves that can be measured by their students' learning and achievement of identified learning outcomes. To build on their new theory by expanding what is published about co-teaching as a form of collaboration as well as to attempt to contribute to filling existing gaps in understanding the professional knowledge of science teachers, they agree that their upcoming research in one or more studies should respond to the following overarching question:

How does co-teaching impact student learning and faculty?

Chapter 14

Phenomenology

Jenny Bossaller, Assistant Professor
School of Information Science and Learning Technologies,
University of Missouri

Introduction to Phenomenology

Is it possible to see the world through someone else's eyes? Is it possible to gain an understanding of the meaning of human experience through research? Phenomenology is a philosophy that states that humans do experience some of the same things and that a universal truth can be derived by processing iterations of conscious experience. The way to know truth is through research: established, rigorous, and defined ways of knowing or methods. Methods can be followed to uncover the truth, and in this case, the meaning of experiences. Phenomenology is a way of understanding self in relation to others in sharing the essence of universal experiences. Unlike, for instance, psychology, which might look at unconscious experience, it is the study of conscious, lived experiences or observable events. Van Manen (2014) breaks down the word, "*phenomenology,* etymologically, which is helpful in that it helps explain the philosophy and method: *phenomenon* means that which appears; the word, *logos,* means word or study" (27). He explains, though, that unlike other "ologies" such as psyche, bios, among others, phenomenology does not have a "subject matter or a subject domain in the sense" that is as easily pinpointed as that of the psyche or living things. Phenome are more difficult to pin down because they cover the range of experience, and experience is ephemeral. However, by combining and giving equal weight to all descriptions of experience because that is all that is available, researchers can hope to find an intersubjective truth of being.

In 1931, philosopher Edmund Husserl wrote that researchers should return to the things themselves. Those things are only available to us through the lens of conscious experience. *How can we know what other people experience? How can we know the truth?* Related are questions about ethics: *How should we relate to the other? How can we know others, enter into communion, and empathize with others?* These are the questions that phenomenologists as philosophers seek to discover. The *how* to do this is the methodology: discovering what the true nature of things *is* by gaining new descriptions of experiences and combining them to see an entire picture; the picture, at the end, is a bricolage of perceptions that reveal the essential truth of the phenomenon.

Phenomenology was established as a philosophy in the early 1900s, though its roots go back to Aristotle. However, it really began to flourish and became widely used during what Denzin and Lincoln (1998) call the "modernist or golden age" of qualitative research (1950–1970). Phenomenology also provided the groundwork for a number of related philosophies, such as poststructuralism and culture critique (van Manen 2014). Cibangu and Hepworth (2016) pointed out that now "phenomenology has pervaded academic research and thinking to such an extent that people hardly realize it" (148). While it is pervasive, it is still somewhat mystifying.

Resources and Background

A researcher who wants to know more about phenomenology has no shortage of resources. The following two short sections will provide a very brief overview of some resources. For more, see The Husserl Page (Phenomenology Online: http://www.phenomenologyonline.com/.)

History and Philosophy

A serious student of phenomenology should tackle the primary texts, as the student shows the philosophical underpinnings and evolution of thinking about knowing, meaning, experience, time, self, and others. Some of the primary texts are Edmund Husserl's *Logical Investigations* (1901) and *Ideas* (1913), Martin Heidegger's *Being and Time* (1927); Jean-Paul Sartre's *Being and Nothingness* (1943), Maurice Merleau-Ponty's *Phenomenology of Perception* (1945), and Levinas's *Totality and Infinity* (1961). Several branches of phenomenology developed over the course of the twentieth century. Creswell (2013, 59) described four different iterations: hermeneutic, empirical, ethical, and transcendental phenomenology. Transcendental phenomenology (Husserl) calls for the researcher to remove himself from his observations—that is, he transcends personal experience in order to gain an objective view of the experience. Later philosophers, such as Heidegger, said that such a state of transcendence is not really possible, but that people can gain a sense of universal experience through empathy, which is a stance that led to the development of ethical phenomenology. Empirical phenomenology says that researchers can know about the world by "borrowing" experiences from other people. Variations in the philosophy focus on relation of self to others, knowing, and what that means for an understanding of truth.

Sokolowski's *Introduction to Phenomenology* (2000) is an excellent comprehensive and accessible overview of the history and philosophers associated with phenomenology. Readers have found Dowling's (2007) article about variations of phenomenology applied to the nursing field to be useful to other human sciences.

Methodology

A number of qualitative textbooks cover the basics of phenomenological methods, among them are Creswell (2013), Patton (2015), and Denzin and Lincoln (1998). A number of excellent books are devoted exclusively to the phenomenological method: Moustakas's (1994) *Phenomenological Research Methods*, Van Manen's (2014) *Phenomenology of Practice*, and Vagle's (2014) *Crafting Phenomenological Research*. Moustakas's 1984 book is very accessible and poetic; it is also applicable across a wide range of disciplines; he included a number of examples of how the method is used in the human sciences. Van Manen's book might prove especially helpful in library and information science (LIS) in relation to studying professionals. Van Manen also provided extensive background on many philosophers of phenomenology.

When Is Phenomenology Useful?

Phenomenology is a philosophy, a way of knowing, or an outlook. Phenomenology is used to explain the essence of a particular human experience, but it is most useful when studying an experience in which the author has an intense personal interest (Moustakas 1994). Almost anything that a person has experienced can be studied using phenomenological methods. For instance, one might study moving to a new country, of entering a shopping mall for the first time, and of gambling, work, or a health experience. As stated earlier, it has been used very often in nursing and healthcare settings. It is concerned with the experiences and meanings of human consciousness rather than the facts or material things that can be counted.

Phenomenology can be used on its own, but it is also very useful as part of a mixed methods study or multiple methods study. Moustakas (1994) wrote a very accessible explanation of phenomenological research methods. He emphasizes that, as with all research, the questions and methods must align:

> The research question that is the focus of and guides an investigation must be carefully constructed, every word deliberately chosen and ordered in such a way that the primary words appear immediately, capture my attention, and guide and direct me in the phenomenological process of seeing, reflecting, and knowing. Every method relates back to the question, is developed solely

to illuminate the question, and provides a portrayal of the phenomenon that is vital, rich and layered in its textures and meanings. (59)

Parts of intended research might be appropriate for phenomenology, while others are best explored with other methods. A multiple methods study would have a research design that uses multiple quantitative or qualitative methods. In this case, it would employ multiple qualitative methods. A mixed method design would use quantitative and qualitative methods such as observations and documentary analysis among others that inform one another, if sequential, or compared in the mixed, or final, stage. Both of these methods will be explained at the end of this chapter. The process of combining research methods can result in a much stronger set of findings, from the reviewer's point of view.

How Can We Use Phenomenology in LIS Research?

Phenomenological studies could be used to influence design or implementation of programs, systems, how one interacts with users, how one structures the break room, or how one designs the physical spaces of our buildings. The main idea is that when one understands how people experience the systems that one builds or implements, when one can empathize with other people, one can make improvements to the system. The experiences of people who use our systems can provide invaluable insight into what is going right and what is not going so well. Admittedly, if a costly change is called for as a result of a phenomenological study, additional, most likely quantitative, data will be called for.

Cibangu and Hepworth (2016) pointed out that "most phenomenological studies in information science are clustered around hermeneutic phenomenology . . . perhaps because of the close relation between information and meaning or cognition" (153). Budd (2005) explains that phenomenology offers a new way for librarians and information professionals to interact with information seekers; it can be about how the seeker interacts with texts and with signs. He says that phenomenology is even more fundamental than that: "If information gives shape to our thoughts and beliefs, what happens within us results in a reshaping?" (49). Through discourse and understanding what other people mean about a specific thing, librarians can more accurately help them find what they are looking for, to intervene or navigate between the internal world and that of generalities, or a created ontology.

Articles in the *Library Literature & Information Science Full Text* database for searches about phenomenology including "phenomenological study," "phenomenological research," "phenomenological analysis" and "phenomenological design" found that researchers are using phenomenological methods to study a variety of topics in LIS. Some recent phenomenological studies in LIS include studies about the public library users; Antell (2004) studied why college students used public libraries, and Pohanjen and Kortelainen (2015) completed a study of transgender information behavior. More studies were about librarians themselves. Some were about librarians' personal lives; for instance, Kendrick and Damasco (2016) studied conservative academic librarians, and Gallin-Parisi (2015) studied librarianship and motherhood. Studies about librarians' professional work were more common. Brown and Duke (2005) studied collaborative instruction between librarians and faculty; Nakhoda and Rahimian (2015) studied the experiences of female librarians in Tehran; Burns and Bossaller (2012) studied experiences of communication in academic libraries; Julien and Genuis (2009) studied emotional labor in librarians' instruction work; and Edwards (2013) studied the experiences of African American women who were in upper management of Information Technology.

How to Do Phenomenological Research

Moustakas (1994) described the research process of phenomenology. It shares some characteristics with other qualitative research methods such as a literature review, an ethics/consent form, and method of data collection but differs in purpose, organization of data, and interpretation. A summary of Moustakas's recommended method is:

(1) identifying the topic, as rooted in autobiographical meanings and values, as well as social meanings and significance;
(2) Performing a comprehensive review of the literature;
(3) Locating appropriate **coresearchers** (more commonly referred to as interview participants);
(4) Going through the proper consent process and ethics review;
(5) Developing a set of interview questions;
(6) Conducting and recording interviews; and
(7) Organizing and analyzing the data.

Phenomenological research is generally completed through long, unstructured interviews. They are most often one-on-one interviews, although some unstructured group interviews might work as well (Denzin and Lincoln, 55).

Phenomenological research is in some respects similar to other qualitative research; it differs primarily in the interviewing process and analysis. Therefore, the following sections will be limited to those processes.

Interviewing for Phenomenology

Van Manen (2014) said of the phenomenological interview, it

> serves the very specific purpose of exploring and gathering experiential narrative material, stories, or anecdotes that may serve as a resource for phenomenological reflection and thus develop a richer and deeper understanding of human

phenomenon. But that is much more difficult than it may sound … it is easier to get a person to tell about an experience than to tell an experience as lived through (315).

The researcher's goal is to ask them to relive the experience, not to reflect on it from the vantage point of the future.

Moustakas (1994) developed a useful set of questions for phenomenological interviews. They are general enough that they could be used in any number of interviews:

(1) What dimensions, incidents and people intimately connected with the experience stand out for you?
(2) How did the experience affect you? What changes to you associate with the experience?
(3) How did the experience affect significant others in your life?
(4) What feelings were generated by the experience?
(5) What thoughts stood out for you?
(6) What bodily changes or states were you aware of at the time?
(7) Have you shared all that is significant with reference to the experience?

Although there is no particular prescribed place to interview, there are some guidelines; it may or may not take place where the experience took place. There must be sufficient time for an unhurried, relaxed interview or even a series of interviews if necessary. Prior to delving into deep discussion, the interviewer must establish trust to draw out personal stories. The conversation should be recorded, because the act of taking notes during an interview would distract both the interviewer and participant, potentially ruining spontaneity and natural conversational flow. The interviewer should encourage the participant to explain what he or she means without reflecting on what it meant; for instance ask, "What did you do next?" rather than, "Do you think that you did the right thing?"

Analysis of Phenomenological Data

A researcher might use several different methods to analyze phenomenological data, but it generally relies upon an initial reading of the data, a close rereading, followed by coding of meaning units, and finally developing an essence description.

Giorgi (2012) explains in detail five steps of data analysis:

(1) Read everything through in order to get a sense of the whole. No further steps can be taken until the researcher has a holistic understanding of the data.

(2) Reread it. This time, mark each transition in meaning. This is the process of constituting parts that are called meaning units.

(3) Transform the data, still basically in the words of the subject, into expressions that are more directly revelatory of the psychological import of what the subject said.

(4) The direct and psychologically more sensitive expressions are then reviewed and with the help of free imaginative variation and essential structure of the experience is written.

(5) the essential structure is then used to help clarify and interpret the raw data of the research. (5)

Applying Phenomenological Methods to the Scenario

Phenomenological methods can be used to answer the question: *How does co-teaching impact student learning and faculty?* Because phenomenology seeks to understand the essence of some phenomenon, the first step is to identify the phenomenon. Within Scenario 6 (Dow), and even within the research question, there is a lot of "noise," methodologically speaking; that is, there is a lot that is not studied using phenomenological methods. For instance, the researcher would not look at measurable impact of student learning in the classroom or students or teachers' reflections on outcomes although in a mixed method study those could be studied; the quantitative results would be combined with the phenomenological findings.

Co-teaching has been explored using phenomenological methods before; Groenewald (2004) interviewed 10 academics and "enterprise representatives" about collaborative educational efforts in adult professional education. He used triangulation, which included unstructured, in-depth phenomenological interviews, memo-ing, and essays to give additional insights into the analysis. As a researcher, you might want to consider additional methods in order to more completely answer the question of impact.

Some aspects of the scenario are very appropriate to study using phenomenological methods. For instance,

1. the experience of what it is like to be a student learning in this situation,
2. the experience of being a faculty member co-teaching with a librarian,
3. the experience of being an embedded librarian,
4. the experience of being a student and writing a problem statement and identifying variables,
5. the experience of conducting experiments.

Phenomenological research is completed through interviews with people who have been involved with the phenomenon under study: in this case, interview students and faculty. Avoid suggestive prompts and avoid any interpretation.

The words of these experiences would only be applicable to this particular instance and strive to have them relive the moment, rather than reflecting on the outcomes. The main idea is to capture what it was like for the participants in order to unearth meaning of the experience.

The Interviews

Reviewing the guidelines stated by researchers in the earlier text, the actual interviews require three questions to be answered: "Who?" "Where?" "When?" Those answers are as follows:

(1) Who? If a researcher is trying to find out how co-teaching impacts student learning and faculty, interview both students and faculty. Get enough data; 10 good interviews should be enough data. Generally, researchers say to interview to the "point of saturation" meaning until there is lots of repetition or the point at which nothing new or significant is being said. The interviews should be conducted with people who both are interested in and invested in the subject; therefore, people who participated in it and who want to talk about it should be interviewed.

(2) Where? The interviews should take place where the coresearchers and participants who might be considered coresearchers, are comfortable and are able to think without being interrupted. Conduct the interviews in their home, office, or another private location. In working with students, researchers would not necessarily want to be in the classroom because that could induce some anxiety. The school library either before or after school or another neutral, relaxed location might be more productive.

(3) When? Conduct the interviews when everyone has plenty of time and is able to relax. It takes time to describe the study, gain trust and then have a conversation about all of the aspects of the experience.

Interview Questions

The researcher should begin with a disclosure of the interview's intent and obtain the coresearcher's consent to use the data. There is no deception in phenomenological research; it is a journey of discovery with the participant, which is why the participant might be called a coresearcher. Interview questions are certainly flexible, but ask the right questions to get started. For teachers, start out with questions such as the following:

(1) What was it like the first time you stepped into the classroom with your co-teacher?

(2) What incidents stood out in the co-teaching experience?

> (3) Was there a particular student who stands out in your memory? Was there an incident that you recall that was meaningful in that students' learning?
>
> (4) What changes in your teaching can you associate with these experiences?
>
> (5) Tell me about an incident that caused you to have strong feelings about teaching and learning while you were co-teaching.

The interviews with students might be more difficult, or easier, depending on the age of the participants. Luckily, the questions should not present any ethical problems, but be prepared to take extra steps in preparing your application for the Institutional Review Board. Once the researcher has explained the study's purpose, and established a rapport with the coresearcher/participant, begin the conversation, some questions to get the interview started are as follows:

> (1) Tell me what it was like going into the classroom when you learned you would have two teachers.
>
> (2) Was there a time when you felt happy/interested in the subject/frustrated with the teachers?
>
> (3) Can you talk about doing experiments in the classroom?

Can you remember a time when you were really excited about learning something new in this class? The point is not to have them reflect on the experience, but rather to ask them to recall particular events that will provide insight into the classroom experience, especially in relation to learning. After you have interviewed a sufficient number of people who participated in the program (10 is often cited as a sufficient number in a study like this), you can begin analyzing your data.

Analyzing the Interviews

In a study, read through each interview, gain a sense of the whole, and begin marking each transition in the interview. Next, compile meaning units—excerpts from interviews that demonstrate what the experience meant for each participant. Finally, review the meaning units and create meaningful categories of meaning. At this point, piece the categories together like a puzzle, which will reveal the main themes of the phenomenon. A main theme for the teachers and a main theme for the students will likely emerge. The end result should be a single idea that is the essence of the phenomenon, which I cannot venture to guess at this point.

In sum, the purpose of phenomenological analysis is to gain universal sense of truth through a collective vision of a particular event, a phenomenon. See Table 14.1 for a summary of this research method.

Table 14.1
Summary Chart: Phenomenology

Overall purpose	Phenomenological studies can be used to influence design or implementation of programs and systems. The main idea is that when we understand how people experience the systems that we build or implement, when we can empathize with other people, we can make improvements to the system.
Advantages	• Rigorous method that controls for bias • Provides deeper understanding of research at an aggregate level • Allows for the application of research to practice • Uncovers gaps in existing research
Disadvantages	• Amount of time required for transcription, reading, and close re-reading for analysis • Requires strong interview skills • Needs comprehensive access to literature • Methodological complexity
Steps in process	1. Identify the topic, as rooted in autobiographical meanings and values, as well as social meanings and significance. 2. Perform a comprehensive review of the literature. 3. Locate appropriate coresearchers (more commonly referred to as interview participants). 4. Develop a set of interview questions. 5. Conduct and record interviews 6. Organize and analyze the data. 7. Present results.
Data collection methods	• Interviewing; comprehensive literature searching • Inclusion/exclusion criteria • Critical appraisal and data extraction from included studies
Data analysis methods	• Content analysis
Support technologies	• Audio and video recording equipment • Field notes • Software for data gathering, analysis, and visualization (e.g., Dedoose, NVivo, and RQDA, a qualitative package for R)

Glossary of Key Term

Co-researchers: Coresearchers are participants in phenomenological research. This is a more appropriate term than subject, although participant might also work. As is appropriate for the method, it purposefully puts the researcher on equal footing with the participant.

Bracketing: Similar to reduction, the process of putting one's own preconceptions aside in order to fully gain an understanding of another's experiences.

Eidetic reduction: "the process by which the person or researcher brings into question their taken-for granted presuppositions, misconceptions, and biases that preclude the fuller acquisition and actualization of knowledge" (Cibango and Hepworth, 150). It helps us to go beyond our own familiarization with the world and see it with new eyes or a sense of wonder.

Epoche: suspending one's own understanding in order to fully understand or enter into an empathetic state with the co-researcher.

Horizontalization: Phenomenology seeks to reveal essential truths about the meaning of human experience; in order to find a complete picture that is unsullied by the researcher's own thoughts or experiences, the process or horizontalization is employed to give each unit of meaning equal weight.

Intentionality: the idea that every act of consciousness is correlated with an object (Sokolowski, p. 8); intending means "the conscious relationship we have to an object" of which we are conscious. Our interpretations of what happens in our life is framed within our own understanding.

Further Reading

Moustakis, Clark. 1994. *Phenomenological Research Methods*. Thousand Oaks, CA: Sage Publications.

Sokolowski, Robert. 2000. *Introduction to Phenomenology*. London: Cambridge University Press.

Van Manen, Max. 2014. *Phenomenology of Practice*. Walnut Creek, CA: Left Coast Press.

Chapter 15

The Case Study

Maria Cahill, Associate Professor
School of Information Science, University of Kentucky
Kyle A. Lee, Doctoral Student
School of Information Science, University of Kentucky

Introduction to the Case Study Method

Case study is a comprehensive strategy ideal for examining a present-day phenomenon within context for the purpose of generating theory or contributing to an existing theory (Yin 2014). Case study can employ both quantitative and qualitative methods and research tools to analyze multiple sources of evidence for the purpose of examining the uniqueness or generalizability of a specific present-day event or phenomenon. Case study itself, however, is not a method but a research strategy (Mills et al. 2010), and "a choice of what is to be studied" (Stake 2005, 443). Unlike other qualitative research methods, case study is defined by the unit of analysis, that is, the case, rather than the focus of the study; thus, it is common for the strategy to be used in combination with another type of study such as ethnography, grounded theory, or narrative (Merriam and Tisdell 2016). Finally, the strategy can be engaged to examine a phenomenon within a single context (i.e., single-case design), or examine the phenomenon across multiple contexts (i.e., multicase design).

Because case study involves multiple forms of data collection, while also requiring the researcher be adaptable to unfolding opportunities and unexpected situations and mindful of ethical considerations related to research with humans, the demands of case study far exceed those of other research methods (Yin 2014). Nevertheless, budding researchers are not excluded from case study. Prior to beginning data collection, however, a logical, well-constructed design is paramount and should include a bounding of the case based primarily upon theory (Elger 2010). Further, it is only through triangulation of multiple sources of data that a phenomenon can be fully understood; thus, sufficient time and expertise with multiple data collection and analysis techniques is prerequisite for sound case study research. Novice researchers may find case study to be a delicate balancing act: they must ensure they collect enough data to allow for adequate analysis, but also must guard against collection of too much data that, in turn, cannot be used (Yin 2014).

Description of Research Method

Dr. Ward and Dr. Neary are experienced scholars and teachers who have recently co-taught a 12-week unit designed to help preservice teachers apply the scientific method to solve authentic problems they encounter in their everyday worlds. The two professors contend that their students have excelled in their learning as a consequence of engaging in a well-designed, co-planned and co-taught unit of instruction, and they wish to research co-teaching to both build upon their new *intensity theory of co-teaching* and contribute to the professional knowledge within the discipline of science education. The question driving the professors' research is "How does co-teaching impact student learning and faculty?"

According to Yin (2014), "how and why questions are more explanatory and likely to lead to the use of case studies and experiments as the preferred research strategies. This is because such questions deal with operational links needing to be traced over time, rather than mere frequencies or incidence" (6). Further, because Dr. Ward and Dr. Neary are interested in exploring a contemporary and bounded phenomenon over which the researchers have little control, case study would be an ideal strategy to employ.

The five steps of case study research design include identifying guiding questions, developing **theoretical proposition** (when appropriate), determining the unit of analysis, illustrating the link between data and propositions, and establishing criteria for interpreting the findings (Yin 2014).

Research Questions

Three sub-questions have been devised to answer the overarching research question "How does co-teaching impact student learning and faculty?" and will guide the design of the case study. Additionally, topics to consider are identified under each sub-question:

1. To what extent does co-teaching impact student learning?

    a. Content learning (e.g., the stated learning outcomes for the project)

    b. Twenty-first century skills

2. How does co-teaching influence student learning?

    a. Affect toward science

    b. Student-to-student relationships

    c. Student-to-teacher relationships

3. To what extent does co-teaching impact faculty?

    a. Affect toward teaching

    b. Faculty-to-faculty relationships

    c. Faculty-to-student relationships

    d. Teaching strategies/pedagogy

    e. Content knowledge

Because "case study fieldwork regularly takes the researcher in unexpected directions" (Stake 1995, 28), the questions at this point are flexible and can be redefined or adjusted as the research progresses.

Theoretical Proposition

Dr. Ward and Dr. Neary's *intensity theory of co-teaching* purports that two educators working together first build maximum intellectual strength in themselves, which, in turn, can be measured by their students' learning and achievement of identified learning outcomes. Thus, the primary proposition guiding this case is that the co-teachers have to recognize and develop their own strengths as collaborative partners and co-teachers in order for the co-teaching to be maximally effective.

Unit of Analysis

As previously mentioned, case study can encompass a single case or multiple cases. Additionally, a research team can employ a holistic design when there are no apparent subunits to consider or when the theory is holistic in nature. However, the overarching research question posed by Dr. Ward and Dr. Neary points to two units of analysis: students and faculty. Thus, an embedded design seems most appropriate in this instance.

Though the two researchers developed their theory based on their own experiences, moving forward they will identify other faculty who are engaged in co-teaching to find relevant evidence to support or counter the proposition that co-teachers must first develop their strengths as collaborators in order for the co-teaching to be maximally effective. Dr. Ward and Dr. Neary must determine whether to delimit the study to a single case or to examine multiple cases.

The inclusion of multiple cases enhances the external validity or generalizability of findings (Merriam and Tisdell 2016); however, if time and resources are limited, a deep examination of a single case would be better than cursory examination of multiple cases. If choosing a single case, it might be advantageous to select an unusual case, and whether single or multiple, they should consider only those cases in which the faculty and students are open to the research team and willing to accommodate the needs of the inquiry (Stake 1995).

Data Collection Procedures

The single most important consideration in qualitative research design is selecting appropriate times, settings, and individuals to provide the information needed to answer the research question (Maxwell 2005). As they move forward, it would be in the researchers' best interest to utilize both purposeful and convenient sampling methods in order to choose participants and venues for the data collection phase. Further, in the interest of construct validity and reliability, the researchers should follow four principles of data collection: use multiple sources of evidence, organize evidence via a database, maintain a chain of evidence, and tread cautiously when collecting evidence from electronic sources (Yin 2014).

Evidence for case studies comes in six different formats: documents, archival records, interviews, direct observations, participant observations, and physical artifacts (Yin 2014). Because the overarching research question and guiding questions consist of the outcomes from the co-teaching model, a variety of data collection methods are available, and appropriate, for the researchers to use during data collection. Thus, for this specific case or set of cases, it makes sense for data collection to occur in the form of direct observations, interviews, and document review.

In addition to labeling each piece of collected data with full identification information, the researchers will also establish an organizational system early in the data collection process. Case study evidence is typically organized by date and/or topic (Merriam and Tisdale 2016). To simplify the organization of various transcriptional codes and **themes** found in the direct observations, interviews, and document reviews, the researchers may choose to use an electronic qualitative data analysis computer software program. McMillan and Schumacher (2010) recommend the following, as they are considered the most popular options for educational researchers: (a) MAXQDA, (b) ATLAS.ti, (c) Ethnograph, (d) NVivo, and (e) HyperRESEARCH.

Direct Observations

Direct observation, a primary source for qualitative data (Merriam 1998), is one of the most common types of field visit methods in case study research (Yin 2014).

Observations enable researchers to understand the context of the case, and they also provide firsthand evidence of behaviors as they are occurring. For this study, direct observations would be best utilized by the researchers during planning sessions of the co-teaching faculty and during lessons where the co-teaching model was being implemented. Naturally, the researchers will be on the lookout for evidence related to the overarching question and sub-questions, and as they are observing, the researches should take field notes related to the physical setting, the co-teachers' and students' activities, interactions, and conversations, as well as less obvious factors such as nonverbal communication, and even the observer's own behaviors (Merriam and Tisdale 2016). It is recommended that the researchers of this study work to develop a consistent observation schedule that allows them to raise questions and develop diverse perspectives related to answering the overarching research question (Yin 2014), and that they write, type, or dictate notes into a narrative format as soon after the observations as possible (Merriam and Tisdale 2016).

Although exposing themselves directly to the research scenario opens access to both the events and groups being studied, there are several concerns associated with observations that the researchers need to keep in mind, mainly that of the reliability of observational evidence gathered by a single researcher. In order to avoid observational bias, the researchers should have more than one single observer conducting observations in the research setting (Yin 2014). Other challenges facing researchers conducting observations include remembering to take detailed field-notes, recording participant quotes accurately, determining what information is most valuable, and keeping one's self from being overwhelmed (Creswell 2007). Although seemingly daunting, when done properly, good qualitative case study observations work to provide an "incontestable description" (Stake 1995, 62) of events in the form of a story to help further clarify, support, and strengthen data analysis. Finally, knowledge of the context and specific observed incidents can serve as reference points for subsequent interviews (Merriam and Tisdale 2016).

Interviews

One of two main principles in case study research is "to obtain the descriptions and interpretations of others" (Stake 1995, 64); thus, interviews should be utilized by the researchers in order to gather data in the form of their personal lived stories and experiences from study participants (Creswell 2007; McMillan and Schumacher 2010). Having direct access to the stories and experiences of both the students and instructors/faculty, in the co-teaching course(s), the researchers will want to perform individual and focus-group interviews to seek out evidence that the researchers would not otherwise be able to directly observe (Patton 2015).

Interviews with the co-teaching faculty could be conducted jointly; however, if the information the instructors have to share is sensitive, that is if the co-teaching experience were not positive for one or both members, that information would be better obtained in individual interviews (Merriam and Tisdell 2016). Whether jointly or individually, the interviews should be conducted in a semi-structured format utilizing a mix of more and less structured questions, to allow the researchers flexibility in their exploration and investigation of the phenomenon. The semi-structured interview would also permit the researcher to "respond to the situation at hand" (Merriam 1998, 74), thus allowing for a consistent flow to emerge from individual and group conversations.

Before embarking on interviews with students, it is important for the research team to recognize the existing power dynamics that may exist between the young adult (and potentially even adolescent) students in undergraduate classes and adult researchers. It might be advantageous for a more closely age-matched graduate student to conduct the interviews, but regardless of the individual interviewer, the research team should ensure that the context in which the interviews occur is natural (Eder and Fingerson 2003). Initially, the interviews should be conducted in a focus-group format, ideally with 6–10 purposefully selected students (Merriam and Tisdell 2016), followed by individual interviews if necessary, and beginning with very unstructured questions that are nondirected and inclusive. After the initial period in which the interviewer allows the process to unfold in a manner that is comfortable for the students, the focus groups and interviews can take on a semi-structured format (Eder and Fingerson 2003).

The most common method for recording interview and focus group data is through an audio recording that is later transcribed verbatim in a format that enables analysis. Audio recording and transcribing can be time consuming and/or expensive; thus some researchers opt to take notes during the interview or to write down as much information as possible immediately after the interview concludes. Because it is impossible to write all pertinent information during the interview or following an interview to remember precisely what had been said, verbatim transcripts are the most ideal recording form in situations where it is permissible (Merriam and Tisdale 2016).

Document Review

Documents are "a ready-made source of data easily accessible to the imaginative and resourceful investigator" (Merriam 1998, 112) that have frequently been underutilized in qualitative research (Merriam and Tisdale 2016). Their primary value is as supporting role in triangulating evidence collected from other sources (Yin 2014). Similar to the semi-structured interview protocol, the researchers should approach document review both organized and open to unexpected evidences (Stake 1995). For this study, it is recommended that for unobtrusive data collection, the researchers refer to documents such as syllabuses, student work, teacher plans, teacher notes, course assessments (both formative and summative), student assessment results, and student records. Additionally, email correspondence between the co-teaching faculty and any text-based discussions conducted in an online learning management system such as Blackboard or Canvas would likely serve as evidence to address the research question and sub-questions. If possible, electronic copies of written documents should be created (Merriam and Tisdale 2016), and to best keep track of the significance and treatment of each document, the researchers should develop an index system or filing method to organize those documents being chosen for examination and usage within the study (Hatch 2002).

Participant Recruitment

"Identifying context for all studies requires selecting settings appropriate to the kind of research proposed and finding environments in which research questions can be answered," (Hatch 2002, 44) and "selecting context and identifying participants are closely related" (Hatch 2002, 48). Because qualitative researchers work to understand the perspectives and lived experiences of participants, the best option for the researchers in this study would be those individuals directly impacted through the co-teaching model, the faculty co-teaching, and the students in those courses. Given the current focus on interdisciplinary collaboration at many institutions of higher education, college-level and unit-level administrators at the researchers' institution are likely aware of and promote cross disciplinary co-teaching; hence, it would behoove Dr. Neary and Dr. Ward to work through administrative channels to identify other co-teaching faculty. Once the researchers compile a list of co-teaching faculty, they should schedule individual meetings to discuss the co-teaching, the present research study, and the faculty's willingness to participate. Based on the outcomes of those meetings, they should select cases in which the faculty are open to the research team and willing to accommodate the needs of the inquiry (Stake 1995).

Prior to beginning the data collection process, the researchers need to develop consent, and possibly assent forms depending upon the age of the youngest students. Additionally, Dr. Neary and Dr. Ward must seek research approval through their university's Internal Review Board (IRB) who will scrutinize the research protocols to ensure that the study abides by regulations governing research with human participants and that the risk associated with participation in the study is minimized. Once the study is approved, the research term should seek informed consent from all participants, as well as parental assent if necessary. Both faculty and student participation should be voluntary with all participants holding the right to remove themselves from the study at any time with no repercussions.

Data Analysis Method

As with most qualitative research, data analysis is considered to be the most difficult stage of case study, and its primary purpose is to bring about full understanding of the case through examination of multiple sources of data (Merriam and Tisdale 2016). Because the researchers should begin to analyze the data during the data collection period, conclusions and inferences about a case can be influenced, thus shifting the researchers' thinking prior to drawing conclusions.

As soon as each field note from an observation, transcription of a focus groups or individual interview, or documents is collected and added to the case evidence, the researchers should read it multiple times to check for accuracy, while also developing familiarity with the data. Beginning with the very first piece of evidence collected and continuing throughout the data collection phase, the researchers will review the evidence and re-view the evidence again and again as additional data are collected. As the researchers begin to notice reoccurring themes and patterns within the data, they will document those by assigning codes. A **code** is "a word or short phrase that symbolically assigns a summative, salient, essence-capturing, and/or evocative attribute for a portion of language-based or visual data" (Saldaña 2013, 3).

Drawing Conclusions

Upon completion of code assignment, the researchers will devise categories or themes that best represent the codes derived from all data collection methods. These categories should give meaning to multiple codes that share similarities and be utilized to represent major ideas about the case being studied (McMillian and Schumacher 2010). The researchers will then begin generalizing and synthesizing the patterns found between categories in order to determine new meanings about the case being studied, thus helping answer the overarching research question. If Dr. Neary and Dr. Ward elect to study multiple cases of co-teaching, they would conduct two stages of analysis. First, they would complete a within-case analysis of each individual case, and then they would complete a cross-case analysis in which they would build a general explanation of the data that fits all of the cases collectively (Yin 2014).

Presenting Results

As with all forms of writing, the first step in constructing a case study report is determining the audience, and because the purpose of case study is to convey understanding of the case, the report will also include a thick description of the case or cases (Merriam and Tisdale 2016). Dr. Neary and Dr. Ward are interested in building on their *intensity theory of co-teaching*; thus, their audience for the initial report will be other scholars of co-teaching and collaboration; however, they should also consider writing an additional report for a practitioner audience.

Though multiple structures exist for case study reporting, Dr. Neary and Dr. Ward are most likely to use the linear-analytic method, which is the standard form and most often employed for journal articles. Following a brief introduction of the problem and a review of the literature on co-teaching, the researchers will provide detailed information about the methodology. Since the researchers put forward a theoretical proposition that the co-teachers have to develop their own strengths in order for the co-teaching to be maximally effective, the report will focus on the findings in relation to that proposition and will be arranged around themes with quotes and evidence from field notes and documents to support the conclusions drawn. Prior to submitting the case study manuscript for publication, the researchers should ask participants to review the draft for accuracy, thus increasing the construct validity of the final report (Yin 2014). Table 15.1 provides a summary of the case study method.

Table 15.1
Summary Chart: Case Study

Overall purpose	A strategy for examining a present-day phenomenon within context for the purpose of generating theory or contributing to an existing theory
Advantages	• Case study can employ both quantitative and qualitative methods and research tools. • Useful for examining present-day, real-world events or phenomena. • Allows for deep examination of a phenomenon within a single or multiple contexts. • Can be used as an evaluation tool.
Disadvantages	• Requires a delicate balance to ensure enough data are collected to allow for adequate analysis, but that too much time and resources are not spent on collecting data that cannot be used. • Sufficient time and expertise with multiple data collection techniques is necessary to fully conduct a case study. • Composing a case study report can be difficult since there is no set formula. • The strategy has not gained acceptance (i.e., it is not valued as a legitimate research strategy) in all academic fields.

(*continued*)

Table 15.1
Summary Chart: Case Study (Continued)

Steps in process	1. Define/focus the question.
	2. Identify a theoretical proposition.
	3. Identify the unit of analysis.
	4. Identify data collection and analysis procedures.
	5. Recruit participants.
	6. Collect data.
	7. Analyze data.
	8. Draw conclusions.
	9. Present results.
Data collection methods	• Interviewing; comprehensive literature searching • Inclusion/exclusion criteria • Critical appraisal and data extraction from included studies
Data analysis methods	• Quantitative and/or qualitative analysis of aggregated data • Meta-analysis or meta-synthesis where able
Support technologies	• Audio and video recording equipment • Field notes • Software for data gathering, analysis, and visualization (e.g., Dedoose and NVivo)

Glossary of Key Terms

Code: Code is "a word or short phrase that symbolically assigns a summative, salient, essence-capturing, and/or evocative attribute for a portion of language-based or visual data" (Saldaña 2013, 3).

Themes: Themes are not codes. A theme is considered the outcome or result of coding, not that which is coded. The code is the label that is given to particular pieces of the data that contribute to a theme. Themes are longer than codes and reflect more conceptual depth (Saldaña 2013).

Theoretical proposition: It refers to a preliminary prediction to guide the design of the case and facilitate the development of the theory being constructed.

Further Reading

Merriam, Sharan B., and Elizabeth J. Tisdell. 2016. *Qualitative Research: A Guide to Design and Implementation*. 4th ed. San Francisco, CA: Jossey-Bass.

Mills, Albert J., Durepos, Gabrielle, and Elden Wiebe, eds. 2010. *Encyclopedia of Case Study Research*. Thousand Oaks, CA: Sage Publications.

Stake, Robert E. 1995. *The Art of Case Study Research*. Thousand Oaks, CA: Sage Publications.

Yin, Robert K. 2014. *Case Study Research: Design and Methods*. 5th ed. Thousand Oaks, CA: Sage Publications.

Chapter 16

Critical Incident Technique

Audrey P. Church, Professor of School Librarianship
Longwood University, Farmville, VA

Introduction to Critical Incident Technique

The **critical incident technique** is a qualitative research method developed from the work of Colonel John C. Flanagan in the Aviation Psychology Program of the United States Army Air Forces in World War II. Flanagan's 1954 seminal article in the *Psychological Bulletin* described the critical incident technique and reported on its early usage in military studies during the war and subsequent use in studies undertaken by the American Institute for Research and at the University of Pittsburgh. As Woolsey (1986) noted, "the two basic principles of the critical incident technique are that factual reports of behavior are preferable to ratings and opinions based on general impressions and that only behaviors which make a significant contribution to the activity should be included" (244).

In most studies utilizing the critical incident technique, participants have lived the experience and report firsthand on critical incidents by participating in interviews, completing questionnaires, or recording incidents on forms as the incidents occur although, depending on the study design, trained observers may also report (Fivars and Fitzpatrick n.d.). "A critical incident report should describe a situation, and an action that was important, significant, 'critical' in determining whether the outcome was effective or ineffective" (Fivars and Fitzpatrick n.d, 1). The situation is the context or setting in which the activities or incidents occur. Participants describe the action/incident that occurred and indicate whether the outcome resulting from that action/incident was positive/effective or negative/ineffective.

The critical incident technique has been utilized in countless studies' conducted in fields as varied as business, counseling, education, government, health care, industry, library and information science, and psychology. In 2001, Fivars and Fitzpatrick published a 301-page bibliography of studies that had used the critical incident technique at that time. A search of the *ProQuest Dissertations & Theses Global* database for "critical incident theory" with date limits 2002 through

2016 yields 1,860 results. In EBSCOhost's *Education Research Complete* database, a search using the same search phrase and date limits yields 211 results. ERIC uses the descriptor, "critical incidents method," with a scope note of "Procedure used to gather examples of effective or ineffective behavior with respect to a designated activity to determine the requirements for its success" (ERIC n.d.); a search of ERIC using this descriptor yields 437 results since 1997 and 319 since 2007. Through the use of the critical incident technique, a researcher can identify specific characteristics that make an incident successful or not.

Description of Research Method

Identifying the Problem and Research Questions

The collaborative instruction occurring between Central State University's Dr. Neary and Dr. Ward in Dr. Ward's introductory level course, Our Physical World, provides an optimum setting for the utilization of the critical incident technique. In this course, Dr. Neary and Dr. Ward have co-taught a 12-week unit that focuses on the scientific process and substantive content knowledge in the physical and biological sciences and which is situated around inquiry-based learning. They have modeled for their students, preservice elementary education science teachers, what collaborative instruction between a classroom teacher and a school librarian should involve. To the partnership, Dr. Ward brings his training on co-teaching which he has used to inform his design of instruction and assignments. Dr. Neary brings her past experience as a librarian working as an instructional partner with teachers at the middle school, high school, and college levels. The two professors have co-taught this unit using face-to-face interactive discussions, and students have designed and completed a control variable experiment grounded in authentic topics and real-world questions.

To further build on and develop their *intensity theory of co-teaching*, Dr. Neary and Dr. Ward have agreed to explore the following overarching question: How does co-teaching impact student learning and faculty? Using the critical incident technique, Dr. Neary and Dr. Ward will be able to identify positive and negative factors that impact their students' view of collaborative instruction as well as their own views regarding collaboration and co-teaching. Findings from their study will both contribute to the development of their intensity theory of co-teaching and, at the same time, provide practical implications for collaborative instruction between classroom teachers and school librarians.

Research questions to be addressed in the research study include the following:

- During the co-taught, collaborative instructional unit in which they took part, did the students experience any critical incidents, either positive or negative, which impacted their view of collaborative teaching?

- During their work to design and complete the control variable experiment assignment, did the students experience any critical incidents, either positive or negative, which impacted their view of collaborative teaching?
- During the time of collaborating and co-teaching this instructional unit, did the faculty members experience any critical incidents, either positive or negative, which impacted their view of collaborative teaching?

The Fit between the Critical Incident Technique and the Research Problem/Question(s)

The first step in using the critical incident technique is to determine the aim of the activity and describe it in clear, simple language because participants will use this description to select incidents that are worthy of reporting (Flanagan 1954; Woolsey 1986). Since Dr. Neary and Dr. Ward are co-teaching the 12-week instructional unit, collaborative instruction is present front and center as the aim or focus of the activity. Using the critical incident technique, Dr. Neary and Dr. Ward can collect key information concerning what makes co-teaching effective or not, about what makes co-teaching work or not work. Use of the critical incident technique is appropriate for this study since CIT "…provide[s] data used to identify factors important in defining criteria for 'acceptable performance' " (Fivars and Fitzpatrick n.d., 1).

Use of the critical incident technique is also warranted since the participants, preservice elementary education science teachers, have lived the experience, participation in the co-taught instructional unit, within the previous 12 weeks. As Flanagan (1954) notes, the more recent the experience, the better, since recall of specific incident details will be stronger and more accurate.

Finally, in the field of school librarianship, work is ongoing to develop a theory of collaboration. As Dr. Neary and Dr. Ward develop their intensity theory of co-teaching, they will contribute to the knowledge bases of both education and library science. Their work in this study will help to define what successful co-teaching looks like, which will have practical implications for study participants in their future careers as elementary school science teachers.

Criteria for Determining/Recruiting Research Participants

Research participants are those "subjects from whom critical incidents will be collected" (Radford 2006, 48). In order to participate in the study, the subject must have participated in the activity in question. Depending on the context of the study, no recruitment may be needed (e.g., a study in the workplace or in a specific class setting) or, at the other end of the spectrum, incentives may be needed in order to encourage participation. Participants in this study include the two groups of Upstart University undergraduate students enrolled in Dr. Ward's introductory level course, Our Physical World, with 28 students in each group and the two faculty members who have provided the collaborative instruction: Dr. Neary and Dr. Ward.

Data Collection Procedures

Data collected using the critical incident technique are "brief, written, factual reports of actions in response to explicit situations or problems in defined fields" (Fivars and Fitzpatrick n.d. 1). Flanagan (1954) outlined four methods of data collection: individual, face-to-face interviews of study participants by trained interviewers; group interviews conducted face-to-face in which participants write their responses; questionnaires; and record forms on which participants record details as incidents occur. Radford (2006) added telephone interviews, email questionnaires, and observation by trained observers who are familiar with the context of the study as other possible methods of data collection. Online questionnaires and online incident reporting forms are now also feasible options.

Radford (2006) advised that, when constructing the questionnaire or interview protocol, the researcher very carefully and deliberately "visualize the final report or paper to be written and think about what questions will help to gather the information needed" (48–49). If demographics will be useful in the analysis and reporting of the data, for example, they should be included as points of data collection. Fisher and Oulton (1999) asserted that "both single and multiple trigger questions have been found to be effective," (123) which gives the researcher some flexibility in constructing the data collection instrument.

Woolsey (1986) suggested that "it can be helpful to orient respondents before the interview," (245) noting that in some studies she and fellow researchers have provided participants information about the aim of the study and a copy of interview questions a few days prior to the interviews so that they could ponder and reflect, stimulating recall. How much data to collect? Woolsey (1986) indicated that "size of sample is determined on the basis of number of critical incidents and not number of people . . . a general rule is to collect incidents until redundancy appears" (246). Radford (2006), on the other hand, suggested that "decisions about how many incidents to collect are unique to each project and depend on such factors as available budgetary and staff resources, purpose and intended use of critical incident results, and target audience for findings" (49).

Methods

In this study conducted by Dr. Neary and Dr. Ward, at the conclusion of the collaborative instructional unit, students will receive an email inviting them to participate in the research study. Following standard research protocol approved by the Upstart University Institutional Review Board, students will be informed that their participation in the study is completely voluntary, that they may choose not respond to any question asked, that their responses will be anonymous, that they may withdraw from the study at any time, and that their participation will not in any way impact their course grade. The email will include brief information about the general aim, context, and purpose of the study and encourage their participation for the purpose of improving teaching and learning. It will contain a link to a questionnaire with two prompts:

Student Prompt #1: Think back to the *instruction* that took place as Dr. Neary and Dr. Ward co-taught the Our Physical World instructional unit. Please describe an incident that occurred during this instruction that helped to form your view of collaborative teaching. This incident could be a positive one, or it could be a negative one. What elements of the incident made you consider it positive/negative?

Feel free to submit information (description of incident, considered positive or negative, elements that made it so) for additional incidents that you consider to be significant.

Student Prompt #2: Think back to your work on the control variable experiment *assignment* in this course. Please describe an incident that occurred during your work on this assignment that helped to form your view of collaborative teaching. This incident could be a positive one, or it could be a negative one. What elements of the incident made you consider it positive/negative?

Feel free to submit information (description of incident, considered positive or negative, elements that made it so) for additional incidents that you consider to be significant.

Since it is important in this study to include the faculty perspective as well as the student perspective, Dr. Neary and Dr. Ward will also respond to a similar prompt in an online questionnaire.

Faculty Prompt: Think back to an incident during the time which you co-taught the instructional unit with Dr. Neary and Dr. Ward. This incident could be a positive one, or it could be a negative one. Please describe the incident and indicate the elements of the incident that made you consider it positive or negative. Feel free to submit information (description of incident, considered positive or negative, elements that made it so) for additional incidents that you consider to be significant.

For the purposes of this study, due to the number of participants (n=58) and the time that would be required to conduct and transcribe individual interviews, the online questionnaire was chosen as the data collection instrument. As Fisher and Oulton (1999) noted, "while there is some evidence that interviewing is the most effective method for producing data, good results have been obtained with the whole range of techniques described by Flanagan" (123). An additional benefit of collecting responses online is that the data, once collected, are immediately ready for analysis.

Data Analysis Methods

Data analysis of the reported critical incidents is primarily an iterative, inductive process, the goal of which is "to provide a detailed, comprehensive and valid description of the activity studied" (Woolsey 1986, 248). Each critical incident is first assigned a unique number. Researchers then read and reread the incidents, coding, sorting the incidents into categories, and ultimately collapsing the categories into themes. Content analysis and theme development require that multiple researchers analyze the data and work to achieve a high level of inter-rater reliability (Radford 2006).

Research questions can guide the data analysis, assignment of codes, and clustering into categories (Radford 2006). Data analysis may also be informed by the review of literature or by a relevant theoretical framework (Radford 2006; Woolsey 1986). The multichromatic analysis technique (MAT) using colored markers and colored paperclips is one manual technique available to analyze the data. Commercial software packages available for data analysis include ATLAS.ti, MAXQDA, and NVivo. In addition to qualitative analysis, critical incidents may be reported quantitatively, indicating the number of times particular activities or actions are mentioned in the incident reports.

Analysis

To analyze the critical incidents reported by students and faculty for the collaborative instructional unit from the Our Physical World course, Dr. Neary and Dr. Ward first download the responses from the online questionnaire. They decide to initially code the data using the framework provided by the research questions with the first code representing the focus of the incident report (Prompt 1: Instruction or Prompt 2: Assignment), the second code indicating a positive or a negative response, and the third code indicating student response or faculty response (see Figure 16.1). Additional codes will emerge as the researchers read and reread the incident reports. Once all data are coded and researchers agree on the coding, they will collapse the data into categories, analyze and come to agreement on those categories, and, finally, agree on emerging themes. They will also include quantitative date in their reporting, indicating the numbers of times actions or activities are mentioned.

Present Results

Results from analysis of reported critical incidents are presented as themes that have emerged from the data. Characteristics and elements that make co-teaching

Figure 16.1
Basic Initial Coding Schemes for Critical Incidents

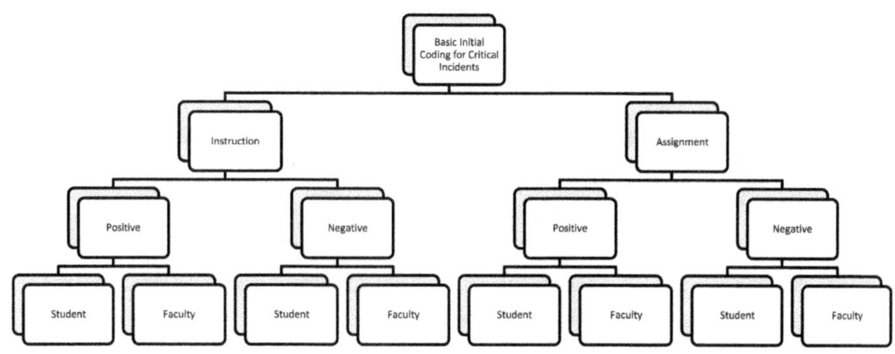

positive and effective are noted as well as characteristics and elements that make co-teaching negative or less effective. Direct quotations from participants are used to illustrate and validate the themes presented. Additionally, critical incidents are reported numerically, indicating the number of times that characteristic or element is mentioned in critical incident reports.

Draw Conclusions and Report

Working to answer their overarching question, "How does co-teaching impact student learning and faculty?" Dr. Neary and Dr. Ward draw conclusions and share their findings, describing what makes collaboration effective and what makes it ineffective. Participants in the study, preservice elementary science teachers, receive an executive summary of the findings that can directly inform their teaching. Dr. Neary and Dr. Ward submit manuscripts reporting on their study to journals in the areas of educational research, science education, library science, and teacher preparation. They also submit proposals to present at science education national conferences, school librarianship national conferences, and educational research national conferences.

In both their writings and their presentations, Dr. Neary and Dr. Ward acknowledge the limitations of their study, noting that it was conducted in one university, in one content area, with a limited number of undergraduate students, and that findings may not be generalizable beyond that context. They encourage future research on the topic of collaboration and co-teaching, at other universities, across content areas, with elementary, middle, and high school preservice teacher candidates, and with both undergraduate upperclassmen and graduate students. Across their writings and presentations, as Flanagan (1954) advised, they emphasize the value of their findings and application to the real world.

Why Use This Research Method

The critical incident technique offers many advantages to researchers. Woolsey (1986) suggested that "critical incident studies are particularly useful in the early stages of research because they generate both exploratory information and theory or model-building" (252). Additionally, "because critical incident data may be analyzed qualitatively and quantitatively, results tend to be more precise, more explicit, and more usable than opinion poll data" (Fivars and Fitzpatrick n.d., 3). Finally, the critical incident technique is applicable across many disciplines. Flanagan (1954) described it as "a flexible set of principles which must be modified and adapted to meet the specific situation at hand" (335).

The critical incident technique also presents some disadvantages. Participants typically self-report either via interview or questionnaire; therefore, data collected are only as accurate or correct as the participants' recall or intent. If the researcher chooses to interview participants, considerable time is spent not only in the interview process but also in the transcriptions of the interviews. Finally, findings, as in most qualitative studies, are not widely generalizable. See Table 16.1 for a summary of this research methodology.

Table 16.1
Summary Chart: Critical Incident Technique

Overall purpose	To describe and identify the most memorable aspects of an incident, either positive or negative
Advantages	• Allows for a "comprehensive and detailed description of a content domain" (Fisher and Oulton 1999, 115). • Grounded in factual occurrence rather than opinion
Disadvantages	• Data are self-reported. • Findings are not typically generalizable.
Steps in process	1. General aims 2. Plans and specifications 3. Collecting the data 4. Analyzing the data 5. Interpreting and reporting
Data collection Methods	• Interviews • Group interviews • Questionnaires • Record forms
Data analysis Methods	• Content analysis • Coding of responses • Developing themes
Support technologies	• Audio and video capture software • Field notes • Transcription software

Glossary of Key Terms

Critical: "To be critical, an incident must occur in a situation where the purpose or intent of the act seems fairly clear to the [participant] and where its consequences are sufficiently definite to leave little doubt concerning its effects" (Flanagan, 1954, 327). "Things which sufficiently affect the outcome" (Woolsey, 1986, 242).
Critical incident technique: "Outlines procedures for collecting observed incidents having special significance and meeting systematically defined criteria" (Flanagan, 1954, 327). "Basically consists of asking eyewitness observers for factual accounts of behaviours (their own or others) which significantly contribute to a specified outcome" (Woolsey, 1986, 242).
Incident: "Any observable human activity that is sufficiently complete in itself to permit inferences and predictions to be made about the person performing the act" (Flanagan 1954, 327). "Things which actually happened and were directly observed" (Woolsey 1986, 242).

Further Reading

ERIC. n.d. *Critical Incidents Method.* Accessed June 27, 2017. http://eric.ed.gov/?qt=critical+incidents+method&ti=Critical+Incidents+Method.

Fisher, Shelagh, and Tony Oulton. 1999. "The Critical Incident Technique in Library and Information Management Research." *Education for Information* 17: 113–25.

Fivars, Grace, and Robert Fitzpatrick. 2001. "12/15/01 Critical Incident Technique Bibliography." Accessed June 29, 2017. https://www.apa.org/pubs/databases/psycinfo/cit-full.pdf.

Flanagan, John C. 1954. "The Critical Incident Technique." *Psychological Bulletin* 5 (4): 327–58. Accessed June 29, 2017. https://www.apa.org/pubs/databases/psycinfo/cit-article.pdf.

Radford, Marie L. 2006. "The Critical Incident Technique and The Qualitative Evaluation Connecting Libraries and Schools Project." *Library Trends* 55 (1): 46–64.

Woolsey, Lorette K. 1986. "The Critical Incident Technique: An Innovative Qualitative Method of Research." *Canadian Journal of Counseling* 20 (4): 242–54. Accessed June 29, 2017. http://cjc-rcc.ucalgary.ca/cjc/index.php/rcc/article/view/1419/1284.

SCENARIO VII

Engaging the At-Risk Student

Sarah A. Chauncey, DPS-IM, Director, Instructional Technology &
Curriculum Development
Student Services Division, Rockland County (NY) BOCES
H. Patricia McKenna, DPS-IM, President
AmbientEase/UrbanitiesLab

Jane Brown is a school librarian in an alternative high school with many students who have classified emotional, behavioral, social, and intellectual challenges. The school's curriculum is rich in creative arts, music, and technology; it is a strengths-based curriculum that centers on student interests in an effort to motivate and engage students who failed to thrive in traditional educational settings. A critical goal of the school's staff is to bolster students' resilience, persistence, participation, and communication skills.

Over the past three years, Jane and her colleagues have provided a safe learning environment that supports student engagement in technology-rich, cross-curricular experiences that include collaborative inquiry, problem-based investigation, socialization, communication, and production of multimedia content. In these learning experiences, "Smart Teams," composed of the school's educators, support staff, and students consider community issues from multiple perspectives; identify challenges and opportunities surrounding the issues; and consider the roles current and emerging technologies might play in addressing various aspects of the issues. Teachers and clinicians have reported that their observations of this school-based collaborative work suggest that the experiences have had a positive impact on student engagement, emotional and behavioral self-regulation, and social interactions among peers and staff.

School leadership is focused on improving school climate, addressing low attendance rates, providing school-to-work initiatives, and developing cross-curricular units of study. In response, Jane and her colleagues are grappling with options to address these organizational issues and strategic objectives and decide to focus on chronic absenteeism as an area of grave concern for a substantial subset of students. Students who are not in school cannot access the curriculum and take advantage of the resources and supports provided to help them achieve to their potential. A critical imperative is reengaging students who are chronically absent; at risk of dropping out; becoming disaffected members of their communities; and potentially engaging in risky behaviors. Jane and her colleagues believe that reaching beyond the school to the community more broadly is key to this particularly complex issue.

Jane would like to build on the success of in-school experiences by creating partnerships with community profit and not-for-profit organizations whose members would join the school's Smart Teams as experts and mentors. She knows that linking with the community is consistent with a critical goal of the high school, to prepare students for life and work in which they will participate and contribute to problem solving in face-to-face and virtual environments. She is also eager to find real-world applications that might draw on the work students have been doing in the school library makerspace including using 3-D printers, robotic toolkits, and virtual reality applications to experiment and design prototypes as solutions.

Collaborative problem solving with community mentors will help students to connect school-based learning to real-world settings. Students will be immersed in teamwork that draws on individual strengths and talents and collegial and positive social interactions that encourage creative thinking and innovation. The program is designed to provide students with school-to-work internship and entry-level jobs. These experiences are intended to reengage students in school-based curriculum with the goal of reducing absenteeism and improving student achievement. Smart Team interactions offer alternative options to evaluate student achievement in the form of artifacts that reflect contributions to the development of prototypes, systems, and processes associated with the resolution of problems. Additionally, business partners, with school staff support, will simulate "employee evaluations" based on student participation in Smart Teams.

Jane drafted the following overarching question that she will share with staff and administration:

What is the impact of collaborative "Smart Teams" on student engagement in technology-rich, cross-curricular experiences?

Chapter 17

Design-Based Research

Marilyn P. Arnone, Professor of Practice
School of Information Studies, Syracuse University
Susan Rothwell, Postdoctoral Researcher
College of Science, Rochester Institute of Technology

Introduction to the Design-Based Research Method

Design-based research is a methodology that allows revision of the research design as the research study progresses, providing flexibility to adapt the research design and interventions based on feedback from researchers and participants. Design-based research is situated in real-life contexts and aims to improve practice by providing a **design**, revising and retesting as the research progresses. Cobb et al. (2003) described this iterative design process as engineering and systematically studying forms of learning within the context defined by the means of supporting those forms of learning. The learning context is tested and revised with successive iterations playing a role similar to systematic variation in an experiment. Bowler (2008) referred to this as a simultaneous merging of research, design and practice. Typically, these three components have been separated, resulting in a much later application of research findings to practice. This gap between research and practice has proven problematic for the library and information science (LIS) field, and some LIS researchers see true promise for design-based research to diminish the divide (Crowley 2005; Rawson and Hughes-Hassell 2015).

The pragmatic melding of research, design, and practice makes design-based research ideal for exploring collaborative, complex educational scenarios such as the impact of Smart Teams. Design-based research promotes iterative improvement of the research design and interventions toward development of an *effective theoretically sound model* of **collaboration** and learning. Using this method, researchers can develop research questions related to a broad question posed in a scenario, with possible solutions implemented and tested not just once but iteratively as we discover ways to improve practices or programs over time. The research design is multiphased with design revisions based on each phase.

McKenney and Reeves (2013) suggested the phases of a design-based research study include (1) analysis and exploration, (2) design and construction, and (3) evaluation and reflection. Zheng (2015) emphasized that multiple iterations on design are necessary to refine a practice model. Bowler (2008) acknowledged that the "design is the hypothesis, the intervention, and the outcome" (40). This fusion of theory-driven interventions and iterations is the heart of the design-based research method. Our outcome will be recommendations and a model for how the program could work in similar situations. Hoadley (2002) summed this up well: Design is purposeful, creative, and open-ended, well-suited to the types of open-ended *how* questions and complex and dynamic context our research scenario addresses. Design-based research can provide reliable, replicable, and valid results that tie theory and implementation to practical educational outcomes.

Why Use Design-Based Research?

The most important advantage of design-based research is its fit for educational classrooms and libraries that are looking for improved or new *products* or *programs* or to *improve learning outcomes* as a result of an intervention or teaching technique. Design-based research allows researchers to continue to improve (and carefully document, of course) those products along the way so that the result is more than the product alone, including recommendations and a model for how the program could work in similar situations. Design-based research is also a good fit with the design practices of librarians. Clarke discusses the need for a broader perspective on design practices in libraries, going beyond designing buildings and spaces to designing successful tools, services, and experiences in order to remain relevant. She states that design thinking and methods are a highly applicable and appropriate approach to librarianship. Design seeks to improve the world as it is: a better fit with what libraries do than science's goal of describing and understanding the world as it is (2015). The power of design-based research is this blending of theory and practice, the melding of design with research.

Another advantage is that design-based research always takes place in the natural, real-world context where learning takes place. Researchers do not have to account for variation in results that may be attributable to a controlled laboratory setting, for example. Researchers can see how students are naturally changing over time. Hoadley (2002) pointed out that collaborative research adds design complexity and is especially sensitive to context changes, requiring time to allow interventions to become more stable. Research-based design applied in context on both technical and social levels can provide valuable insight.

Finally, the greatest strength of this participatory and iterative research approach is the opportunity to partner dedicated educators with researchers to solve real problems in an authentic learning context. This dedicated collaboration is key to the success of the method.

Methodological Limitations and Concerns

All research methods carry certain dilemmas. In the case of design-based research, controversy has existed for more than two decades on the reliability and validity of the method. There is concern for the effect that the researcher has on the process, team, and intervention he or she is embedded in. The researcher, if reflective, journals every interaction and carefully documents every design and intervention iteration; this may result in a more descriptive and rich account of how the educational program or learning intervention achieved results, contributing to design principles produced as study results. Hoadley (2002, 2004) stated that the researcher is obligated to provide full design narrative descriptions of perspectives and starting points, tools built, context in which tools are studied, any plausibly relevant intervention strategies used by participants or researchers, activities and practices offered to users, and especially evolution of context over time in response to the tools. Strong design narrative for design-based research supports replicability, reliability, and in the longer term, systemic validity: Does the research really inform the questions that motivated the research?

Application of an iterative design process is generally expected to produce a higher quality end product (Adams 2001, 2002; Banathy 1987; Dow et al. 2012). Iterative design in context is an effective means of uncovering unanticipated consequences and adapting to local culture (Hoadley 2002). Use of external evaluation or assessment can provide additional reliability and validity to balance concerns about involvement of the research team.

Careful concern needs to be paid to the questions asked in design-based research. Most often, the questions are posed as *how* questions, as in how to accomplish a particular learning or motivational outcome. Many of the questions posed to explore our assigned scenario are, in fact, *how* questions. The design-based researcher may be hopeful that the intervention yields success, yet it is entirely possible that other aspects of the situation under study may be responsible for results. The broader overarching *how* question may require a number of smaller sub-questions and much empirical support to be able to say that the *intervention* is, at least to a great extent, responsible for the *outcomes*.

Differences between Formative Research and Design-Based Research

Though both research methodologies in part focus on revising research design, there are distinct differences between formative research and design-based research. According to Reigeluth and Frick, formative research is a type of developmental or action research targeted at improvement design theory for the design of instructional practices or processes. Formative research evaluates an accurate application of an instructional design theory or model, applying formative evaluation and looking for weaknesses in the application that may reflect weaknesses in the theory. Potential improvements for the application may also reflect potential improvements to the theory. The goal of formative research is to contribute to generalizable design knowledge (1999).

Design-based research targets revision of the research design as the research study itself progresses. The goal is to iteratively evaluate and improve the research design throughout the duration of the research study, adjusting the research design process and interventions as needed to produce a quality end product. Improvements and weaknesses are identified in the research design process and educational interventions. Hoadley (2002) states that design-based research leads to locally grounded results that require application by experienced practitioners in other contexts to determine how localized or generalizable the findings really are.

Identifying and Addressing the Research Problem

The problem described in the scenario is the high rate of absenteeism by a subset of the high school population. It is assumed that problem-based learning and a Smart Team Approach including community business mentors and current and emerging technologies will be the solution. The Smart Team Approach as stated is an ill-defined solution missing theoretical or philosophical grounding and a social dimension. Smart Teams alone are helping somewhat, but it is not known what else may help. A basis for expanding Smart Teams to the community is necessary. In addition, Jane and the research team will need to determine the cause of the high rate of absenteeism to improve the chances of creating a successful intervention. The following modifications to the research scenario are suggestions to better ground the study:

> Jane and the research team investigated options to strengthen the conceptual framework of the study. They decided to combine design-based research and **connected learning** strategies as the best fit. Design-based research allows revision of the research design as the study progresses, providing flexibility to adapt to the needs of challenged students. Connected learning is an educational approach advocating learning that is socially embedded, interest-driven and oriented toward educational, economic or political opportunity (Ito et al. 2013). The combination of design-based research and connected learning has been used successfully in library new media-oriented programs to engage teens and promote interest in science, technology, engineering and

mathematics (STEM) via a participatory culture with the librarian as the connector. Public and school libraries are embracing connected learning, in part with support from the Young Adult Library Services Association (Ahn et al. 2014; Subramaniam 2016). A front-end assessment will determine the cause of the high rate of absenteeism.

Modifying the Smart Team Approach to include a connected learning framework incorporating current and state-of-the-art technologies in the evolution of a makerspace library environment with focus on career-oriented authentic learning opportunities is expected to increase social involvement of peers and community, build on student interests, establish the librarian as the connection, improve **engagement** and achievement, and reduce absenteeism.

The social aspects of connected learning are particularly important to create a sense of belonging and purpose and build trust and rapport between students and teachers, librarians, peers, and business mentors on interest-driven and relevant projects in their own community. Smart Team projects connect to educational content across multiple classes and content areas such as math, science and technology, social studies, writing, speaking, listening, and computer and information literacy.

The Smart Teams intervention design will be multiphased with revisions based on each phase. Baseline data including reasons for absenteeism, student achievement and interests, what motivates **curiosity** in students, and future career aspirations, will inform the initial design and drive the theoretical basis for research strategies and interventions. Research questions may expand or evolve as the research team learns more about what works and does not work with the Smart Teams intervention.

Researcher involvement will provide ongoing, iterative, research design process improvement with flexibility to meet evolving student needs and project requirements. What is known about curiosity, interest, and engagement will help drive the theoretical basis for design of the interventions and strategies the research team employs. This fusion of theory-driven interventions and iterations is the heart of design-based research.

Relationships between technology, curiosity, interest, and engagement can be complex, another reason why design-based research is a good fit for Jane's research scenario. Curiosity, if satisfied, can trigger development and deepening of interest and consequent engagement that can result in deep learning and effective participation. Unresolved curiosity may lead to lack of perceived competence, anxiety, frustration, withdrawal, and disinterest (Arnone et al. 2011). Interest can re-trigger curiosity and, if sustained, interest may evolve into a maintained situational interest. This could lead to emerging individual and group interest with potential to grow into well-developed interest. Interest also supports varying levels of engagement (Hidi and Renninger 2006). Renninger et al. describe three types of engagement: participative engagement involves learning because of an imposed goal such as by a parent or teacher with little intrinsic need to learn. Affective engagement occurs simply because the experience is enjoyable and may trigger interest. Cognitive engagement may occur when an individual or group is fully and intrinsically committed to learning more about a phenomenon (Renninger, Sansone, and Smith 2004). Engagement and support can foster self-efficacy (Eccles and Wigfield 2002) and sustain and deepen interest (Csikszentmihalyi, Rathunde, and Whalen 1993; Eccles et al. 1993; Renninger and Hidis 2002). Social and technological context may influence if, or the extent to which, curiosity is acted upon and whether interest and engagement emerges and is sustained. Certain technologies may help students focus their curiosity-inspired learning through goal setting and planning; others may help sustain curiosity, interest, and engagement as projects progress (Arnone et al. 2011).

Research Participants

Research participants include students designated by the alternative high school to participate in the Smart Team Approach, associated educators and support staff, the school librarian, and selected local business partners/community mentors. It is anticipated that these participants, working together in Smart Teams, will provide diverse yet comprehensive perspectives on student and Smart Team performance.

Research Questions

Jane and the research team developed research questions with respect to participation in the Smart Team within a connected learning framework, including individual, collaborative, and technological factors, as demonstrated in Table 17.1. The research questions are predominantly *how* questions (as discussed by Hoadley 2002) and are designed to capture big-picture, social, and personal perspectives that are not readily captured by short-term or purely academic evaluations.

Table 17.1
Research Questions for a Research-Based Design

Overarching research question: What is the impact of modifying the Smart Team Approach to include a connected learning framework on attendance and engagement in technology-rich, cross-curricular, socially embedded, interest-driven, and career-oriented experiences?

(*continued*)

Research Sub-questions

Reducing absenteeism	How does participation on a student's selected Smart Team affect absenteeism?
Increasing achievement	How does participation on a student's selected Smart Team affect achievement across the curriculum? *As tracking extent of participation would be complex/time consuming for students, impact of participation vs. attendance on increased achievement is a topic for future research.*
Interest matching	Is there a match (definite, partial, not as stated) between students' curiosity and interests and the specific Smart Team into which they self-select?
Collaboration quality	*Smart Team:* How do students' perceptions of the quality of the collaboration between student/mentor and student/team compare with their satisfaction with their Smart Team experience? *Collaboration quality is based on frequency, technology access, responsiveness, supportiveness, trust, rapport, creativity stimulation, and so on.* *Librarian support:* How do student's perceptions of the school librarian's approachability and support of their ideas and autonomy affect participation in Smart Teams *(use the Perceived Autonomy Support for School Librarians measure)*? *Social connectedness:* How do students' perceptions of their overall social connectedness vary as the projects progress (connections with community, peers, teachers, librarian, and mentors)?
Personal relevance	How do students' views of their participation on Smart Teams as relating to their personal curiosity and future career interests affect duration of their participation on their Smart Team?
Increasing persistence	*Significance:* How do students' perceptions of the significance of the community problems they address in their projects impact the completion rate of the projects? *Makerspace investment*: How do students' perceptions of their involvement in improving the library's makerspace environment (i.e., contribution to ideas and implementation) impact their willingness to continue working with their Smart Team as the project progresses?
Technology	*Access:* How do students' perceptions of access to their preferred technologies impact their satisfaction with the Smart Team experience? *Enabling curiosity:* To what extent do students who have greater access to technologies report being able to better "act" on their curiosity and interests?
Product ratings vs. engagement	How do mentors' ratings of students' final products compare to students' level of engagement in their Smart Teams?
Researcher impact	What impact will the researcher have on the improvement of Smart Team iterations?

Data Collection Methods

Design-based research generally requires quantitative and qualitative data collected from multiple sources over time, especially for studies involving collaboration. Time is required to observe how interventions reach a more stable condition as individual and team practices adapt to change and possibly reach equilibrium (Anderson and Shattuck 2012; Hoadley 2004). For Jane's scenario, data will be both qualitative and quantitative, collected from multiple data sources to permit triangulation of the data over a time frame of two school years. Required digital tools for researchers include laptops or tablets with Microsoft Office, web design tools, video/audio and photo capture and editing software, video conferencing, scheduling and messaging tools, and qualitative and quantitative data analysis software.

Baseline data on student attendance and Smart Team performance will be obtained via document analysis of student records prior to beginning research interventions. Data on potential community contacts and resources will also be collected prior to beginning research interventions via Internet research and discussion with the school librarian and guidance counselor, faculty and support staff, the local chamber of commerce, and local public librarians.

Data for formation of Smart Teams will be collected from mentors and students to establish a baseline on student motivational factors, explore student and mentor interests, and match students with mentors. Expert mentors will be recruited via interview, based on their industry/agency, project-related interests, and familiarity with technologies, including participation in a makerspace information session. Mentors will be debriefed after the makerspace session to obtain data on ideas/ suggestions, questions/concerns, necessary skills for students, and possible future internship or entry-level positions. Students and mentors will then have an introductory meeting and field trip to community businesses/agencies to familiarize students with mentors and potential opportunities, followed by a debriefing. Data obtained will be used to plan multiple Smart Teams of four to five students, with one mentor and project topic per Smart Team, self-selected by interest. Faculty and support staff will be shared across Smart Teams. Sample Smart Team project topics include ergonomics and robotics, environment and innovation (reduce waste, improve community attitude, design a nature space), and coding (create a just-in-time app).

Research data will be collected during the following three terms including attendance, engagement, achievement, and social connectedness from school records, focus group meetings, mentor debriefings, results of simulated employee evaluations, Smart Team peer reviews, weekly student project journals, faculty feedback, student interviews, student project presentations to the community including student discussion of what they learned, and design process tracking. Smart Team focus groups will meet weekly, involving all Smart Team members and the school librarian, with community experts included as required. Focus group meetings will be a primary platform for discussion of project status, what is working, what is not working, and general questions, all of which will feed into refinement of the research design. Student opinions on their learning, reasons for absenteeism, and enthusiasm for the current Smart Team program will be elicited using an online motivational questionnaire administered for baseline data and repeated at regular intervals to obtain longitudinal data.

Data on the research design will be collected throughout the study as a basis for ongoing, iterative revision of the study design, as shown in Table 17.2. For this project, as is typical for design-based research, careful monitoring of the learning context, students and their Smart Teams, social aspects, project progress and problems, and opportunities for improvement is critical for design and implementation of effective and timely interventions. Bowler and Large (2008) use of this design data to create and test interventions as the project progresses helps users (i.e., Smart Teams) to choose, understand and use information.

Table 17.2
Research Design Data

Design and process improvement	Learning and workforce development	Technologies
What can be confirmed.	Identification of skills and knowledge that are lacking, and ways to incorporate those into the program and determine effectiveness.	Makerspace opportunities and evolution.
What can be better targeted.		What may increase curiosity and interest.
Solution/product match.		
Problems identified and encountered.		Future use of the technologies and training on the technologies.
Problems and solutions/ interventions.	What are students getting out of this?	
Changes to the program.	What are mentors/ companies/agencies getting out of this?	Use of collaborative technology.
What can be improved in the next iteration.		
What worked and what did not work.	Student and team performance based on researcher observations and project data.	
Lessons learned and suggestions for improvement.	Ways to improve social connections.	
	Ways to better prepare future workforce.	

Data Analysis Methods

Data will be both quantitative and qualitative and will be analyzed using multiple methods as is typical for design-based research (Anderson and Shattuck 2012), with triangulation when feasible. Examples of possible digital data analysis tools include Microsoft Excel, Qualtrics, IBM SPSS, NVivo, MAXQDA, Wordle, and online tools such as SurveyMonkey and DataCracker.

Data from identification of community businesses, agencies, and resources will be used to identify community matches and who to work with in the community. Quantitative data from questionnaires and surveys will be analyzed to determine counts and frequencies and compare student and community interests and needs for formation of Smart Teams. Qualitative data from interviews, surveys, questionnaires, student project journals, debriefings, and focus group meetings will be analyzed using deductive and inductive content analysis with intercoder reliability checks. Results may include narratives, frequencies, quotes, questions/concerns, problems, and suggestions for improvement.

Longitudinal data analysis is necessary to look at changes over time for achievement, absenteeism, engagement including comparison with baseline data, persistence, and the research-based design. Averages, medians, and mode will be determined and compared. Regression analysis will be used to investigate the relationship between engagement and attendance, engagement and achievement, and attendance and achievement. Longitudinal meta-analysis of all collected data will be used to answer the overarching research question on the impact of modifying the Smart Team Approach to include a connected learning framework. See Table 17.3 for a summary of this research methodology.

Potential Reporting Venues

Potential reporting venues include Association for Library and Information Science Education conferences and publications, American Library Association conferences and publications, Association for Information Science and Technology conferences and publications, and the *School Library Research* journal. Results, recommendations, and best practices could also be shared via workshops or seminars involving local educators, librarians, and key members of the community.

Table 17.3
Summary Chart: Design-Based Research

Overall purpose	To iteratively evaluate and improve the research design throughout the duration of the research study, adjusting the research design process and interventions as needed to produce a quality end product

(continued)

Table 17.3
Summary Chart: Design-Based Research (Continued)

Advantages	• Good fit to improve products, programs, and learning outcomes via interventions or teaching techniques in real-world, complex, dynamic contexts • Good fit with design practices of librarians • Partnering of educators and researchers to solve authentic problems
Disadvantages	• Concerns for effect that researcher has on the process, team, and intervention; may require use of external evaluation or assessment • Requires thorough documentation, at least two iterations, and a number of research sub-questions with empirical support to adequately tie interventions to outcomes
Steps in process	1. Initial research design 2. Collecting and analyzing data, including data on the research design 3. Ongoing, iterative evaluation and revision of the research design
Data collection methods	Document analysis, Internet research, discussion, interviews, online motivational questionnaire, debriefings, focus groups, simulated employee evaluations, peer reviews, student project journals, faculty feedback, project presentations, design process tracking
Data analysis methods	Matching, counts, frequency analysis, deductive and inductive content analysis, longitudinal data analysis (averages, medians, modes, regression analysis), longitudinal meta-analysis.
Support technologies	• Varies. For the given scenario, including the makerspace: • Laptops or tablets with Microsoft Office, web design tools, video/audio and photo capture and editing tools • Scheduling, messaging, and video conferencing tools • Qualitative and quantitative data analysis software, survey tools

Glossary of Key Terms

Collaboration: It is a joint effort reflecting experiences and viewpoints of persons who intentionally work together to produce a mutually agreed-upon end result (Holsapple and Joshi 2002).

Connected learning: It is an educational approach advocating learning that is socially embedded, interest-driven and oriented toward educational, economic, or political opportunity (Ito et al. 2013).

Curiosity: Curiosity with respect to new media environments is a desire for new information or experience. Curiosity includes a trigger or multi-trigger scenario evoked by dynamic environments, reaction (which may involve multiple new media skills), and resolution (satisfied/not satisfied). A curiosity episode, if resolved satisfactorily, initiates new learning. Curiosity can trigger and be triggered through the development and deepening of interest and, consequently, the forms of engagement that result in deep learning and effective participation, collaboration, and affinity (Arnone et al. 2011).

Design: It refers to the creation of engineered systems that satisfy specific human and societal needs within a context (Suh 2013).

Design-based research: A methodology that allows revision of the research design as the research study progresses, providing flexibility to adapt the research design and interventions based on feedback from researchers, participants and others involved in the research project.

Engagement: To want to participate, to participate, or to be involved with at length/in depth is called engagement.

Iteration: Iteration is the repetition of a process or procedure to try to move closer to a goal.

Social learning: attitude change through learning from direct personal experience.

Further Reading

Clarke, Jody, Chris Dede, Diane Jass Ketelhut, Brian Nelson, and Cassie Bowman. 2006. "A Design-Based Research Strategy to Promote Scalability for Educational Innovations." *Educational Technology* 46 (3): 27–36.

Kelly, Anthony E., Richard A. Lesh, and John Y Baek, eds. 2008. *Handbook of Design Research Methods in Education: Innovations in Science, Technology, Engineering and Mathematics Learning and Teaching*. New York: Routledge.

Chapter 18

Longitudinal Research

Carol Collier Kuhlthau, PhD
Professor Emerita in the Library and Information Science
Department Rutgers, the State University of New Jersey
Leslie Maniotes, PhD
Curriculum Specialist and Educational Consultant
on Inquiry Based Learning
Jannica Heinström,
Associate Professor in Information Studies
Åbo Akademi University, Finland,
and Docent at the University of Borås, Sweden

Introduction to Longitudinal Research

Longitudinal methods involve repeated data collection with the same subjects over a period of time. All longitudinal studies require extensive investigation over the course of time. Some longitudinal studies track people over many years, returning to them at intervals. Multiyear studies are not uncommon. Some studies may even extend over a lifetime. Due to practical considerations, however, most studies encompass a shorter time span, perhaps several days, weeks, or months.

Longitudinal studies make observing changes possible and more accurate. These methods are particularly suited to research in psychology and sociology that strives to compare different points in an individual's experience and development. Longitudinal studies are applied in various practical fields, such as medicine, social services, and education, where determining impact is the goal. Longitudinal methods allow researchers to distinguish short-term effects from long-term phenomena, which is not evident in single-incident studies that are limited to examining one point in time. By following people over time, with multiple points of data collection, the longitudinal approach offers extended observation of change in a problem, experience, or process.

Longitudinal studies often include a cohort, a group of people who share a common event, sometimes referred to as a panel. A cohort can be studied as a group, as individuals within a group, or some combination of these. Cohort studies are particularly suited to research in educational settings where students are organized in class groupings and grade levels. Educators who serve students in the same school over several years have continuing contact with the same students as they pass through different grade levels. In schools, teachers often systematically collect longitudinal data on students in the course of their teaching. They assess student progress to determine the need for further instruction. They regularly apply longitudinal methods to evaluate student work to assign a grade. Teachers and school librarians are therefore uniquely positioned to have access to cohorts over time and to return to the same students at a later time.

Longitudinal research that addresses a specific problem requires intentional, systematic application of these methods for collecting and analyzing data to determine findings that indicate a solution. Longitudinal studies can be retrospective, using existing data, such as student accumulative records that go back in time. Teachers have access to student information that helps to gain a background picture of progress and challenges. They work under a system of professional practice that requires ethical and responsible use of student data. Confidentiality is essential in using this data. This information can provide valuable baseline data as a starting point for longitudinal study. Retrospective data can also offer important comparison when investigating improvement and impact.

An important, unique characteristic of longitudinal research is the combination of a wide range of data collection methods that open a problem for extensive investigation, not available in short-term studies. Both qualitative and quantitative methods may be employed in longitudinal studies. Qualitative methods, such as interview, journals, and observation, can provide **case study** analysis of individuals within a **cohort.** The case study researcher needs to be skilled in remaining interested but neutral during interviews and observation. Where perceptions are elicited, participants' recollections and reactions are accepted as true without value judgments or correction imposed by the interviewer.

Quantitative methods, such as **surveys** administered at different points in the course of a study, can provide data for statistical analysis of a large cohort over time. Quantitative methods may be used to verify qualitative case study findings and vice versa. The combination of qualitative and quantitative methods in the context of extensive **longitudinal** study reveals findings of impact not possible in short-term, single method studies.

Longitudinal studies are uniquely suited to revealing a process over time. Repeated observation has more power than single point observational studies for opening a process for investigation and to detect change. Therefore, longitudinal methods are particularly useful in studying the learning process of students.

By identifying a starting point and an end point, data can be collected in between to reveal students' experience, progress, and challenges within that time period. Disadvantages of longitudinal studies are that they take a lot of time and can be very expensive. Therefore, they are often not convenient.

Example of Application of Longitudinal Methods

Kuhlthau's studies of information search process (ISP) provide an example of longitudinal methods. Following is her explanation of applying these methods in a series of studies of students' experience in the process of information seeking and use in school assignments (Kuhlthau 2004).

I needed to understand more about students' experience in the process of learning from a variety of sources in an extensive research project. I noticed that there was a time, early in a research project, when many students had difficulty moving ahead. They had stalled in their progress and their interest was diminishing. My research questions were: What do students experience as they progress through in a research project? How do their thoughts, feelings, and actions change in the process? Why does their interest and engagement seem to diminish at certain times?

A class of 25 high school seniors was selected to serve as a cohort for a year-long study within two research assignments, one in fall semester and one in spring. Longitudinal methods were chosen to capture changes in the students' thoughts, feelings, and actions as they progressed through their projects. The study was composed of qualitative data collection instruments:

- Journals—Students kept journals of their thoughts, feelings, and actions throughout the project.
- Search Logs—Students recorded all relevant sources in search logs with an assessment of useful, most useful, and not useful.
- Check-in at three points—Students composed short pieces of writing on their topic at the beginning, midpoint, and completion of the project.

In addition, eight individual interviews were conducted with six students throughout the process. After the closing interview, each of these students was asked to chart on a timeline their experience along the way and a flowchart of sources they had used.

- Conversations—Eight 30- to 40-minute **semi-structured interviews** were conducted with each of the six students selected for case study.
- Charts—Each case study student drew a timeline and flowchart describing his or her process at the completion of the study.

Data were analyzed for patterns of change in thoughts, feelings, and actions throughout students' research projects. The findings revealed a dynamic holistic process of fluctuating engagement and interest in six stages, described as the ISP. In **initiation** and **selection,** when the project was announced and topics chosen, feelings of interest were moderate and externally motivated—"what does the teacher want?" This was followed by two stages, **exploration** and **formulation,** that were the major new findings of the study. In **exploration,** interest and engagement unexpectedly decreased when students had difficulty making sense of conflicting and confusing information. This was the point that they often became frustrated, anxious, and stalled. The students who were able to work through their confusion to form a focus for making sense moved on to **formulation,** the turning point of their search process. Once they had formed a personal perspective, they were more internally motivated with their interest and engagement increasing. With a clearer idea of what they were learning, they could move on to **collection** and **presentation.** Many students expected to skip over **exploration** and **formulation** and to move directly to **collection** once they had selected their topic. But their thoughts, feelings, and actions revealed increasing uncertainty and decreasing confidence with mounting anxiety and frustration until they formed a focus for their work. **Formulation** resulted in rising personal interest, engagement, and ownership that increased through the remainder of the project. Figure 18.1 provides an overview of the ISP.

These findings were verified in numerous studies over several decades, all of which applied longitudinal methods in order to capture the process. Here, Kuhlthau briefly describes two verification studies, one a qualitative follow-up with the same cohort and the other a larger-scale quantitative study of a diverse population of students.

Twenty of the original 25 students responded to a mailed survey after four years of college. Their perceptions were compared with those they held in high school for changes that had taken place over the four years. Where the original longitudinal study offered insight into the perceptions of the subjects over an extended search process, this study revealed their perceptions of the process at two different points in their lives as students. At this point they were found to view research as a process of evolving and changing thoughts and feelings that contribute to the success of the outcome (Kuhlthau 2004).

The other component of the four-year follow-up was with the case study subjects that were part of the earlier study. Four of the six high school case study subjects were available for further study. Individual semi-structured interviews were conducted. In this study, Case study participants revealed an understanding of

Figure 18.1
Information Search Process (Kuhlthau 2004, 82)

Model of the Information Search Process (ISP)						
	Initiation	Selection	Exploration	Formulation	Collection	Presentation	Assessment
Feelings (Affective)	Uncertainty	Optimism	Confusion Frustration	Clarity	Sense of direction/ confidence	Satisfaction or disappointment	Sense of accomplishment
Thoughts (Cognitive)	Vague ——————→ Focused				Increased interest		Increased self-awareness
Actions (Physical)	Seeking relevant information				Seeking pertinent information		
	Exploring				Documentir.		

stages in the search process and a tolerance for the ambiguity and uncertainty of the earlier stages. They had gained an awareness of their own pace in the ISP, a sense of ownership in the process, and an expectation of creativity in the process (Kuhlthau 2004). One of the case study subjects remained in the longitudinal study for two more rounds of five year intervals moving from novice to expert in the workplace (Kuhlthau 2004).

Another verification study was conducted with 147 high school students, longitudinal methods were applied by administering a survey to elicit thoughts, feelings, and actions at three points in an extensive research project (Kuhlthau 2004). The underlying concept of the information search process (ISP) was verified indicating stages in a process of learning moving from vague thoughts and low confidence to clearer thoughts, increased interest, and raised confidence. A later longitudinal study including 385 participants further verified earlier findings (Kuhlthau 2004). The ISP continues to be increasingly valuable with advancing information technology (Kuhlthau, Heinstrom, and Todd 2008).

The ISP reveals that interest increases with the formulation of personal perspective and point of view at some time in the middle of the inquiry process. At this midpoint phase, motivation for learning can shift from external (what they want me to do) to internal (this is my work). Ideally, learning experiences heighten student interest into the flow of their own work (Csikszentmihalyi 1975).

With this description of longitudinal methods and actual examples of how these methods have been applied, let's now turn to the problem introduced in the scenario to see how longitudinal methods fit in this context.

Identify and Refine Problem

Jane, a school librarian in an alternative high school, reports that the school is experiencing a problem of chronic absenteeism and lack of student engagement. Thus, the school is having difficulty meeting its two goals:

1. To motivate and engage students who failed to thrive in traditional education settings
2. To bolster students' resilience, persistence, participation, and communication skills

Over the past three years, the school has been able to provide a safe learning environment and a curriculum that centers on student interests. An initiative that seems to hold promise is school-based collaborative work in "Smart Teams" that is providing learning experiences on community issues. Teachers sense that these are having a positive impact on student engagement, emotional and behavioral regulation, and social interaction. Still the problem of low attendance and chronic absenteeism persists.

School leadership is focused on further improving the school climate to reengage students in school-based curriculum with the goal of reducing absenteeism and improving student achievement. The idea of drawing community mentors into the Smart Teams is being suggested to help students connect school-based learning to real-world settings. Jane and her colleagues believe that community partners joining the school's Smart Teams as experts and mentors can be the key to this complex problem. Authentic methods to evaluate student achievement that reflect resolutions of actual problems in work and life outside of school may also heighten engagement. Jane will share with staff and administration the need to study the impact of collaborative Smart Teams on student engagement in technology-rich, cross-curricular experiences.

Fit between Longitudinal Methods and Problem

Since investigation of impact will require study of change over time, longitudinal methods are appropriate for this study. The scenario describes underlying assumptions that also indicate the usefulness of longitudinal methods to investigate this problem. The first assumption is that absenteeism may relate to lack of student engagement. Second is that student engagement may improve with connection to real-world problems. And third is that Smart Teams with the addition of community mentors may be key to increasing student engagement. Maniotes (2005) research supports these assumptions. In longitudinal study of third space, she found that student engagement was high when the students' world outside of school (first space) and the curriculum (second space) joined to create a powerful learning space (third space).

These authors recommend longitudinal study to reveal the fluctuation of student engagement in the phases of learning experiences and how this compares to attendance. Identification of phases in learning experiences will be essential for tracking changes in student interest. To support systematic investigation over time, a phased framework is recommended for designing engaging learning experiences, data collection instruments to track student engagement in these experiences, data analysis methodology to elicit engagement in the phases and a means to report results.

Guided inquiry design (GID), based on the ISP, provides a framework for tracking students through the phases of learning in curriculum units. The GID approach is a good match for addressing the critical problems described in the scenario (Kuhlthau, Maniotes, and Caspar 2015). It provides learning experiences in the five kinds of learning the school is seeking to achieve: inquiry, problem-based investigation, socialization, communication, and production of multimedia content. It uses a team approach that includes community experts. It provides a framework to design cross-curricular units that are specifically intended to raise

Figure 18.2
Guided Inquiry Design Process (Kuhlthau, Maniotes, and Caspari 2012)

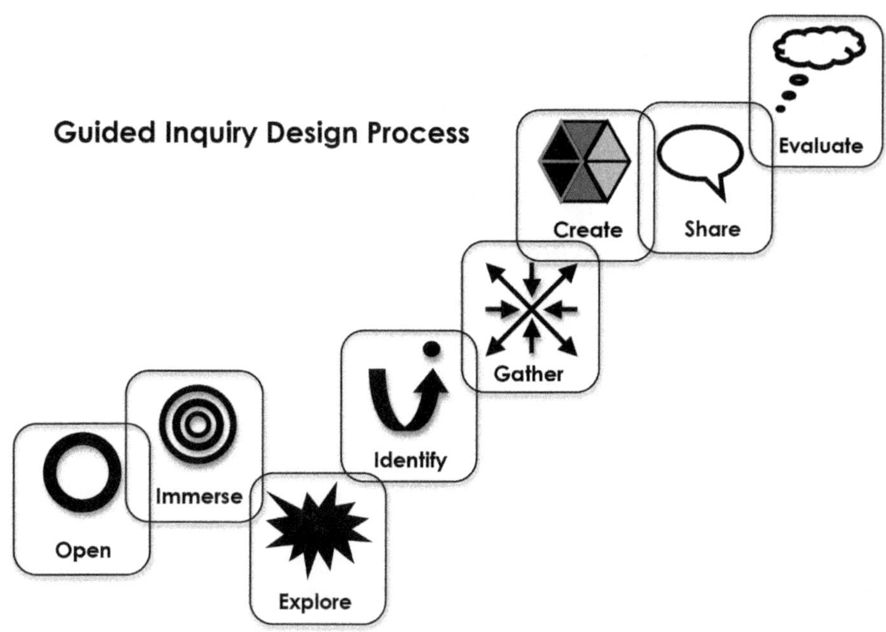

and sustain student curiosity, engagement, and interest throughout the learning process. It centers on school-based learning applied to real-world settings for addressing community and life issues that matter to students and applies authentic methods to evaluate student achievement.

In the first step in the longitudinal study, Smart Teams meet to design learning experiences in cross-curriculum units related to community and life issues in real-world settings, using the GID framework.

Figure 18.2. GID Process (Kuhlthau, Maniotes, and Caspari 2012)

The framework is specifically designed to foster engagement and self-motivation, increased interest, and confidence in eight phases of the learning process: Open, Immerse, Explore, Identify, Gather, Create, Share, and Evaluate (Kuhlthau, Maniotes, and Caspari 2012). Workshops may provide support and time for Smart Teams to work together to design learning experiences for each phase of GID.

Community experts are identified and invited to join Smart Teams. These experts are selected to provide expertise to support the learning and serve as mentors through relationships with students.

Criteria for Determining Participants

The next step is to identify the classes of students that form cohorts for study as they progress through the learning experiences in cross-curricular units.

Cohorts are selected that have the best prospect for tracking in a single semester or over one academic year. Study in the school provides an opportunity to both repeat with several cohorts and to return to same cohorts at later time, as shown in the ISP studies. Cohorts in ninth or tenth grade may be chosen with the intention of tracking students over several years of their high school education. Established Smart Teams will have valuable advice for selecting cohorts that are already working with evidence of success.

Data Collection Procedures

The next step is to review the overarching research question and underlying assumptions and to develop data collection procedures to investigate these questions.

The overarching research question is:

- What is the impact of collaborative "Smart Teams" on student engagement in technology-rich, cross-curricular experiences?

This question is elaborated by three underlying assumptions that help to operationalize investigation of the overarching question.

- Absenteeism may relate to lack of student engagement.
- Student engagement may improve with connection to real-world problems.
- Smart Teams with the addition of community mentors may be a key to increasing student engagement.

A combination of quantitative and qualitative methods is applied in this longitudinal study. The quantitative component consists of two instruments. One for tracking the attendance of the students in the cohorts during the study, as well as collecting their prior attendance records for comparison. The other instrument is the School Library Impact Measure (SLIM) survey (Table 18.1) adapted to elicit the specific changes in levels of engagement sought in this study, to be administered at three phases in the curriculum units. Survey can be created in Google Forms so that data are more easily accessed by all team members and analyzed.

The qualitative component consists of journal writings in response to **prompts** to draw out explanation of changes in engagement and interest, as well as their reactions to real-world issues in the curriculum units, and influence of community experts and mentors (Table 18.2). Each student within the study cohorts will be required to write in a journal during each of the eight phases of the inquiry process. Journals can be created in Google documents so that the learning team can more easily access and code these documents. A date stamp on each entry will

Table 18.1
SLIM Reflection Tasks 1,2,3

1. What is the main topic that are you learning about in this unit of study?	
2. How interested are you in this topic?	❑ Not at all interested
Check one box that best matches your level of interest.	❑ Slightly interested
	❑ Interested
	❑ Very interested
	❑ Extremely interested
3. Rate your interest level related to the statement.	❑ Strongly disagree
My interest is motivating me to want to work on this	❑ Disagree
project.	❑ Neither agree nor disagree
	❑ Agree
	❑ Strongly agree

Table 18.2
Prompts for Student Journals

	Prompt	GID phase when prompt is presented to students
Interest and engagement	List some things that are interesting about this topic. Write what makes them interesting.	Open
	What is the most interesting thing that you are learning? In what way does what you are learning connect to your own interests?	Immerse
	What are you finding interesting enough to consider learning more about? What is motivating you in this work?	Explore
	How interested are you in the topic you chose to pursue? Describe your interest and how that makes you feel.	Identify
	How is your interest in this topic changing? Write about your motivation to work on this project. What's motivating you, and how?	Gather through Evaluate
Real-world connections	Describe any connections to real life (or your life) that you are making. What are your reactions to these connections?	Each Phase
Community	What are you learning from your mentor? How are you connecting with your mentor?	Open through Identify
	What are you finding useful about your connection with your mentor?	Gather through Share
	What was the best part of having mentors as a part of this process?	Evaluate

support the cross-analysis between attendance data and responses to these questions across time. Although they may be encouraged to expand on these writings on their own, in-school time will be provided for journal writing in response to the following prompts:

Data Analysis Methods

Attendance of students in each cohort will be charted and mapped onto the GID phases. District tools such as Infinite Campus and/or other attendance tracking programs can provide data on student attendance in multiple formats. Access to these tools and working with school administrators will be necessary. Attendance charts aligned with the learning process will be examined for evidence of patterns of increased or decreased interest at each phase. In addition, attendance patterns prior to study will be compared for evidence of change during the study.

Responses to SLIM surveys collected at three points in curriculum unit will be collated and analyzed for evidence of change in interest and engagement at beginning, middle, and conclusion of the learning experiences. Responses also will be analyzed for evidence of positive influence of the inclusion of real-world issues and to the presence of community mentors.

Results of the SLIM survey will be the basis for identifying further explanation, elaboration, and illustration in student journals kept in each of the eight phases of the process. Journal writings will be coded for themes of engagement and personal interest, evidence of student reaction to real-world problems, and experience with community experts. Results that show fluctuating interest and engagement will be examined for evidence of what may have prompted any decrease and what may have stimulated reengagement when interest had decreased. Analysis of journal writings will seek students' explanation of their experience in each phase of the learning experiences, specifically related to fluctuating engagement, influence of real-world issues, and relationships with community experts.

Present Results

Charts of attendance patterns, themes that emerged in the SLIM survey, and anecdotal comments and quotes from student journal will be prepared to share these results with staff and administration. Results will be organized to respond to each of the following questions.

- Is there evidence that absenteeism relates to lack of student engagement?
- Is there evidence that student engagement improves with connection to real-world problems?
- Is there evidence that Smart Teams with the addition of community mentors increasing student engagement?

Results from the combined analysis from the longitudinal data collected in the three instruments applied in the study will reveal a comprehensive picture of the situation in the school. The study will provide evidence for answering the overarching question posed in the scenario: What is the impact of collaborative Smart Teams on student engagement in technology-rich, cross-curricular experiences? It will also give some indication of next steps for reengaging students in school-based curriculum with the goal of reducing absenteeism and improving student achievement.

Draw Conclusions

Chronic absenteeism is likely to have many causes that the school has little control over. However, the school staff are proceeding to concentrate on what they can do by seeking to improve engaged learning. They see student engagement as related to low attendance.

They are working in Smart Teams incorporating in real-world community and life issues that matter to students with community mentors and experts. This longitudinal study uncovers where interest may diminish in the phases of a curriculum unit and if this occurs at a time of increased absenteeism. In this study, longitudinal methods are designed to provide insight into students' engagement in the real-world curriculum initiatives and suggest how community mentors can be used to help engage students. The results can contribute substantial evidence for making informed decisions on how to proceed to reengage students with the prospect of breaking cycles of chronic absenteeism.

It is likely to take several years to see the kind of change the school is looking for. Longitudinal methods will enable them to continue studying the problem and to repeat the study at intervals over a number of years. Additional data collection instruments accompanying the GID framework, which are not applied in this study, may be useful in further longitudinal studies in the school. These include logs, charts, small group conversation, and large group interaction for sharing multiple perspectives and ideas (Kuhlthau, Maniotes, and Caspari 2012). These integral tools for learning also provide authentic means of evaluation and assessment. The advantage of these instruments is that they support engaged learning across the process and, therefore, they are neither intrusive nor do they require extra time and effort.

Advantages and Disadvantages of Longitudinal Methods

One problem applying longitudinal methods is inherent in the very problem the study is addressing: chronic absenteeism. A disadvantage of this method with this population is that student absenteeism may cause gaps in the data collection that make analysis incomplete (Kuhlthau 2004). In order to gather consistent data across the study, it is important that the instrument be administered to each student in the cohort at each point in the data collection. The application of both quantitative and qualitative methods may help to alleviate this problem somewhat. However, flexibility on when the data are collected is likely to be essential to gather data on each student in this population throughout the entire learning process. This will need to be built into the study design. The use of technology such as Google Forms, Google Classroom and Google Documents will provide access at a distance to school journals, questionnaires, and assignments or readings presented in class, allowing absent students an opportunity to engage with the work even when not at school. All students may not have access to technology at home, but public libraries and other access points may need to be considered. In order to elicit responses, technology in the form of prompts on students' cellphones may be used. It is also important that completing both the SLIM survey and the student journal are considered an inherent part of the curriculum, needed for completion of the course. A summary chart of this research methodology is included in Table 18.3.

Table 18.3
Summary Chart: Longitudinal Research

Overall purpose	• Development over time • Understanding connections on a timeline
Advantages	• Robust evidence of development • Evidence of change over time • Deeper understanding of development than obtained through short-term research
Disadvantages	• Time consuming • Practical challenges, such as following people who may move and change schools • Evidence is not immediate but available over time
Steps in process	1. Develop research question 2. Determining population as well as time line for data collection and prompts 3. Collecting data 4. Qualitative and quantitative data analysis 5. Conclusions 6. Present evidence
Data collection methods	• Content analysis of journal entries and SLIM responses • Statistical analysis of quantitative replies on SLIM and attendance

Table 18.3
Summary Chart: Longitudinal Research (Continued)

Data analysis methods	• Content analysis of journal entries and SLIM responses • Statistical analysis of quantitative replies on SLIM and attendance
Support technologies	• Google Classroom • Online data collection in Google Documents, Google Forms • Qualitative content analysis in NVivo, Atlas.ti, or similar • Statistical analysis in SPSS or similar • Prompts on student smartphones

Glossary of Key Terms

Case study: It is an in-depth investigation of persons or groups over time to study developments as they happen.

Cohort: This term refers to a group of people who share a common event, sometimes referred to as a panel.

Longitudinal: It refers to repeated study of the same subjects over a period of time.

Prompts: Questions or statements to elicit a response are called prompts.

Semi-structured interview: An interview organized around a series of prompts that elicit responses and open further conversation is called a semi-structured interview.

Surveys: Surveys are questionnaires administered to a group of participants.

Further Reading

Glaser, Barney, and Anselm Strauss. 1967. *The Discovery of Grounded Theory: Strategies for Qualitative Research.* New Brunswick, NJ: Aldine Transaction.

Kuhlthau, Carol. 2004. *Seeking Meaning: A Process Approach to Library and Information Services.* 2nd ed. Santa Barbara, CA: Libraries Unlimited.

Maniotes, Leslie. 2005. *The Transformative Power of Literary Third Space.* PhD Dissertation, School of Education, University of Colorado, Boulder.

Todd, Ross, Carol Kuhlthau, and Jannica Heinström. 2005. *Impact of School Libraries on Student Learning.* Institute of Museum and Library Services Leadership Grant Project Report. Accessed June 27, 2017. http://cissl.comminfo.rutgers.edu.

Yin, Robert. 2014. *Case Study Research: Design and Methods.* 5th ed. Thousand Oaks, CA: Sage.

SCENARIO VIII

Envisioning a Library of the Future

Charles O'Bryan, Director
James M. Milne Library at SUNY Oneonta
Molly Brown, User Experience and Outreach Librarian
DuPont Ball Library, Stetson University

The Christopher Robin Library at New York College is staffed by eight full-time equivalent (FTE) tenured or tenure-track (UUP union) librarians, one professional line librarian, 18 (CSEA union) support staff, and 45 work-study students. Academic support is provided to the college's 5,800 undergraduate students, 259 FTE, and 234 part-time faculty.

Significant increases in student usage of the library have come to the attention of the campus administration, thus leading to their desire to bring two more groups out of the mainstream of the library into the mix. Student Disabilities Services and the Center for Academic Development and Enrichment are now slated to enter the picture, which will increase student usage of the library and demand for library services.

"I realize that we are understaffed, yet without more data to inform our decisions, the choices we make may work out; however they will not be representative of our constituents and their needs," library director Gene Parks remarked. "And we need to be aware of our users' needs." Gene was waxing reflectively about his need for a new type of librarian in his house, a user engagement or user experience (UX) librarian. He had recently read an article that said that, in order to be successful, academic libraries need to focus on satisfying user needs and meeting their expectations.

"Let's be realistic here," remarked Mia Signet, associate director and head of Access Services, "We don't have the staffing or hiring lines to support new librarians or to allocate existing time to other duties." Gene nodded, yet could not drop the idea that a fundamental shift was occurring in academic libraries and that, as always, they found themselves coming to this scene a bit late. Nevertheless Gene understood the library needed to be in the game.

"Why a UX librarian?" Mia questioned. "We already do assessment of library instruction; keep bi-annual counts of usage of space; and do marketing and outreach. We have always done these, for the past 35 years. Why do we need a dedicated person to do this? We have standing committees spelled out in our library bylaws for marketing and outreach and have always done assessment of instruction and bi-annual observations of where students study. We don't need to change anything."

Gene replied, "Mia, although our commitment to serve our patrons continues to be our main focus, the *way* in which we serve them has changed significantly over the last 35-years. It is now important for us to think how the users *interact* with the library, considering not only the physical space, but also the suitability of all our systems to the audience being served. Libraries are no longer static spaces due to the ever-rapid change in technology and thus we need to begin to create spaces both physically and virtually that are innovative, inviting and intuitive. The UX Librarian would assess all the services and service points a patron interacts with, both our physical space(s) and our web presence. The feedback we would be able to obtain would be remarkable and we would be able to fashion a library that is focused on the users of the material, not the material itself."

"I still don't understand why we need to change anything. The library is always full of students," Mia replied.

"But are they using it for the computers and printing?" Gene asked, "Or, are they using it because our library is responsive to their needs. Are we offering an inviting space whether it is for studying or relaxing, a website that easily gets them to the sources they want, or outreach programs that excite the campus community? Ultimately, what we are aiming for is a library that is resilient and 'future-proof' and by having a librarian dedicated to the needs and desires of the users of the library who informs us of changing trends and needs is a valuable addition to our team; and one that is long overdue."

"The traditional services, such as reference and instruction are not being abandoned," Gene assured her. "We see the need is increasing. But in addition to these services, we need to broaden our view and envision the library as the central location on campus where scholarship and serendipitous interactions occur in a space that works for our users. And in order to maintain this vision for the library, we need to have a UX librarian who continuously assesses patrons' needs. I would like to investigate aspects of this overarching question:

What is the vision for the college library of 2020 and what are the implications for space utilization?

Chapter 19

Survey Research

Rebecca Teasdale, Doctoral Student
Educational Psychology, University of Illinois at Urbana-Champaign

Introduction to Survey Research

Surveys are a research approach used in the social and educational sciences to conduct descriptive studies of large populations. Familiar examples include the U.S. government decennial **census**, public opinion and political polls, and customer satisfaction surveys in retail and hospitality industries. In libraries and schools, surveys are an important tool in our toolbox for gathering information about our communities.

Surveys allow researchers to gather information from a group of individuals that is too large to be observed directly. A survey presents each individual with a set of standardized questions and/or asks him or her to respond to a set of statements. Together, these questions and statements are referred to as survey items. By using standardized items, surveys enable researchers to aggregate data and describe the characteristics of a large group of respondents.

Surveys are a very flexible research method that can be used to gather information about attitudes and opinions as well as factual information and descriptions of behavior. However, survey information is self-reported; that is, the respondents report information about themselves. This can be a benefit to researchers seeking to understand respondents' perceptions and opinions, but it can be a limitation to researchers who seek to understand respondents' actual behavior.

Survey research can be conducted in one of two ways: as a census or as a **sample survey**. A census is a survey that is administered to a full population of potential respondents. This type of survey is often used in library contexts—for example, when library staff members administer an annual survey to every library cardholder. In contrast, a sample survey is administered to a fraction of the population and responses are used to draw inferences about the full population. Sample surveys are commonly used when it would be impractical to administer the survey to the full population—for example, when researchers seek to measure the opinions of the entire U.S. population. In that case, researchers use probability sampling and statistical weighting to draw inferences about the full population even though data were gathered from just a fraction of the population.

The use of survey methods requires expertise in several areas: item design, overall survey or instrument design, instrument testing, survey administration, data analysis, and, when applicable, sampling. It is rare for a single staff member in a library or a school to possess all of the necessary skills, so it is typically helpful to work with a team whose members each bring expertise in one or more of the required areas. Expertise can also be found beyond the library or school. Many colleges and universities include experts in survey methods within the departments of sociology, educational psychology, marketing, public health, and public policy. Some universities also operate survey centers that provide assistance to educational and not-for-profit organizations at a reduced price.

Description of Research Method

In the scenario that precedes this chapter, library director Gene Parks is seeking to understand the ways in which students at New York College are interacting with the Christopher Robin Library, as well as the students' larger needs and desires. Survey methods are well suited to this scenario for two reasons. First, Gene and his team need to gather data directly from a student body that is too large for library staff to personally observe or interview. Survey methods will allow library staff to direct their data collection efforts toward all 5,800 undergraduates. Second, Gene and his team need to understand trends and issues across the entire student body. Other research methods would allow them to develop a deep understanding of the experience of particular students or groups of students but would not enable them to grasp the general experience of all students. Survey methods are specifically designed to provide this type of insight about a broad population.

It seems likely that Mia Signet, associate director and head of Access Services, will lead this survey research project. To begin, Mia should form a small survey research team (SRT) made up of faculty and staff with expertise in item design, instrument design, instrument testing, survey administration, and statistical analysis. Once this team is assembled, its first task will be to develop specific, clearly defined research questions that the survey will seek to answer. These are not the actual items that will appear on the survey instrument, but rather the broad, overarching questions the team seeks to answer by conducting their research effort.

Next, the SRT will need to determine the best survey mode to reach their target group: online, by text message, in person, by mail, or by phone. It seems likely that an online survey will meet the needs of the Christopher Robin Library; however, each survey mode presents both strengths and limitations to consider. Online surveys are administered through a website that can be displayed on library computers, loaded on tablets in the library, or, most often, distributed by emailing a link to the survey page. Several free or low-cost web-based survey platforms are available, and it is likely that New York College also provides a more high-powered platform for faculty and staff use.

Online surveys can be very convenient for respondents because they can be taken at any time from nearly any Internet-enabled device. They offer a great deal of flexibility in design, including the ability to implement **skip logic,** which allows questions to be limited to certain respondents based on their answers to previous questions, and the option to randomize the order of questions or response choices. Most online survey software platforms also employ responsive design that adapts the survey display to the size of each respondent's screen. As the software captures data as individuals enter their responses, no additional data entry is required.

Many software platforms also perform basic analytic procedures, such as calculating simple descriptive statistics. Responses can be anonymous when administering an online survey, and the impersonal nature lowers the risk that respondents will provide answers that they think will please the researchers rather than providing their true options. This phenomenon is called *social desirability bias* and can cause survey findings to be less trustworthy.

The utility of online surveys, however, is limited to those audiences that have Internet access, are comfortable responding to a survey online, and can be reached electronically. In this scenario, these limitations are unlikely to present a problem since undergraduates tend to be tech-savvy and likely to view an online survey as convenient and easy to complete. In addition, it is expected that New York College supplies an email address to all of its enrolled students. This would allow the SRT to draw a current, complete list of email addresses to use in disseminating the survey. Another limitation of online surveys is that they have a relatively low rate of completion compared with other modes of administration. Mia and the SRT may wish to address this by offering an incentive for completing the survey.

Next, the team can begin developing the survey items, which can be broadly categorized into two groups: close-ended and open-ended. Close-ended items are those that provide a predetermined list of response choices from which respondents make their selection. Examples of close-ended questions are **dichotomous items**: multiple-choice items, rating scale questions, and ranking tasks. Since the purpose of survey research is to gather quantitative data that can be summarized statistically, the vast majority of survey items should be close-ended. This presents a possible limitation, however, since researchers must know the appropriate response choices in advance. If the SRT is uncertain about what response choices may be appropriate for certain survey items, they may need to conduct exploratory research prior to drafting their survey items.

In contrast to close-ended items, open-ended items invite respondents to enter an unstructured response such as a number, a few words, or one or more sentences.

Although primarily focused on quantitative data, a survey can include a limited number of open-ended items, although research has shown that respondents are more likely to skip open-ended items compared with close-ended items (Reja et al. 2003). If the team finds that they want to include many open-ended items in their survey, that may be an indication that they would be better served by conducting individual or group interviews rather than or in addition to administering a survey.

In order to obtain valid, reliable information, survey items must be written in such a way that respondents understand the question, have the knowledge necessary to answer the question, and have the appropriate response choices available to them. Specifically, SRT should do the following:

- *Use simple, clear language.* If respondents don't understand exactly what an item is trying to communicate, it is more likely that they will make mistakes, choose the wrong answers, or give up on the survey entirely. Items should be written in short, complete sentences that are free of jargon and acronyms. Negative items should be avoided, as these are easy for respondents to misinterpret.
- *Limit each item to a single thought or idea.* Poorly written survey items sometimes include more than one thought or idea embedded in them. When that happens, respondents may answer one but not both parts or their answers for the two parts may be in conflict, leaving them unsure about which answer to select.
- *Avoid bias in the wording of the items and response choices.* Biased items are those that encourage respondents to answer in a particular way. For example, the SRT might write an item in such a way that it reveals their own opinion or they might refer to what "most people" think or believe. These items would be biased because respondents may be inclined to answer in a way that agrees with the stated opinions.
- *Ensure response choices are exhaustive and mutually exclusive.* Response choices should be comprehensive so that every respondent can find a response that reflects his or her experience or opinion. As the SRT writes its questions, the group should reflect on different situations and circumstances that would influence respondents' answers, strive to consider respondents who will be an exception to the rule, and then include response choices for those individuals. They should also include "None of the above" and "Other (specify)" choices as needed. When structuring response choices, the SRT should also ensure that response choices are mutually exclusive, that is, that the responses don't overlap.
- *Focus on respondents' personal experiences and perspectives.* Respondents must have the knowledge necessary to answer the questions being asked. This means that items should be focused on respondents' personal experiences and perspectives rather than asking them to speculate on the experiences and perspectives of others or of students in general. In addition, items should not require respondents to recall details of past behavior or to project future actions.

- *Randomize response choices whenever possible.* Research has shown that respondents are more likely to select response choices near the top of the list (Galesic et al. 2008; Krosnick et al. 1991). To offset this bias, the SRT should employ the randomization feature of the survey software that presents response choices in varied, random order.
- *Avoid drop-down menus.* Although response choices can be presented using drop-down menus, research has shown that these items are more likely to be skipped and that respondents are more likely to accidentally select an unintended answer or to select response choices toward the top of the list (Best and Harrison 2009).
- *Balance rating scale items.* Depending on the nature of the item, SRT may want to include equal numbers of positive and negative response choices to avoid encouraging respondents to provide a positive or a negative answer. In addition, the instructions for the item should be balanced as well. For example, the instructions might read, "Please indicate the extent to which you agree or disagree with the following statements" rather than "Please indicate the extent to which you agree with the following statements." Research is ongoing to determine the importance of offering a neutral response choice, the optimal number of response choices, and whether response choices should be labeled with numbers and/or words. (See, for example, Preston and Colman 2000; Weathers et al. 2005; Weijters et al. 2010.)

After the SRT drafts its items, the group will need to organize the items into a survey instrument. The instrument should begin with an introduction in which the SRT explains who is conducting the survey and why, describes how long the survey is likely to take, explains what incentive, if any, is being offered, and provides any consent information or process required by New York College's institutional review board if applicable. Next, the body of the survey will include the SRT's survey items. Items should be arranged in a logical order, which will most likely be grouped by theme or topic. When possible, it is recommended to begin with the item that will be most interesting to respondents so that the survey captures their attention and piques their interest in responding. It's important to note, however, that early items can influence responses to later items. Randomizing is not recommended as a solution since it can result in a jumble of topics that can be confusing to respondents.

Demographic items should follow the body of the survey. These are placed near the end of the instrument because they are typically the most sensitive information that is requested. The SRT should take care to only ask for demographic information that it needs and will use. Finally, in the closing section, the SRT should thank respondents for their time and responses.

No matter how much care and skill goes into creating a survey, there will always be some mistakes such as spelling errors, ambiguous wording, or a question that respondents are not able to answer. For this reason, it is critical that

SRT members test their survey and revise it based on what they learn. To begin, they should ask several colleagues in the library or from around campus to review the instrument for content and clarity (Presser and Blair 1994). These reviewers should check for errors as well as opportunities to clarify and simplify items. Reviewers should also consider the format of the instrument since a poorly organized or formatted instrument can confuse respondents, result in respondents missing items, and/or cause them to abandon the survey altogether. Since this survey will be administered online, respondents won't have an opportunity to ask questions; therefore, the instrument needs to be relatively self-explanatory and provide clear instructions (Evans and Mathur 2005).

After making the revisions that reviewers identify, the next step in testing will be cognitive interviewing or "think aloud" testing in which members of the SRT would ask a few undergraduate students to voice their thoughts aloud, either while taking the survey or immediately after completing it (Presser et al. 2004; Willis and Miller 2011). This can provide insight into how the target audience interprets the instructions and survey items and whether any response choices are missing. Following any revisions that result, the SRT will be ready to conduct a pilot test. During this phase, it will administer the survey to a small portion of the target audience. This will allow the team to identify problems with its data collection procedures and with the performance of individual items on its survey. The SRT should send the survey to about 30 randomly selected students following the exact procedures that will eventually be used in fielding the survey to the full student body. As the data are collected, SRT members should monitor whether they are being stored as expected in the survey software and should also watch for unexpected patterns in the responses. For example, if they observe that all of the respondents select the same response for a question, it could indicate that there is an error in the response choices that are listed or that the item isn't sensitive enough to distinguish among respondents' different opinions or experiences. If no data are recorded for a particular item, this could indicate that the skip logic malfunctioned and didn't offer that question to any of the respondents. Pilot testing will also reveal how long it takes respondents to complete the survey. If any problems are identified and corrected, the data from the pilot test must be discarded. If no changes are made, the pilot test data can be combined as part of the full sample.

After a successful pilot test has been completed and the instrument has been finalized, the SRT will be ready to field the survey. At this point, it will not be able to make any further changes to the instrument in order to maintain standardization across respondents. As the survey is fielded, the SRT should turn its attention to ensuring a strong response rate in order to obtain the most meaningful data possible. In any survey, it is expected that there will be differences between individuals who choose to respond to a survey and those who don't. SRT may be able to speculate about some of those differences in relation to its survey. For example, students who have a positive impression of the library may be more likely to take the time to complete the survey than students who have a negative impression of the library. More importantly, however, there are likely to be differences between respondents and nonrespondents that will be unknown to the researchers. These unknown differences can lead to **nonresponse error** in survey findings. To minimize this error, the SRT should invest effort in obtaining a high response rate.

Research indicates that the most important factors for a high response rate are that the survey be short, relevant, and of interest to the target audience (Evans and Mathur 2005). The timing of the survey is also important for maximizing the response rate. Data collection should fall within the middle of fall or spring semester. October, February, and April are popular months for data collection because the semester is well under way and there are typically no school breaks scheduled. In addition, an email should be sent out in advance of the survey to alert students to be expecting the survey, and the actual survey invitation should be sent out midweek rather than on Monday, Friday, or a weekend. The SRT should also send a reminder email approximately one to two weeks after the survey invitation has been sent. Incentives can also boost response rates. Research seems to indicate that cash is a stronger incentive than gift cards, that an incentive provided to every respondent is more effective than being entered in a prize drawing, and that a prepaid incentive has a stronger effect than an incentive provided after completing the survey (Birnholtz et al. 2004; Millar and Dillman 2011; van Veen et al. 2015; Warriner et al. 1996).

When the data collection period ends, the SRT should close the survey so that no additional data are recorded. The data can then be exported to quantitative data analysis software such as Excel, SPSS, or R. SRT members will then compute basic descriptive statistics, primarily means and frequencies, for each survey item. It will be important for them to remember that most rating scale data are categorical in nature; that is, respondents choose a category into which their response falls. These data should be analyzed as frequencies as it is not appropriate to convert these categories to numbers and compute means. It is also likely that the SRT will want to conduct subgroup analysis to compare the responses of key groups of students. For example, they may wish to compare the responses provided by freshman and sophomores with those provided by upperclassmen to determine if there are differences of opinion across different groups. Similarly, they may wish to compare the responses of students majoring in arts and humanities with the responses of students in math and sciences. Statistical testing can help the SRT determine which differences it discovers are statistically significant and which are due to normal variation in the data. Responses to open-ended items can be analyzed by grouping responses according to themes and counting the number of responses that correspond to each theme in order to identify patterns within the data.

It is expected that some respondents will skip individual items on the survey. This is called **item nonresponse** and results in "missing data" for that particular item. If 5% or less of the data are missing for a given item, they can usually be ignored since that level of missing data is unlikely to change the statistical analysis overall. As the amount of missing data increases, however, it becomes increasingly problematic since the SRT will not know how the missing data may differ from the responses that were obtained. If the percentage of missing data becomes high, the SRT should omit the affected item(s) from its analysis. It may also become necessary to impute or estimate missing data, and, if that is the case, the team should consult the statistics department on campus for assistance.

The final step in the research process will be for the SRT to interpret its findings and take action based on what it has learned. In this step, the SRT must guard against the tendency to make inferences from the survey responses to the entire student body. Instead, the survey findings only apply to those students who actually took the survey. Findings from the survey can be used to develop new services, adjust collections, refresh existing services, focus staff development activities, and more. Mia and the SRT should share what they have learned with key **stakeholders** beyond the library as well. The SRT should also document their entire research process and findings to make it easy to revisit them in the future.

Why Use This Research Method?

Survey research is very useful for gathering quantitative data from large populations that the researcher would be unable to observe or interview directly. Some of the power of survey methods lies in their flexibility; surveys can be used to examine attitudes, opinions, and reported behavior and can be administered online, by text message, in person, by mail, or by phone. In the case of Christopher Robin Library, survey research can be relatively low cost for the library and impose a low burden for respondents since an online survey is well suited to its needs.

Survey research also presents several limitations. First, developing strong instruments that yield valid, reliable data requires specialized skills and knowledge. While it is relatively easy to develop and field a survey, the quality of the data it yields is directly related to the quality of the survey items and the instrument overall. In addition, researchers must know all of the response choices that need to be included for each item. If some or all of these are unknown, the survey will not yield meaningful information. Finally, surveys generate self-reported information. While this type of data aligns well with certain research questions, self-reported information about behavior may be less trustworthy than behavioral data obtained through other research methods. Table 19.1 summarizes this research methodology.

Table 19.1
Summary Chart: Survey Methods

Overall purpose	Description of large population
Advantages	• Enables data collection from a large population • Flexible method that can be used to examine attitudes, opinions, and reported behavior • Can be relatively low cost and impose a minimal burden on respondents
Disadvantages	• Requires expertise in numerous areas • Need to know appropriate response choices • Reliance on self-reported information
Steps in process	• Determine research questions • Develop survey items • Prepare survey instrument • Conduct testing • Collect data • Analyze data • Take action based on findings
Data collection methods	• Descriptive statistics • Inferential statistics for subgroup analysis and when seeking to make inferences from a sample to a population • Thematic analysis for open-ended items
Data analysis methods	• Descriptive statistics
Support technologies	• Online survey software • SMS survey software • Statistical analysis software

Glossary of Key Terms

Census: Survey that collects information from all members of a population is called census.

Dichotomous item: It refers to a survey item with two possible responses such as Yes/No or True/False.

Item nonresponse: This indicates a situation in which a respondent answers some or most survey items but does not respond to one or more items.

Nonresponse error: It refers to error in survey findings that arises because some individuals in the population or sample do not respond to the survey.

Sample survey: Survey that collects information from a subgroup of a population is called sample survey.

Skip logic: It is a feature of survey software in which a respondent is presented with certain survey items based on his or her responses to prior items.

Social desirability bias: It refers to bias in survey findings that arises when respondents provide answers that are hoped to please the researcher or place the respondent in a favorable light.

Stakeholders: Individuals who have an interest in the findings of research or are affected by those findings are called stakeholders.

Further Reading

Babbie, Earl R. 2013. *The Practice of Social Research*. 13th ed. Belmont, TN: Wadsworth, Cengage Learning.

Dillman, Don A., Jolene D. Smyth, and Leah Melani Christian. 2009. *Internet, Mail, and Mixed-Mode Surveys: The Tailored Design Method*. Hoboken, NJ: John Wiley & Sons, Inc.

Fowler, Floyd J. 2009. *Survey Research Methods*. 4th ed. Thousand Oaks, CA: Sage Publications, Inc.

Chapter 20

The Delphi Method

Jami Jones, Associate Professor
East Carolina University

Introduction to the Delphi Method

Many decision makers face, at one time or another, a lack of information when data are incomplete or faulty or perhaps too many intangibles make it difficult to determine the best way to proceed. For such occasions of uncertainty, a research method named after Pythia, the Delphic oracle who was able to foresee the future, was developed in the 1950s by mathematicians at the Rand Corporation, a global nonprofit policy and decision-making organization originally formed by the Douglas Aircraft Company to offer research and analysis to the U.S. Armed Forces. Its first use was to "obtain the most reliable **consensus** of opinion of a group of experts" regarding "selection from the point of view of a Soviet strategic planner, of an optimal U.S. industrial target system and to the estimation of the number of A-bombs required to reduce the munitions output by a prescribed amount" (Linstone and Turoff 1975, 3).

The Delphi method is best used to ferret out opinion and gain consensus in situations of uncertainty where information is not available and the problem does not lend itself to precise analytical techniques, but could benefit from subjective judgments on a collective basis. It is a research process that is "highly conducive to producing preliminary insights into the subject matter at hand" that cannot be researched in other ways; although there is no way to know what will occur until events unfold (Dalkey and Helmer 1962, 17).

Delphi is also useful when the time and cost of bringing together a group of experts are improbable. Similarly, when the **expert panel** members represent diverse backgrounds with respect to experience and expertise, it is unlikely they would normally gather in a common space such as a conference, but could engage in research via email or Internet communications.

According to Rowe and Wright (1999), four key features characterize the Delphi method:

1. Anonymity of Delphi participants
2. Iteration that allows participants to refine their views based on the progress of the group's work from round to round
3. Controlled feedback by the **facilitator** that informs participants of other participants' perspectives and allows participants to change their views
4. Quantitative analysis of the group response and interpretation of data

Dalkey and Helmer (1962), cocreators of Delphi, posited that this iterative method of anonymous consensus of participants avoids the "disadvantages associated with more conventional uses of experts, such as round-table discussion or other milder forms of confrontation with opposing views," leading to the "hasty formulation of preconceived notions," (2) closed mindedness, the unwillingness to consider novel ideas, and the tendency to defend a stance once taken. These authors contend that the process of anonymity circumvents domination by strong personalities, and outlier opinions and judgments have a greater chance of consideration.

Since its inception, Delphi has been used successfully in many situations calling for long-range planning in areas of health, education, and economics. In the library and information science field, Delphi has been used for the purpose of forecasting, exploration, and long-range planning; the examination of these studies is a rich source of information regarding design and implementation. In library science, the method has been used widely to identify and explore topics such as the following:

1. Key issues and challenges of bibliographic records (Zhang and Salaba 2016)
2. Models of academic library websites (Wijayaratne and Singh 2015)
3. Essential reference sources to introduce in basic Library and Information Science (LIS) reference courses (Rabina 2013)
4. Dispositions of exemplary school librarians (Bush and Jones 2010)
5. Future of the academic library and academic librarian (Feret and Marcinek 2005)
6. Library as place (Ludwig and Starr 2005)
7. The use of databases by high school students (Neuman 1995)

Considerations in Using Delphi

On the surface, Delphi seems a simple and easily conducted research technique to collect expert opinion for purposes of decision making and forecasting. However, design considerations and the technique's inexactness can make Delphi a particularly challenging method to implement for the reasons discussed below.

The Role of the Facilitator

The skills of the facilitator, who is the designer and implementer of the research project, are crucial when applying this method to questions that are not easily quantified and to categorizing and consolidating statements without misinterpreting their meanings. One challenge is that it is only possible for the facilitator to develop the initial scenario and first-round research questions; latter **rounds** depend on panelist member's input in the form of estimates, rankings, and comments. Although the iterative process typically consists of three rounds, also referred to as sequential questionnaires, the facilitator must decide at the end of each round to continue or to conclude the study based on information provided and consensus reached. Too few rounds and the facilitator and expert participants may not have delved deeply enough into the topic; too many and experts may drop out as the process becomes too lengthy. Contributors to the literature on the Delphi method caution that too many rounds can lead to panelists leaving the study as well as bias being introduced. Scheibe, Skutsch, and Schofer (1975) wrote that the cut-off point is difficult to discern "since there is no underlying statistical theory . . . no true statistical level may be set as might, for example, be possible with a statistical change in variance test" (278).

Although the study is planned, information from each round leads to design decisions for future rounds, for which the facilitator must remain open. Common reasons for the failure of a Delphi study are as follows:

1. Imposing an overly specific Delphi structure and not allowing for the contributions of other perspectives
2. Poor techniques on the part of the facilitator in summarizing and presenting the group's responses
3. Ignoring and not exploring disagreements, so that discouraged dissenters drop out and an artificial consensus is generated

The Uniqueness of the Expert Panel

Unlike other research methods, the Delphi does not depend on a statistical sample that is representative of any population. Rather, the method relies on an **expert panel** whose knowledge and opinion are valued to complete iterative questionnaires. Panelists are qualified experts in the field with deep understanding of the issues and "relevant knowledge and experience of a particular topic" (Thangaratinam and Redman 2005, 120), who are selected on the basis of their workplace experiences, professional activities, and contributions to the field through research, publication, service, and idea generation. In addition to knowledge and experience with the issues under investigation, Adler and Ziblio (1996) urged that the following to be considered as well: capacity and willingness to participate, sufficient time to participate, and effective communication skills. Readers are warned that experts should not be selected on the basis of acquaintance with the researchers; however, compliance to this recommendation may be difficult in intensely specialized areas.

It has been described in the literature that heterogeneous groups, characterized by panel members with widely varying personalities and substantially different perspectives on a problem, produce a higher proportion of high-quality solutions than homogenous groups (Delbecq, de Ven, and Guftafson 1975). It is suggested that panel members be recruited from varied backgrounds in order to guarantee a wide base of knowledge and divergent opinions.

There are no hard or fast rules regarding the size of the Delphi panel which has been reported in the literature to range from four experts to 3,000. Seven to 20 expert participants seems to be a typical range (Linstone and Turoff 1975), but participation varies according to the scope of the problem and the resources involved.

Delphi Is Time Consuming

Delphi method is time consuming for the facilitator who organizes and summarizes comments as well as for the expert panel members who respond to research questions and rank and weight the information. It is important to explain to potential panel members the process, projected time commitment, and turnaround in replying to and submitting questionnaires. As emphasized above, a common reason for the failure of a Delphi project is to underestimate the time commitment by panelists who might drop out if the effort seems too great.

Perceived Lack of Statistical Rigor

Perhaps the greatest criticism of the Delphi technique is its lack of perceived statistical rigor compared to quantitative research methods that are systematized and "experimentally confirmed propositions of the natural sciences" (Dalkey 1969, 2) or the social sciences (Fischer 1978). Its lack of sampling, the impossibility of accounting for unseen events, and the absence of clearly defined procedures and processes for conducting Delphi studies are just a few of the features that differentiate it from controlled scientific methodologies (Ludwig and Starr 2005, 316). Sackman (1974), in his critical analysis and evaluation of the Delphi technique, noted that the "accuracy of the technique ... is necessarily suspect as long as Delphi questions are not empirically linked to objective and independently verifiable external evaluation criteria" (v).

Although Dalkey and Helmer (1962) recognized Delphi's lack of reliability and shortcomings, they lauded the method as being "highly conducive to producing preliminary insights into the subject matter at hand on which a more effective research program may be based," (17). They hoped that "a carefully contrived opinion consensus would often turn out to be an acceptable substitute for direct empirical evidence when the latter in unavailable" (17).

Delphi Methodology

Since the 1950s when the first Delphi research was conducted, and 1963 when the definitive paper about the method was published, the method has undergone an "abundance of methodological interpretations," resulting in what Powell (2003) referred to as its "different guises" (376). Even though Delphi has been applied flexibly, the three basic elements initially described by Dalkey and Helmer (1962) have been retained:

1. "Repeated individual questioning of the experts"
2. "Avoids direct confrontation of the experts with one another"
3. "Interspersed . . . controlled feedback" (2)

Skulmoski, Hartman, and Krahn (2007) presented a useful 11-step framework based on the classic Delphi technique developed and implemented by Dalkey and Helmer (1962) that has been successfully utilized by their graduate students of information systems. Skulmoski, Hartman, and Krahn (2007) cautioned that the "typical Delphi process that we follow . . . is a general guide rather than a template" (5).

Each of these steps will be applied to the scenario that is described below.

1. Develop the research question.
2. Design the research.
3. Identify and select members of the expert panel.
4. Develop Delphi Round One questionnaire.
5. Conduct a pilot study to test and adjust the Delphi questionnaire to "improve comprehension, and to work out any procedural problems (Skulmoski, Hartman, and Krahn 2007, 4). The facilitator can also pretest subsequent questionnaires. The authors write that it is "especially important for inexperienced researchers who may be overly ambitious regarding the scope of their research or underestimate the time it will take a Delphi research participant to fully respond to the Delphi survey" (Skulmoski, Hartman, and Krahn 2007, 4).
6. Release and analyze the Round One questionnaire. These responses become the basis for the Round Two questionnaire.
7. Develop the Round Two questionnaire.
8. Release and analyze the Round Two questionnaire.
9. Develop the Round Three questionnaire.
10. Release and analyze the Round Three questionnaire.
11. Verify, generalize, and document research results.

Applying Delphi to the Scenario

The charge to authors is to apply the Delphi method to the Christopher Robin Library at New York College that is facing tremendous growth in student usage. In this scenario, library director Gene Parks notes that ways the library interacts with patrons have not changed significantly over the last 35 years, yet he senses that the library's future landscape needs to be explored and understood. He is interested in an intriguing new position that he has read about—the User Experience (UX) librarian, whose focus is to identify users' needs and expectations in order to fashion a library responsive to these changes. Although Parks is receiving pushback from members of his staff, he is not deterred by this lack of enthusiasm, but is eager to collect information about ways "users interact with the library, considering not only the physical space, but also the suitability of all our systems to the audience being served." Parks seeks to obtain expert opinion to understand the future and to make informed decisions about the Christopher Robin Library.

From this scenario, several Delphi designs are possible, ranging from simple to complex. For a less-complex Delphi, one panel of experts with experience in the field would be selected to respond to whatever number of research questions are identified—two, three, or more. However, a more complicated Delphi design could be crafted by asking these questions to multiple panels, each populated by experts with specific views and experiences with the library such as administrators, LIS faculty, collection development or reference librarians, college students, and subject faculty, and the results of these panels would be compared.

The Research Questions Identified by Director Parks

Parks begins this research by reading broadly about the topic, discussing with colleagues the ways users interact with the library, and browsing through the literature to understand the different ways that Delphi projects are designed. He pulls together a small collaborative research team, from now on called facilitators, to identify the research questions and to design the process. After much discussion, the facilitators decide to ask open-ended questions as this is the most authentic way to gather opinions that are more creative, and not hindered, or confined, by already expressed thoughts. It should be noted by readers that even though open-ended questions are "recognized to increase the richness of the data collected," it is not unusual for the first-round questionnaire to be based on results of a literature review, or even previous research such as surveys (Powell 2002, 378).

The Research Questions

The research questions selected for the first round were as follows:

RQ 1: What is the vision for the college library in five years?

RQ 2: How will users interact with the library in five years? Think broadly about this interaction and consider space utilization, the learning environment, technology and web presence, the collection, personnel, and programs and services. Feel free to identify additional categories of user interaction.

RQ 3: What will users expect from the library in five years? Think broadly about these expectations and consider space utilization, the learning environment, technology and web presence, the collection, personnel, and program and services. Feel free to identify additional categories of user expectations.

Selecting the Expert Panel for the Christopher Robin Library's Delphi

The facilitators begin the process by identifying and selecting the expert panel members. Okoli and Pawlowski (2004) suggested following a multistep iterative approach in choosing members of the expert panel, and advocate using the Knowledge Resource Nomination Worksheet to identify categories of expertise so as not to overlook any important group of experts. In considering membership to the expert panel, the facilitators would identify the following categories from which to choose: varied work experience of librarians in administration and departments throughout the library such as reference, instructional services, technology, collection development; LIS faculty; professional activities; service to the profession through committee leadership and involvement with professional organizations such as the American Library Association and the Association of College and Research Libraries; and contributors to the library literature through research and publication of books and articles. In addition, the facilitators might consider space utilization planners and users of the library such as students and faculty members in subject disciplines.

The facilitators populate the categories with actual names of potential experts. Each category represents a different lens for identifying and considering experts, which is a necessary process to ensure that responses are varied and as heterogamous viewpoints are expressed. It is also possible to contact identified experts to ask them to nominate their colleagues who would become potential experts. The last step in this process is to rank the experts by qualifications based on the categories previously identified, which becomes the pool for the study. The facilitators select and invite the agreed-upon number of experts to join the study.

For Delphi research regarding high school students' use of databases, Neuman (1995) asked seven national experts in this field to submit lists of potential panelists. Library media specialists whose names appeared on one of more of these lists were asked to participate. For Bush and Jones's (2010) Delphi on dispositions of school librarians, members of library publishing boards and editors of journals were asked to participate. Zhang and Salaba (2009) identified experts who either had published on the topic of Functional Requirements for Bibliographic Records or were instrumental in its development. They write that "123 individuals met the selection criteria and were invited to participate in the study; thirty-three of these accepted the invitation to form the panel for this study" (237).

Pretesting the Delphi

It is good research design to pretest research projects, but it is especially critical to identify ambiguities in word meanings or phrases in the first round of Delphi. Pretesting improves the likelihood that responses address the research questions, and is recognized as an "important reliability assurance for the Delphi method" (Okoli and Pawlowski 2004, 19).

The facilitators decide to pretest the first-round survey with a small group of the experts who will be used solely for this purpose, and will not become part of the larger study, to ensure the reliability of the questions, and to hone their skills at aggregating responses and feeding these back to the experts. The first time Delphi researcher may want to practice the entire 11-step process with a small group of experts before embarking on research with the entire panel.

Date Collection and Analysis

The Delphi method requires a minimum of two rounds or three if the first round is open-ended. Beyond that, the number of rounds is not clear-cut. Feedback is provided after each round of the Delphi in the form of aggregated group responses, qualitative information such as justifications, and numerical or statistical data, but the type of data analysis depends on the round being analyzed.

Data Collection

The order of data collection falls into three categories (Schmidt 1997):

1. Phase 1: Brainstorming
2. Phase 2: Narrowing down
3. Phase 3: Ranking

Round One

The creative stage of the Delphi study occurs in the first round, which is likened to brainstorming, by soliciting opinions from participants in the form of open-ended responses. Managing these opinions in the form of ranking and weighting in later questionnaires involves mostly judgmental opinion (Okoli and Pawlowski 2004).

After experts have completed and returned the first-round questionnaires, the facilitator analyzes responses, removes identical and full consensus responses, records on a consolidated list the number of panelists that initially suggested each item or idea, and groups these items and ideas conceptually into categories. This information is fed back to participants to confirm if their ideas and comments have been captured correctly, and becomes the basis of the second round questionnaire. For instance, in Round One of Zhang and Salaba's (2009) Delphi, experts were provided a direct link to an online survey and asked to suggest three or four major critical issues facing Functional Requirements for Bibliographic Records (FRBR).

Round Two

In the second round, the narrowing down phase, experts are asked to organize, group, prioritize, and discuss what is meant or implied by the first-round responses. The facilitator may quantify these second-round responses by identifying the mean, median, and standard deviation. The results are presented back to the experts.

For instance, in Round Two of Zhang and Salaba's (2009) Delphi, experts were provided a direct link to an online survey and were instructed to rate using a ten-point scale the importance of the FRBR issues raised during the previous round and to introduce additional items as well.

Round Three

In the third round or ranking phase of a three-round Delphi, the facilitator asks panel members to rank order or weight those factors identified and selected in previous rounds. The facilitator may calculate arithmetic mean and median scores, standard deviations, and could assess consensus using Kendall's Coefficient of Concordance (W), which is a nonparametric test to analyze data that is ordinal, ranked, subject to outliers, or measured imprecisely (Schmidt 1997). For instance, in Round Three of Zhang and Salaba's (2009) Delphi, FRBR issues were ordered by mean score and rationales were given for this ordering. Experts were asked to rate these issues previous round.

If necessary, a third or fourth round is conducted to obtain consensus. Most Delphi research is conducted in three rounds as the technique becomes increasingly ineffective after three rounds. However, the number of rounds and what occurs in these rounds depends on the design of the project and information and feedback from expert panel members.

The Presentation of the Data

Results of each round of the Delphi are presented in various formats: tables; figures such as bar and pie charts; or lists. Depending on the round and the data collected, facilitators will display ranking and weights, comments of panel members, and numerical or statistical measures.

The Delphi literature provides cogent examples of data presentation. For example, Zhang and Salaba (2009) presented the results of the three rounds in table format by ranked issue, and for each round the mean rating and standard deviation were identified. In the final column, the authors identified whether greater consensus was reached in Round Three. In Ludwig and Starr's (2005) Delphi study on library as place, the 78 opinion statements were presented in table format with columns identifying consensus ranking, agreement percent, disagreement percent, statement, and desirability and impact. In Feret and Marcinek's (2005) Delphi study on the future of the academic library and the academic librarian, the authors illustrated results using bubble and column charts.

Table 20.1 summarizes the advantages and disadvantages of Delphi, steps in the process, data collection and analysis methods, and support technologies.

Table 20.1
Summary Chart: The Delphi Technique

Overall purpose	To gather expert opinion to improve decision making
Advantages	To achieve consensus in situations of uncertainty or where information is not available, but expert opinion is valued; to provide preliminary insights into the topic to support further research and actions; and the stimulation of new ideas
Disadvantages	Not considered a rigorous research methodology; few clearly defined procedures and processes for conducting Delphi studies; and requires researcher to correctly interpret comments and refrain from bias
Steps in process	Multiple beginning with identification of research questions, selection of expert panel members, and 3–5 rounds in which comments are fed back to panelists
Data collection methods	Questionnaires in which experts respond to open-ended questions and then sort, rank, and weight information.
Data analysis methods	Content analysis, central tendency (mean, median, mode), dispersion of scores (standard deviation), and/or Kendall's Coefficient of Concordance
Support technologies	Email and web-based applications such as Qualtrics and Survey Monkey advantageous to anonymous communication

Glossary of Key Terms

Consensus: It is an identified percentage amount in which participants agree with each other. Although there seems to be no firm rules for establishing this percentage, failure to offer an interpretation of the meaning of consensus is considered a research design flaw.

Expert panelists: Individuals chosen by their work and credibility to respond to the research questions, or questionnaires, identified by the facilitator are called expert panelists. There is no set number of the number of experts chosen to participate on a panel; the range varies from 4 to 3,000.

Facilitator: The person responsible for designing and coordinating the Delphi study. The facilitator selects the panel of experts, sends out the research questions, or questionnaire, for panelists to respond to, and collects and analyzes their responses.

Multiphase design: multiple methods are used in multistages.

Rounds: The Delphi iterative process is conducted in rounds, also identified as sequential questionnaires.

Further Reading

Dalkey, Norman, and Olaf Helmer. 1963. "An Experimental Application of the Delphi Method to the Use of Experts." *Management Science* 9 (3): 458–68.

Linstone, Harold A., and Murray Turroff. 1975. *The Delphi Method: Techniques and Applications*. Reading: Addison-Wesley Publishing Company.

Luo, Lili, and Barbara M. Wildemuth. 2009. "Delphi Studies." In *Applications of Social Research Methods to Questions in Information and Library Science*, edited by B. M. Wildemuth, 83–92. Westport, CT: Libraries Unlimited.

Chapter 21

Mixed Methods Research Design

Dabae Lee, Assistant Professor
Department of Instructional Design and Technology,
The Teachers College, Emporia State University

Introduction to Mixed Methods Research

The term "mixed methods" describes research that mixes quantitative and qualitative methods. One research method is often insufficient to fully address a complex research problem in a real setting because there are so many components, people, and contextual factors associated with the research problem. Mixed methods research integrates quantitative and qualitative research methods to allow for a better understanding of the research problem by collecting multiple sources of quantitative and qualitative data. Because quantitative and qualitative research methods have their unique advantages and disadvantages, mixed methods research aims to maximize the advantages of both while offsetting the disadvantages.

Five types of mixed methods designs blend quantitative and qualitative data in different ways to better address unique situations (Creswell and Plano Clark 2011). A research design uses quantitative and qualitative research methods in different ways at different times. Figure 21.1 illustrates the five types of mixed methods designs.

Convergent Parallel Design

As Figure 21.1 suggests, with a **convergent parallel design**, the researcher performs quantitative data collection and analysis and qualitative data collection and analysis simultaneously and compares the results to develop a more complete understanding of a research problem. This design is usually used when the research problem is multifaceted, and when it is necessary to examine the problem from multiple perspectives. For example, a researcher would use this approach to study how playing an educational game influences students' attitude, behaviors, and learning outcomes. Gaining insight into the influence of gaming would

Figure 21.1
Mixed Methods Research Design

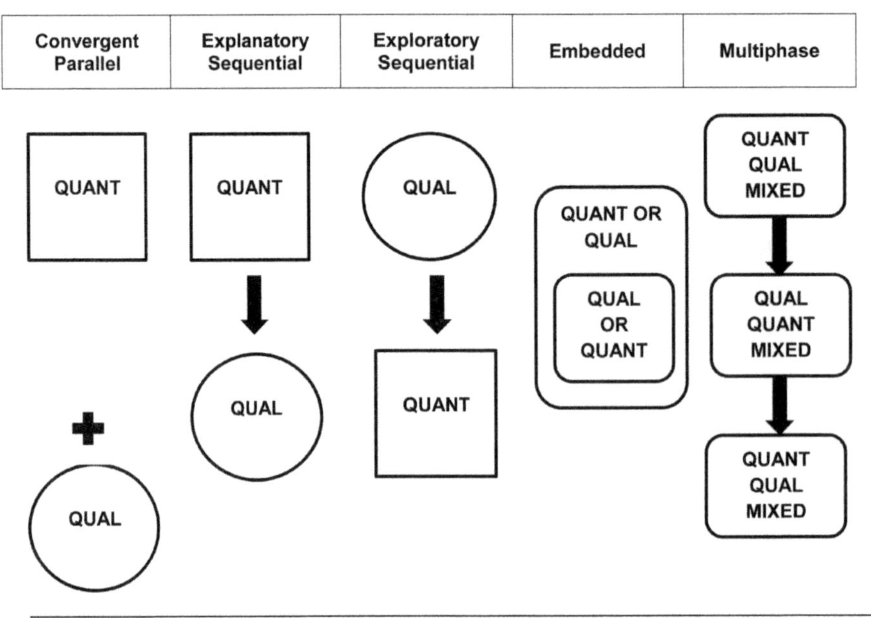

require the researcher to collect students' game-playing data, measure students' attitudes with a survey, observe students' behaviors, and measure learning outcomes using a test.

Explanatory Sequential Design

In an **explanatory sequential design**, the researcher uses a qualitative approach to explain quantitative results, typically done, as Figure 21.1 suggests, in a two-phase design where a quantitative method follows a qualitative method. The researcher first collects quantitative data to identify some phenomenon that requires in-depth investigation and then chooses a qualitative design based on the nature of the phenomenon of interest. An example of this design is understanding teachers' student-centered classroom approaches. The researcher identifies those who are using a student-centered approach via survey responses and then conducts direct observation of how they implement student-centered learning in their classrooms.

Exploratory Sequential Design

The purpose of the **exploratory sequential design** illustrated in Figure 21.1 is to investigate whether a phenomenon observed in qualitative data can be generalized to a bigger population in a two-phase design in which qualitative data are collected and analyzed and a quantitative approach is used to investigate the findings from the qualitative data. Suppose that, through interviews, a researcher has identified a need for a training program on a certain technology. To learn how many people want such a program, the researcher would then conduct a survey with a bigger population.

Embedded Design

In the **embedded design** shown in Figure 21.1, one method is nested within another method, with a quantitative design embedded in a qualitative design or a qualitative design embedded in a quantitative design. The embedded method can take place before, during, or after the main design. For example, a researcher can conduct an experimental study on the effects of a training program and qualitatively investigate the participants' changes in behaviors before and after the training program.

Multiphase Design

The final method depicted in Figure 21.1., the **concurrent triangulation design,** is a combination of sequential and convergent designs. Typically, this design takes place in multiple stages so that a qualitative or quantitative study informs another quantitative or qualitative study. Then the researcher designs another mixed methods study. A **multiphase design** can use any combination of the other four types of mixed methods designs. Because this approach takes multiple stages and multiple data sources, the design requires sufficient resources, time, and effort. For this reason, this design is used in a large-scale, multiyear project with sufficient funding.

Description of Research Method

Identifying the Problem

With the increasing student usage of the library, Director Gene Parks wants to understand the needs and expectations of the library patrons to better serve them. This needs analysis is different from library instruction assessment and biannual observations of where students study; while the assessment and observations investigate the current services, Gene's purpose is to capture what the users want that the library does not currently offer. Therefore, the needs analysis will help the library staff form the vision for the future.

Because patron needs keep changing, Gene wants to hire a User Experience (UX) librarian who will continuously assess users' needs and inform their decisions regarding physical and virtual space utilization of the library. The UX librarian may employ a mixed methods research design to address this challenge.

Understanding user needs entails a multifaceted process. While Gene wants to understand which specific things users want or expect from the library, he also needs to know how many people want or need those things and how important new services are in relation to one another. Therefore, Gene and his UX librarian will need to use both qualitative methods to elicit in-depth descriptions of their needs and quantitative methods.

Determining Research Participants

As in any type of research that aims at generalization, obtain a sample that is representative of your population to generalize your study results; the research question will guide which participants should be included in the study. For example, if Gene or his UX librarian only conveniently recruits research participants from library users, they will lose the perspectives of potential users. Gene needs to understand why some community members do not use the library and how to get them to use the library. Likewise, if Gene only recruits participants from those who visit the library website, he will fail to capture the perspectives of patrons who visit the library in person.

To get a representative sample, first define the population. The population in this scenario is the students and faculty of the college. There are 5,800 undergraduate students, 259 full-time faculty, and 234 part-time faculty. For the sample to be proportionally representative of the population and there should be about 10 times more students than faculty in the population. So, you want to make sure there are about 10 times more students in your sample.

Then, you want to think about if there are other characteristics of population you need to consider. For students, you may consider their disciplines, grade levels, or whether they are in residential or online programs. For faculty, you may consider whether they are full-time or part-time, their college, and so on. Once you decide on the important characteristics to make your sample representative, you want to randomly select your participants. For example, assuming that you want 1,000 student participants. If 10% of the student population consists of business majors of 580, which is 10% of 5,800, then 10% or 100 of the 1,000 in your sample should be recruited from students majoring in business. The 100 students should be randomly selected from the total number of 580 business students.

Choosing a Research Design

To conduct the research presented in the scenario, for the various types of mixed methods research designs available, the exploratory sequential design or the explanatory sequential design would be most appropriate for the research purpose. Gene and his UX librarian might operationalize these approaches as follows:

Exploratory Sequential Design

In the exploratory sequential design, Gene and his UX librarian would first collect and analyze qualitative data to gather users' perceptions, and then collect quantitative data to explore whether these perceptions represent those of a bigger population. In the context of Scenario VI and using this design, the following steps would be taken.

First, select a small group of users and ask them their current experience with the library's virtual and physical space and what they want to see more in the future. This qualitative method would allow Gene to understand the very specific needs of library users. For example, an interviewee may say, "My instructor gives a lot of group projects to be completed outside the classroom. I need a space where I can work with my group members, where I can talk freely with them and collaborate around a computer because we use Google Docs." Or another interviewee may say, "I think the current interface of the library website is not very user-friendly. I usually go to the website to search for books or articles. I have learned where to go, because I have done it many times, but I wish the search option is just right there when I enter the library website." These are very specific needs.

The next step in the exploratory sequential design is to explore how many people have those needs through a survey to a large sample of users. In the survey, Gene or his UX librarian will list the identified needs and ask your survey respondents how strongly they agree with the listed needs. For example, they can ask, "How often would you use a group space with a computer in the library?" If survey respondents share their answers on a 4-point scale, 1 being never and 4 being always, then this survey data will provide insight on how many people would use a group space, how often they would use it, whether the group space will be needed, and whether group space should receive a higher priority than other needs.

In sum, Gene's exploratory sequential design would proceed in these steps:

1. Investigate users' needs through one-on-one interviews or focus-group interviews with a small group of users.
2. Analyze the interview data and identify what needs exist.
3. Administer a survey with a large sample.
4. Analyze the survey data and determine how many people share the same needs and how strong these needs are.

Explanatory Sequential Design

As opposed to exploratory sequential design, explanatory sequential design model collects the quantitative data first and qualitative data is collected to explain the quantitative data. Steps to be taken in our scenario follow.

First, Gene and his UX librarian would design a survey to understand overall usage and experience of the users that includes questions about how often users come to the library on a 4-point scale, 1 being almost never and 4 being almost every day. Also, they can ask how satisfied they are with the library on a 4-point scale, 1 being very dissatisfied and 4 being very satisfied. This survey data will help them identify individuals who use the library very often and those who use the library very rarely as well as individuals who are very satisfied with the library and those who are very dissatisfied with the library.

The next step is to select individuals for an interview one-on-one or in a focus group interviews. In the interviews with patrons who come to the library almost every day, Gene can ask why they come to the library almost daily, what they use, and which services they would like to have. In the interview with survey respondents who reported rarely using the library, Gene can ask why they do not come to the library very often and how the library can be redesigned to satisfy their unmet needs. These data will help Gene and his UC librarian what is maintained and what needs to be changed.

In sum, Gene and the UX librarian can follow this explanatory sequential design process:

1. Investigate the overall usage and experience of the users through a survey with a large representative sample.
2. Analyze the survey data and identify individuals to invite for an interview.
3. Conduct interviews and ask specific questions.
4. Analyze the interview data and find out their specific needs.

The two designs have different focuses, and they are good for different situations. The exploratory sequential design is good if Gene and the UX librarian are ready to redesign the library space and want to know which specific changes to make. So, if there is already approved budget and the library wants to start a renovation of the library, the exploratory sequential design would provide Gene with useful data. On the other hand, the explanatory sequential design is good when Gene and the librarian want to learn about library users' experiences and closely investigate specific reasons for the overall experience. Also, an explanatory sequential approach would be a means for Gene to gather data to write a proposal for a budget to renovate the library and need to justify the budget request.

Data Collection Methods

One of the strengths of mixed methods research is it is not limited to a particular data collection method. A researcher can use any data collection method or source to answer appropriate for the research question including survey, one-on-one interviews, focus group interviews, direct observation, existing documents, or system data from the library website. Refer to Chapter 19 (XXX) for more about how to collect and analyze survey data and Chapter 4 (XXX) for more about to how to collect and analyze interview and focus group data.

Data Integration

Conducting mixed methods research entails having multiple types of data to analyze, interpret, and report on your research questions. This requires you to integrate different kinds of data—usually both qualitative and quantitative—in order to arrive at meaningful and complete answers to your questions. There are three approaches to data integration introduced by O'Cathain, Murphy, and Nicholl (2010): (1) mixed methods matrix, (2) following a thread, and (3) triangulation.

Mixed Methods Matrix

One of the benefits of mixed methods research is that you can have both qualitative and quantitative data for the same cases. For example, in our scenario, if Gene employs an explanatory sequential design where he is to identify individuals from a survey and conduct interviews with them, he would have the interviewees' survey responses, as well as their interview transcripts. To analyze these data, he can summarize data by each case and display the summaries in matrix as in Table 21.1. This matrix is called a *mixed methods matrix*, which allows him to easily compare each individual's responses collected using different methods in order to see if there are any surprises and/or contradictions. Also displaying the data in a matrix helps him to look for patterns across cases in each data collection method and compare them across methods.

Following a Thread

Another data integration approach in the analysis stage called *following a thread* is theme-based, rather than case-based, unlike the mixed methods matrix approach. In this approach, you begin with initial analysis of one dataset to identify key themes, just as you would do in qualitative research. Then, you take one theme at a time and follow it across the other datasets, which creates a "thread." This process is repeated until the key themes are exhausted. For the initial

Table 21.1

One-on-One Interviews vs. Focus Group Interviews

	One-on-one interviews	Focus group interviews
Number of subjects	Individual subject at a time	Group of subjects
Interview time	The entire time devoted to the individual	The subjects should share the assigned interview time
Advantages	Provide in-depth data on a topic from individual subjects	Efficient Prompt one another and spur conversation
Disadvantages **Good for**	Time-consuming Sensitive and personal topics	Peer-pressure Idea-building Nonsensitive topic A topic that needs multiple perspectives

analysis, it is advisable to select a dataset wisely, because the themes identified in the initial analysis direct your analyses of other datasets.

In our scenario, if Gene employs the exploratory sequential design, he would first analyze the interview transcripts and identify key themes there. Suppose that one of the themes is *Faculty want to use the library to meet with collaborators.* Then Gene would take this theme, turn to the survey data, find relevant survey questions, and see if the theme is supported, complemented, or contradicted. Survey responses may enrich the finding by adding information, such as how many people would want such spaces, how often the group work spaces will be utilized, or where they prefer to have those spaces.

Triangulation

It should be noted that **triangulation** here should be differentiated from the same term used in qualitative research. In qualitative research, triangulation refers to a strategy that employs multiple methods, data sources, or researchers to enhance validity of qualitative research findings. In contrast, triangulation for mixed methods research refers to a specific strategy to integrate data analysis results at the interpretation stage.

Triangulation entails analyzing each dataset separately and comparing findings from different methods; in other words, you will analyze quantitative and qualitative data separately as you would do in a quantitative or qualitative study. Then list findings from each dataset on the same page to compare if findings (1) agree, (2) complement each other, (3) disagree, or (4) diverge into two very different directions. You may be surprised (or even disappointed) to see disagreements

Table 21.2
Usage Frequency

	N	**Mean**	**SD**
Group space	987	3.8	0.5
Quiet study	985	3.5	0.7
Computer lab	985	3.5	0.7
Books	983	3.2	0.5
Rest area	980	2.9	1.4
Cafeteria	980	2.7	1.7

or divergences, but finding inconsistencies is an important part of mixed methods research, as it allows you to explore possibilities that you may have not considered and helps you better understand the phenomenon of your study and come to a more solid conclusion.

In both of Gene's exploratory and explanatory sequential designs, he has survey responses and interview data. Using the triangulation strategy, he would first analyze the survey responses and interview data separately, and display all findings in one place to find which findings agree, complement, and disagree. For example, suppose we have displayed all relevant findings as in Table 21.2.

The theme relating to faculty collaboration and question responses indicates that the idea that not only are group spaces needed, but also that more student quiet study workspace is necessary. In addition, combining the theme relating to students' desire for group workspace with its complement that faculty also desire workspace and students request for more individual workspaces may lead Gene to a conclusion that there is a need for flexible spaces that can be utilized as both group spaces and individual spaces for both students and/or faculty.

As Figure 21.2 shows, comparing the findings from each dataset can often quickly identify areas of agreement, disagreement, complementarity, and divergence. While mixed methods matrix and following a thread integrate data at the analysis stage, triangulation integrates findings at the interpretation phase after analyzing each dataset separately.

Potential Reporting Venues

Results of the research study may be of interest to fellow librarians or teachers and administrators in reports or articles in journals or in presentations at local, national, or international conferences. Also, findings could be shared in your library's or school's website.

Figure 21.2
Example of Findings Triangulation

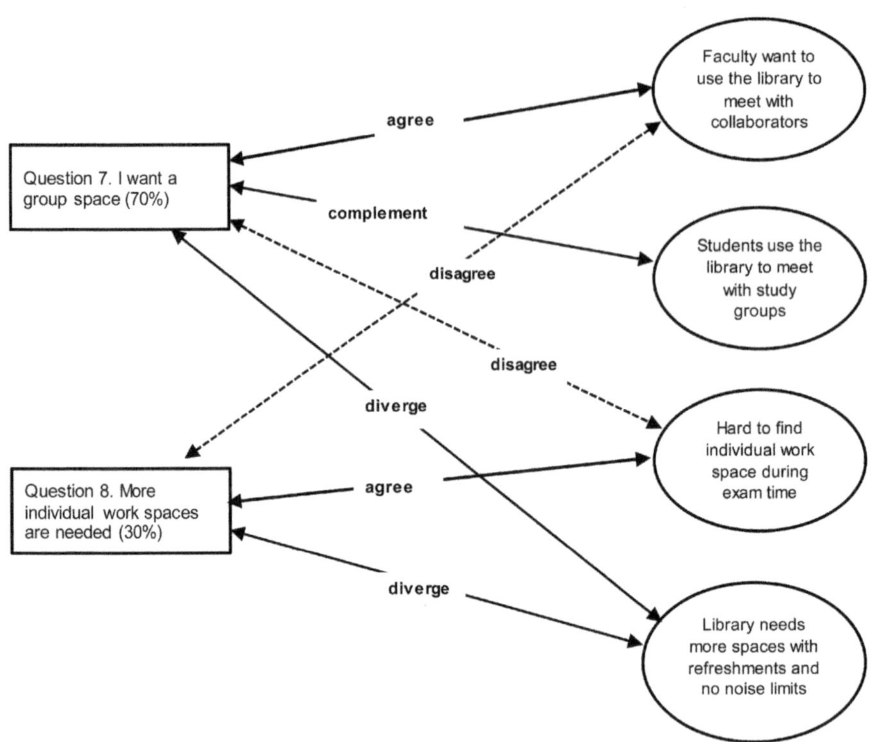

Why Use Mixed Methods?

Advantages, Disadvantages, and When to Use

Because mixed methods research uses both quantitative and qualitative research methods, it has the advantages of both. The researcher is able to gain breadth of a research problem by using quantitative methods. In our scenario, a survey method was used to investigate a large number of people's opinions and usage. At the same time, the researcher can take an in-depth approach to the problem. In the scenario, conducting interviews allowed us to take a close look at users' needs. Therefore, it allows the researcher to take a holistic approach to the research problem.

Another advantage of mixed methods research is that researchers can triangulate or corroborate your findings from multiple sources of data. Because the researcher is collecting data using multiple methods from multiple sources, for example, from different people, existing documents, or system data, the research findings are more trustworthy and reliable than those from research conducted using a single method.

Table 21.3
Summary Chart: Mixed Methods

Overall purpose	Mixes qualitative and quantitative methods to gain breadth and depth of a research problem
Advantages	Takes advantages of the both research methods and corroborates research findings
Disadvantages	Requires expertise in both methods and time, effort, and money
Steps in process	Depending on the nature of a research issue, qualitative and quantitative methods can take place concurrently or sequentially
Data collection methods	Any data collection method and data source can be used including surveys, interviews, direct observations, system data, archived data, or documents
Data analysis methods	Any data analysis method can be used that is appropriate for data types
Support technologies	Any technology can be used to collect and analyze data such as web-based survey tools, video-conferencing tools for interviews, Word or Excel, statistical packages, or qualitative analysis software

However, these advantages come with disadvantages. Because mixed methods research uses more than one research method, it requires expertise in both as well as time, resources, and effort to collect and analyze multiple types of data. Therefore, when a researcher needs to make a quick decision, conducting and integrating multiple methods may significantly delay deriving results needed for decision making.

Mixed methods research is good when a research issue is complex and one research method is insufficient to address the issue. Given the advantages and disadvantages of mixed methods research, a mixed methods approach is best when the researcher needs to gain both breadth and depth of insight into the research problem; when the researcher needs to make sure the research results are reliable and trustworthy; and when the researcher has enough resources to conduct the mixed methods research. For a summary of mixed methods research, see Table 21.3.

Glossary of Key Terms

Convergent parallel design: This refers to conducting quantitative and qualitative methods concurrently and comparing the results.
Embedded (nested) design: One research method is embedded within another research method.

Explanatory sequential design: A quantitative research method is performed followed by a qualitative research method.

Exploratory sequential design: A qualitative research method is performed followed by a quantitative research method.

Following a thread: It is a data integration strategy that takes place at the analysis phase of a study in which key themes are identified in an initial analysis of one dataset and researchers take one theme and follow it across all remaining datasets.

Mixed methods matrix: It is a data integration strategy that takes place at the analysis phase in which researchers create a matrix that organizes data summaries by cases and data collection methods.

Multiphase design: Multiple methods are used in multistages.

Triangulation: It is a data integration strategy that takes place at the interpretation phase after analyzing each dataset, in which researchers display all relevant findings in one place and see if the findings agree, complement, diverge, or disagree.

Further Reading

Creswell, John W. 2014. *A Concise Introduction to Mixed Methods Research.* Thousand Oaks, CA: Sage Publications, Inc.

Creswell, John W. 2013. *Research Design: Qualitative, Quantitative, and Mixed Methods Approaches.* 4th ed. Thousand Oaks: Sage Publications, Inc.

Creswell, John W., and Valeria L. Plano Clark. 2011. *Designing and Conducting Mixed Methods Research.* 2nd ed. Thousand Oaks, CA: Sage Publications, Inc.

Chapter 22

Conclusion: Shared Research Strategies and Tools for Educators and Librarians

Marcia A. Mardis
Florida State University

In this book, we aimed to explore ways in which librarians and educators might use a variety of quantitative and qualitative research methods to explore problems that may occur in their organizations and communities. Myriad policy and social pressures affecting schools have created a prime opportunity for fresh academic exploration of the flow and effect of information for learning, teaching, and administration. Educators are faced with choices resulting from sweeping changes in their practice and culture; libraries are at the nexus of these changes and librarians are pressed to respond. Indeed, calls are coming from within the educational establishment to reclaim the energy children are directing at learning activities outside of classroom (Cilesiz 2009) by designing time in school with more unstructured time that allows children to explore their interests and build prior knowledge (Archibald 2006; Bolliger 2006; Hirsch 2006).

We began by outlining general principles that underlie effective research: ethical orientation this book (Chapter One, Small), problem identification and question formation (Chapter Two, Hughes-Hassell), and literature grounding (Chapter Three, Brettle and Koufogiannakis). We then proposed a series of eight scenarios in response to which esteemed researchers envisioned responses centered on various research methodologies; in many instances, the chapter authors highlighted the flexibility of methods to fit specific contexts and needs. In other instances, chapter authors pointed out cautions to using the research methods in the scenario context (e.g., Chapter Thirteen, Pribesh and Gregory) or the unsuitability of certain research methods for particular types of research problems (e.g., Chapter Ten, Maylone).

Schools and Libraries as Research Contexts

As the scenarios directly addressed and included for further consideration in this book suggest, schools and libraries are compelling research contexts at the intersection of information and communications technology; effective teaching and learning; and information creation, provision, and use. The chapters in this volume illustrate the parallel and linked problems and research needs of both environments. Determining research intent is a key element to selecting a research approach.

Researching a problem can begin with an in-depth, systematic analysis of existing documents and data, as Suzanne Stauffer detailed using historical methodology in Chapter Six and Carol Kulthau, Leslie Maniotes, and Jannica Heinstrom discussed in Chapter Eighteen's description on longitudinal research. Maria Cahill's description of case study techniques in Chapter Fifteen offered another way in which the past can be reexamined to inform future decisions.

When the research problem is centered on documenting the present, researchers have many strategies available to them, ranging from interview and focus group research (Chapter Four, Waugh and Subramaniam), participant observation (Chapter Seven, Gross), phenomenology (Chapter Fourteen, Bossaller), correlational research (Chapter Eleven, Maylone), causal research (Chapter Thirteen, Pribesh and Gregory), critical incident technique (Chapter Seventeen, Church), survey research (Chapter Nineteen, Teasdale), and many of these methods in mixed designs (Chapter Twenty-One, Lee).

Researchers may also select methods based on the intended use of the research results; although all research documents help stakeholders, some techniques are better suited for informing immediate, iterative improvements in practice (formative research, Chapter Ten, Kim and Charles; evidence-based practice, Chapter Twelve, Todd) and student learning (action research, Chapter Five, Farmer; assessing learning with rubrics, Chapter Eight, Oakleaf; formative assessment, Chapter Nine, Stefl-Mabry; and design-based research, Chapter Seventeen, Arnone). Research can also be used to define future actions, such as the Delphi method described in Chapter Twenty (Jones).

Practice Meets Research: A Framework
for Educators and Librarians

In his influential book *Pasteur's Quadrant: Basic Science and Technological Innovation*, Donald Stokes (1997) argued that scientific research falls into quadrants, as depicted in Figure 22.1.

Each of these quadrants can be represented by the research of a particular scientist and whether that work advanced theory or use. The upper-left quadrant contains pure basic research that is not meant to have immediate use in the real world. Research like that of theoretical physicist Niels Bohr is placed in this

Figure 22.1

Basic and Applied Scientific Research as Proposed by Stokes (1997)

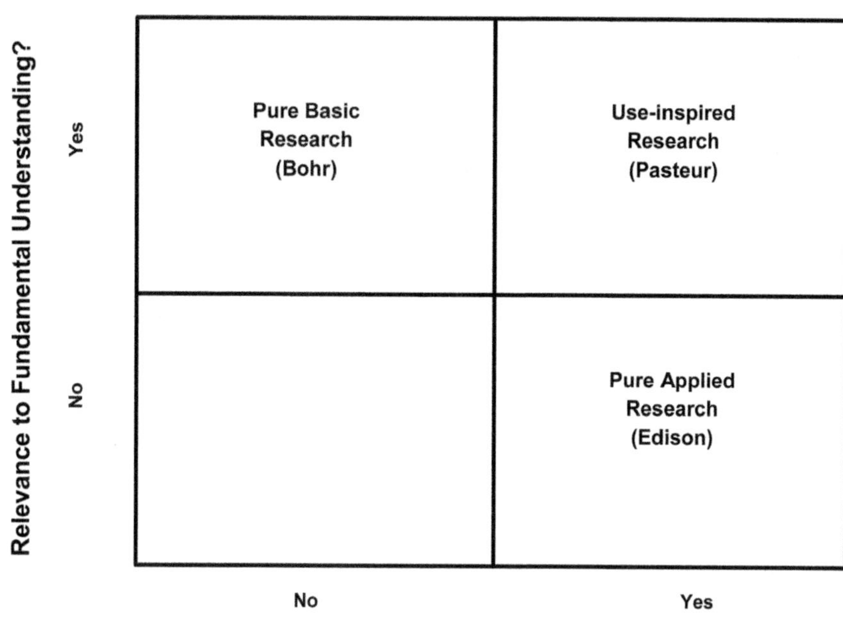

quadrant. In contrast, the lower-right quadrant is represented by the work of scientific entrepreneur and inventor Thomas Edison. Edison's work was pure applied research because he was primarily interested in its application to market. The lower-left quadrant contains work that is neither theoretical nor applied, but is not driven by the desire either to advance knowledge or to find practical solutions. Classification or taxonomy work fits into this quadrant. The upper-right quadrant contains "use-inspired basic science," a dialogic and interdependent blend of research and application, like the disease prevention work of Louis Pasteur, hence Stokes's title of *Pasteur's Quadrant*. Stokes's illustration of Pasteur's quadrant was important to the scientific academy because it gave context to applied science and put value on research that led to application.

Stokes's model is a useful template for examining research methods for librarians and educators. Figure 22.2 illustrates a possible relationship between research and practice.

As Figure 22.2 shows, some of the research methods addressed in this book require researchers to study practice to inform knowledge in education and/or librarianship while other methods require researchers to gather and analyze data with an aim of improving practice. The upper quadrant includes pure research that is designed only to further knowledge of a discrete phenomenon in education and

Figure 22.2
The Relationship between Research and Practice in Education and Librarianship

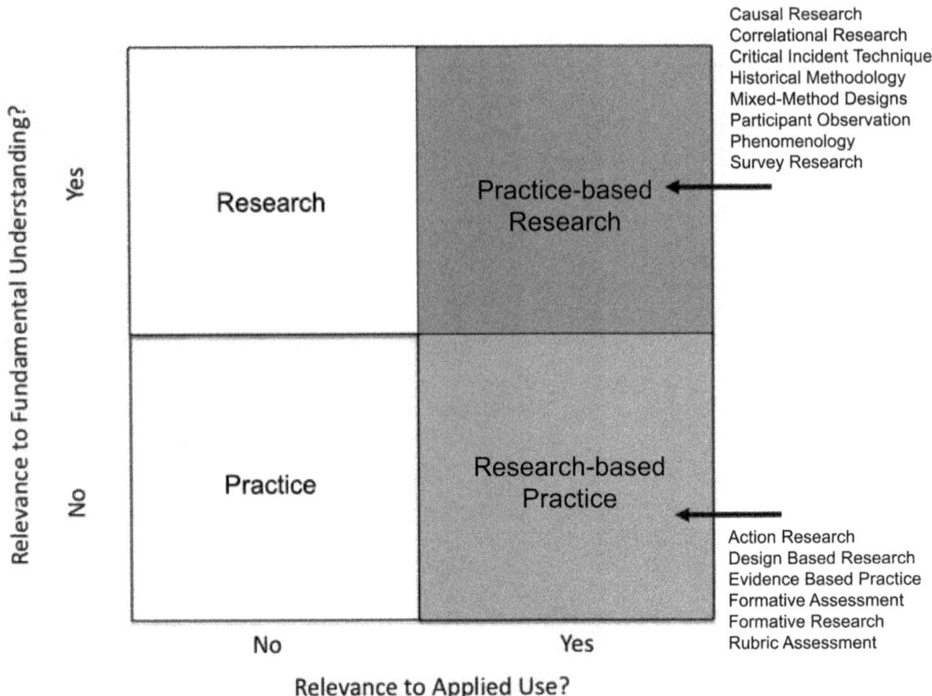

librarianship that is not intended for practical application. Likewise, the lower-right quadrant contains practice that is not meant to further research in library and information studies. The upper-right quadrant includes research-based practice and, very importantly, its converse, practice-based research. This quadrant includes activities that pertain to data derived from practice as well as research performed separate from, yet brought to bear on, practice. All areas of practice in librarianship have a research "face," and all areas of research have an application or practice face.

Libraries are as varied as the communities their schools serve. Librarians are prepared for and guided by principles that emphasize collaboration with educators and community members; contribution to the overall excellence of the organization; development of children's leisure and academic interests; promotion of career possibilities; facilitation of creative expression; and support for student learning (ALA LLAMA 2017). These important roles demand examination, investigation, and understanding.

This book is intended to be seen as a starting point for intellectual leadership, interdisciplinary research, and agenda-setting necessary to ensure that educators and librarians engage in research about and because of practice. Greater awareness of schools and libraries as viable microcosms for exploration can help to strengthen practitioners' research face and dialogue between educators and librarians.

APPENDIX A

Practice Scenarios

W e hope that this book has piqued your interest in research and provided you with the basic information for determining how you might conduct research in your library or institution. If you'd like some practice in applying what you have learned to some additional problem scenarios, we've included five additional scenarios from a variety of contexts to stimulate your thinking about the research process.

PRACTICE SCENARIO #1

Demonstrating the Value of Public Libraries Situated in Schools

Anne Ledford, School Liaison
District of Columbia Public Library, Washington, DC

Hannah Chrysler is the school liaison for the Southeast Public Library (SEPL) system, an urban public library system of 20+ branches serving almost 500,000 residents. Her role focuses on the needs of school-age students and teachers and creating broader access to SEPL resources. One of her primary responsibilities in the current school year was to open a school library within a charter school in the Southeast Public School District.

Already having a close relationship with Southeast Public Schools, SEPL was looking for ways to also work more closely with Southeast's charter schools. The school library pilot project came out of a million-dollar budget allocation from the Southeast City Council that was earmarked by SEPL to go toward a special collaboration with the Southeast Public Charter School Board. When the council increased the SEPL collection budget with the allocation, the executive director of SEPL came up with the idea to create a library in one of the many charter schools serving low-income families that would also serve as a gateway to public library usage.

SEPL selected Southeast's Priority Elementary School, a charter school located in one of the lower-income wards of Southeastsouthwe. The school has approximately 400 students, grades preschool to 3rd. The school was suggested by the Southeast Public Charter School Board to receive the library because its building was recently renovated with a space for a library but had only a few hundred books contained in two bookshelves and no school librarian.

The school library opened to students last year. The library is part of the school's daily activities, supporting the school's curriculum with high-interest nonfiction and reflecting a diverse and culturally relevant range of topics and authors. During the school year, the library is open 10–20 hours a week and staffed by a children's librarian from the neighboring public library branch, located three blocks away from the school. Each homeroom class is able to visit the library twice a month.

This school library is essentially a satellite public library branch within a school. The library contains 5,000 books that are circulated through Southeast Public Library's citywide catalog system. The books are checked out from the school library and can be returned at any SEPL location. Every student at Priority Elementary School was given a public library card to use at school at and at all SEPL branches.

This is the first partnership of its kind in the district with high-profile interest. In order for the school library to continue to have adequate staffing, more funding is needed. Hannah will need to submit a report to the city council to demonstrate the value of the library to the school and community and is looking for a method for collecting data to present to the city council to demonstrate the impact of the school library on student achievement and student quality of life at Southeast Priority Elementary.

Hannah has reached out to a professor at a nearby college to see if there are any graduate students interested in the project who could develop a research study dedicated to investigating the value of a public library in a charter school. She is hopeful that with the help of an academic researcher, she can demonstrate the value to the community of this school partnership. Hannah has come up with an initial overarching research question:

What is the impact of public library services within a charter school on student achievement?

<u>PRACTICE SCENARIO #2</u>

Public-School Library Collaboration For Motivating Lbrary Use By Underserved Populations

Tom Spector is the director of the Oakdale Public Library, located in an upscale, largely middle- to upper-middle class, professional suburban community with a population of approximately 4,400. Approximately 14% of the population represents racial and ethnic minorities, including African Americans (6%), Vietnamese immigrants (3%), and people with disabilities (5%).

Many of the library's most frequent users are stay-at-home moms with toddlers, retired professionals, and school children who use the library on weekends to do their homework assignments and for recreational reading. However, in the past three years, approximately 400 families (parents and school-age children) have been drawn to the public library's makerspace program.

The library is situated in a new, modern building, located in the center of town and containing, in addition to rooms with print collections and computer workstations a children's room, two meeting rooms, and a "Fab Lab" space for the 3-D printer and some robots, used for the makerspace and other special technology-based programs.

The staff include 16 librarians and approximately 20 part-time volunteers from the community. There is also an appointed board of trustees that consults with the administration on matters of policy.

Tom has been director of the Oakdale Library for the past 11 years. He has brought a number of innovations to the library, and, while the number of people using the library has increased almost 25% during his tenure, Tom is concerned that only about 1% of the minority population in Oakdale uses the library on a regular basis. He would like to conduct some research to determine why that is so and what the library and information needs of this minority population are.

Over the years, Tom has worked closely with the six school librarians in each of Oakdale's schools (two librarians in the high school and one in each of the two middle schools and two elementary schools). Tom started thinking about how he could get the information he needs to determine how and when to attract more minorities to the library's programs and services. When he shared his thoughts in a meeting with the school librarians, they tell him that they have found that, in general, the students in their schools from Tom's target population have been active and enthusiastic users of their school library, which makes the issue even more puzzling to Tom who wonders why the students' active use of the school library does not transfer to the public library.

The school librarians are excited to collaborate with Tom on this research project and all six librarians are forming a research team to explore the problem through research. The librarians begin thinking about questions they might want to answer with their research and have come up with one overarching research question:

What are the library and information needs of the minority populations of Oakdale?

PRACTICE SCENARIO #3

Identifying the Technology Needs of a Rural School and How Those Technologies Impact the Greater Community

Abby Harris is the school librarian at Glendale School, a small rural K–8 school in an upstate farming community. The teaching staff include 11 classroom teachers, six special subject teachers, and one librarian. The 326 students at Glendale come from mostly middle- and lower-middle-class families, and about 20% of students qualify for free lunch. Approximately 11% of the student body comprises minorities and 6% qualifies as having disability and have individualized education programs.

During the first week of school in the fall, Abby learned that the library was awarded a $25,000 grant by the school district to invest in technology. Francis Welker, Glendale's principal, wants Abby to spend the money in a way that will be most beneficial to the entire school community. Since Glendale is a rural school, many parents use the school computers before and after school. Some of the possibilities include upgrading the public computers throughout the library, which are out of date and frequently used by students, teachers, and parents; investing in a 3-D printer and other tools to establish a community makerspace; or purchasing some new technologies that the library doesn't currently have.

Abby had spent a sizable portion of last year's regular school budget on technology tools for the grade 6–8 students at Glendale, including iPads, snap circuits, video recorders, microphones, and music and video editing software. At the end of the year, Abby asked the middle-school teachers if these tools have had an impact on their students' proficiency with technology. The responses she received were mixed and Abby wasn't even sure she had asked the right questions in order to get the information she needed.

Abby started thinking about how she could get the information she needs to make a good decision about her grant. First, she could review the curriculum to see where technology plays a major role. Last year, she had conducted a curriculum-mapping exercise with all of the teachers in her school to determine what was being taught, when it was being taught, and what activities and assignments were included. Though the curriculum map, she was able to identify where and when her inquiry skills lessons and the library's technology and resources might be needed.

Abby also used the curriculum map to identify opportunities to collaborate with teachers on planning, teaching, and evaluating lessons for students in which she would teach important inquiry skills so students could successfully complete their research assignments. The 6th grade social studies teacher, John Smithee, was particularly open to collaborating with Abby. John had come to Glendale from the high school three years ago and had collaborated with his librarian on a regular basis.

Last year, Abby collaborated with John on four different units. They worked together to plan their lessons and cotaught the lessons in the library. Abby was also invited to attend the students' presentations on their research projects and to use the assessment rubric that she and John had developed. While several other teachers were willing to collaborate with Abby, they would only coplan but not coteach, and they saw no reason to include Abby in the evaluation of student work.

One of the 7th grade English teachers, Barbara Stiles, who had been at the school for 12 years, told Abby she didn't believe in collaborating and didn't think there was anything Abby would teach the students that she couldn't teach herself. (Barbara only lets her students come to the library when they needed to get books to complete assignments but not to do research or other assignments.) Two other teachers at Glendale, Sarah Lawson, a first year 3rd grade teacher, and Bob Thornton, an 8th grade science teacher who had been at the school for 14 years, told Abby they would like to explore expanding the role Abby played in their collaboration activities, beginning the following fall.

At the teachers' meeting during the first week of school, Abby told the teachers about the grant and told them that she would be investigating how best to spend the money. Several of the teachers suggested ways in which they thought the money should be spent but Abby wanted to collect data in a more purposeful and scientific way, as well as study the impact that technology had on the school and the greater community. She also knew she wanted to work with at least one teacher to explore solutions to this problem in more depth. She began to think about what information she needs and came up with a potential overarching research question:

What are the technology needs of teachers and students at Glendale School and how does meeting those needs impact the greater community?

PRACTICE SCENARIO #4

Measuring Transfer of Research and Writing Skills
from in Higher Education

Fillmore Community College is a two-year, publicly funded institution providing the equivalent of the first two years of a four-year higher education curriculum, as well as continuing and adult education, to the citizens of Fillmore County. It also serves as a gateway for some students to enter nearby Zachary Taylor State University. There are approximately 13,000 students enrolled at Fillmore, 48% full-time and 52% part-time students.

Janet Martino has been a tenured professor in the well-respected history department at Fillmore for 23 years. Her specialty is American history. Janet works closely with Paula Cooper, the American history librarian at Fillmore on a range of teaching and research projects. They often coteach a two-semester research and writing skills course which is required of all students in the American history department.

In addition to teaching, Janet is part of a research center on campus that brings together faculty, librarians, and students to explore a variety of policies, programs, and practices that shape the college experience for Fillmore's faculty and students. Janet's research has largely centered on how students make the transition from community college to four-year universities, focusing on how and how well their research and writing skills in history courses transfer from community college to a research university setting.

Janet and Paula have collaborated on a series of research studies investigating the acquisition and use of research and writing skills by American history majors at Fillmore. They have found that 85% of American history students demonstrate a significant improvement in their research and writing skills after taking Janet and Paula's collaborative research-writing course. Now, they are interested in taking their research a step further to determine whether and how well American history students, who graduate from Fillmore and enroll at Taylor, transfer those skills to their research assignments at Taylor State and what skills seem to be the most critical.

Currently, there are approximately 3,800 Fillmore graduates enrolled at Taylor, including 49 American history majors. All 49 students have taken the research-writing skills course at Fillmore. Janet and Paula discuss how they might approach this research study, what research questions will shape their research, and what methodology(ies) they will use. They agree that their overarching research question is:

In what ways do students' research-writing skills learned in collaboratively taught community college American history courses transfer to the quality of their research and writing assignments required by American history courses in four-year institutions?

PRACTICE SCENARIO #5

The Relationship of Collaborative, Technology-rich Teaching Affects Research Skills Learning and Attitudes by High School Students

Sarah Burns teaches English at Madison Technical High School (MTHS), one of five high schools serving more than 12,000 students in the Madison City School District, a diverse, urban public school district. The district has a high school dropout rate of 11%, compared to a national average dropout rate of 5%. In addition, 13% of students are eligible for special needs services, and 10% are English Language Learners. All high schools in Madison rank below or near the state averages in mathematics, English, and college readiness. However, approximately 75% of MTHS students go on to either a community college or a four-year college or university.

Sarah teaches 9th grade English classes at MTHS. She finds the students' ability to formulate research questions, to seek relevant information to help them answer their questions, and to critically assess the quality of the information they find (largely from the Internet) to be poor and underdeveloped. In addition, she notices that very few students demonstrate any curiosity about or interest in learning or using these skills both in and out of school.

Over the past two years, Sarah has been attending workshops, taught by Jim Davis (the school librarian) on how to use a range of media and technologies for teaching and learning. Mr. Davis has also taught students how to use a variety of technologies, from databases to presentation software, for completing class research assignments. Sarah is hoping that these technologies will motivate and engage students to improve their reading, writing, and researching skills for their assignments but has no documentation as to whether this has happened.

Sarah has experimented with the use of some of these technologies in her teaching and notices that her students seem to be more attentive when she teaches with certain technologies. She and Jim discuss the possibility of collaborating so they can coteach the 9th grade students a unit on the research process, including essential research and critical thinking/reading skills. In addition, they want to infuse their lessons with motivational strategies that stimulate students' curiosity and interest.

Jim and Sarah work together to plan and coteach the unit sessions and assess student learning. While assessments indicate that the students have done quite well in learning the skills taught, Sarah has also anecdotally observed that some of her students are asking more and better questions in class, requesting library passes, taking more books out of the library to read, and using computers to pursue research on topics of interest to them in and out of class more than before but she doesn't have any actual scientifically gathered data to support that, nor does she know whether students who go on to college have learned these skills and developed their motivation for exploration in ways that transfer when they go on to higher education or to the workplace.

Sarah meets with Jim to see if he has any more formal data that might support her informal observations. While he does not, Jim tells her that he has also been thinking about doing some research on whether students' research skills have improved with the use of technology and whether their collaborative teaching on several units during the school year makes a difference in their attitudes toward pursuing research to explore questions about topics that interest them.

They agree that this will require a more formal research effort and are excited to work together on it. Their first task is to determine an overarching research question and have come up with at least a tentative one:

In what ways do students' research and critical thinking skills improve when learned in collaboratively taught high school English courses using a variety of technologies and how these new skills affect students' attitudes toward research and the quality of their completed research assignments?

Glossary

All of the glossary of key terms included in this book's chapters have been collected and are presented in alphabetical order below. Each term is followed by the chapter number (in brackets) in which it appears.

Analytic rubric: Analytic rubrics "divide . . . a product or performance into essential traits or dimensions so that they can be judged separately—one analyzes a product or performance for essential traits. A separate score is provided for each trait"(Arter and McTighe 2001). Analytic rubrics can be further divided into two subcategories: task/performance and developmental. [8]

Assessment (the product or outcome): information on the extent to which intended learning outcomes have been attained [9]

Assessment (the process & instrument): the means by which information on the extent of attainment of learning goal is obtained. [9]

Bracketing: Similar to reduction, the process of putting one's own preconceptions aside in order to fully gain an understanding of another's experiences. [14]

Case study: It is an in-depth investigation of persons or groups over time to study developments as they happen. [18]

Census: Survey that collects information from all members of a population is called census. [19]

Closed-ended Questions: These are questions with a clear answer, such as Yes/ No, or concrete information (e.g., "What is your job title?"). [4]

Code(s): These are words or phrases that describe a piece of data in relation to the research question, prior to a scholarship or a new finding. [4] Code is "a word or short phrase that symbolically assigns a summative, salient, essence-capturing, and/ or evocative attribute for a portion of language-based or visual data" (Saldaña, 2013, p. 3). [15]

Code book: The complete list of codes for a given study can be found in the code book. [4]

Cohort: This term refers to a group of people who share a common event, sometimes referred to as a panel. [18]

Collaboration: It is a joint effort reflecting experiences and viewpoints of persons who intentionally work together to produce a mutually agreed upon end result (Holsapple & Joshi, 2002). [17]

Concurrent triangulation design: This design is a combination of sequential and convergent designs that typically takes place in multiple stages, leading to another mixed methods study.

Connected learning: It is an educational approach advocating learning that is socially embedded, interest-driven, and oriented toward educational, economic, or political opportunity (Ito et al., 2013). [17]

Confounding variables: These are variables that have not been controlled by the researcher and thus negatively impact the internal validity of the experiment. [13]

Consensus: It is an identified percentage amount in which participants agree with each other. Although there seems to be no firm rules for establishing this percentage, failure to offer an interpretation of the meaning of consensus is considered a research design flaw. [20]

Control group: It refers to the group of participants who do not experience the treatment. [13]

Core capability: A capability that contributes to concurrent and subsequent learning and/or has powerful application to the world outside of the learning environment. [9]

Coresearcher: Coresearchers are participants in phenomenological research. This is a more appropriate term than subject, although participant might also work. As is appropriate for the method, it purposefully puts the researcher on equal footing with the participant. [14]

Convergent parallel design: This refers to conducting quantitative and qualitative methods concurrently and comparing the results. [21]

Correlational research: It is a research approach that attempts to establish a relationship between or among variables. Correlational research can never establish causation (see "Experimental research"), but it can suggest it. [11]

Correlational coefficient: It is a value between -1.0 and $+1.0$, generated by use of an appropriate statistical program, and indicative of the strength of a correlation. A correlational coefficient of 0.0 indicates no relation between the variables under consideration. Correlational coefficients near −1.0 or +1.0 are considered strong. Coefficients may also be weak, moderate, or perfect. The most common version of a correlational coefficient is the Pearson product-moment correlation. [11]

Co-researchers: Coresearchers are participants in phenomenological research. This is a more appropriate term than subject, although participant might also work. As is appropriate for the method, it purposefully puts the researcher on equal footing with the participant. [14]

Critical: "To be critical, an incident must occur in a situation where the purpose or intent of the act seems fairly clear to the [participant] and where its consequences are sufficiently definite to leave little doubt concerning its effects" (Flanagan, 1954, 327) "Things which sufficiently affect the outcome" (Woolsey, 1986, 242). [16]

Critical incident: "To be critical, an incident must occur in a situation where the purpose or intent of the act seems fairly clear to the [participant] and where its consequences are sufficiently definite to leave little doubt concerning its effects" (Flanagan, 1954, 327). [12]

Critical incident technique: "Outlines procedures for collecting observed incidents having special significance and meeting systematically defined criteria" (Flanagan, 1954, 327) "Basically consists of asking eyewitness observers for factual accounts of behaviours (their own or others) which significantly contribute to a specified outcome" (Woolsey, 1986, 242). [16]

Curriculum: A structured set of learning goals [9]

Curiosity: Curiosity with respect to new media environments is a desire for new information or experience. Curiosity includes a trigger or multi-trigger scenario evoked by dynamic environments, reaction (which may involve multiple new media skills), and resolution (satisfied/not satisfied). A curiosity episode, if resolved satisfactorily, initiates new learning. Curiosity can trigger and be triggered through the development and deepening of interest and, consequently, the forms of engagement that result in deep learning and effective participation, collaboration, and affinity (Arnone et al., 2011). [17]

Data saturation: This is the point at which the researcher sees the same themes emerging from multiple sources, interviews, and so on. [4]

Dependent variable: Dependent variable, also called outcome variable, is influenced by independent variable. [13]

Design: The creation of engineered systems that satisfy specific human and societal needs within a context (Suh, 2013). [17]

Design-based research: A methodology that allows revision of the research design as the research study progresses, providing flexibility to adapt the research design and interventions based on feedback from researchers, participants and others involved in the research project. [17]

Design theory: A design theory offers means to accomplish a goal or set of goals in different situations. [10]

Designed case: It refers to a case that was created or managed using a design theory. [10]

Dichotomous item: it refers to a survey item with two possible responses such as Yes/No or True/False [19]

Educational evaluation: The use of information to improve (increase the value of) an educational program [9]

Educational program: Any intentional effort directed to the attainment of one or more learning goals. [9]

Embedded (nested) design: One research method is embedded within another research method. [21]

Engagement: To want to participate; to participate; to be involved with at length/in depth is called engagement. [17]

Eidetic reduction: "The process by which the person or researcher brings into question their taken-for granted presuppositions, misconceptions, and biases that preclude the fuller acquisition and actualization of knowledge" (Cibango and Hepworth, 150). It helps us to go beyond our own familiarization with the world and see it with new eyes or a sense of wonder. [14]

Epoche: suspending one's own understanding in order to fully understand or enter into an empathetic state with the co-researcher. [14]

Evidence for practice: It refers to evidence that examines and uses the best available formal empirical research and methods to form practices and inform current actions, and to identify best practices that have been tested and validated through empirical research. [12]

Evidence in practice: It refers to evidence that focuses on integrating available research evidence with deep knowledge and understanding derived from professional experience, as well as implementing measures to engage with local evidence to identify learning dilemmas, learning needs, and achievement gaps to make decisions for continuous improvement. [12]

Evidence of practice: It refers to evidence derived from systematically measured, primarily user-based, data. [12]

Executive summary: It is a short summation of a longer work designed to give a top-level overview of the study [4]

Experimental group: It refers to the group of participants who experience the treatment; also called treatment group. [13]

Experimental research: It is a research approach in which one variable (the "independent variable") is isolated and manipulated to observe any effect on a second variable (the "dependent variable.") In experimental research, an attempt is made to control the environment so that consideration of other variables can be eliminated. Experimental research attempts to establish *cause and effect* ("causation"), and stands in contrast to correlational research. [11]

Expert panelists: Individuals chosen by their work and credibility to respond to the research questions, or questionnaires, identified by the facilitator are called expert panelists. There is no set number of the number of experts chosen to participate on a panel; the range varies from 4 to 3,000. [20]

Explanatory sequential design: A quantitative research method is performed followed by a qualitative research method. [21]

Exploratory sequential design: A qualitative research method is performed followed by a quantitative research method. [21]

Facilitator: The person responsible for designing and coordinating the Delphi study. The facilitator selects the panel of experts, sends out the research questions, or questionnaire, for panelist's to respond to, and collects and analyzes their responses. [2]

Field notes: These are notes taken by researchers during or after observations of the phenomenon being studied. [7]

Focus group: It refers to a small group of people (typically six to eight) who meet together with a facilitator to share information, experiences, or opinions about the research question. [4]

Following a thread: It is a data integration strategy that takes place at the analysis phase of a study in which key themes are identified in an initial analysis of one dataset and researchers take one theme and follow it across all remaining data sets. [21]

Formative assessment: Assessment is a process carried out to form or inform an educational program for currently participating learners [9]

Full model rubric: Full model rubrics are the most descriptive type of rubric. Formatted in a chart or table, full model rubrics include "criteria" or indicators of a performance down one column and levels of performance across the top row of a table (Callison 2000). [9]

Grading and grades: Aggregating disparate source of information e.g. assessments, tests, attendance, student behavior into an overall value referred to as a grade, e.g. midterm grade, course grade [9]

Grey literature is research produced by organizations outside of the traditional commercial or academic publishing and distribution channels. Common grey literature publication types include reports, working papers, government documents, white papers and evaluations. The standard of quality, review and production of grey literature can vary and it may be difficult to discover, access, and evaluate without sound search strategies (Bates and Maack 2010). [3]

Holistic rubric: Holistic rubrics provide one score for a whole product or performance based on an overall impression. [9]

Horizontalization: Phenomenology seeks to reveal essential truths about the meaning of human experience; in order to find a complete picture that is unsullied by the researcher's own thoughts or experiences, the process or horizontalization is employed to give each unit of meaning equal weight. [14]

Hypothesis: It is a suggested explanation for phenomena based on limited or incomplete evidence. A *null* hypothesis is one that assumes there will be no significant relationship between two variables. [11]

In vivo **naturalistic case:** It refers to a case that was not designed or managed using a design theory and that is being studied while it happens. [10]

Incident: "Any observable human activity that is sufficiently complete in itself to permit inferences and predictions to be made about the person performing the act" (Flanagan 1954, 327) "Things which actually happened and were directly observed" (Woolsey 1986, 242). [16]

Independent variables: These are variables that are manipulated in an experiment in order to determine possible change in the dependent variables, also called predictor variables. [13]

Inference: It refers to a data-driven conclusion that links causes to effects. [13]

Institutional Review Board (IRB): This is a committee that reviews, approves, and monitors research involving human subjects in order to ensure that research is conducted ethically and participants' rights are protected. [13]

Instruction: An instruction is anything that is intended to help learners attain learning goals. [9]

Instructional collaborations: It means where a team of educators work together and share expertise to plan, design, implement, and assess an instructional unit to meet curriculum standards and school goals. [12]

Instructional worthiness: Educators need to constant ask themselves: *"Is this an activity worthy of instructional time?"* If the answer is no, then valuable time should not be spent on the activity. Instructional time is wasted and learners experience frustration when they are asked to perform tasks that have little connection to what is being taught and has little value beyond the completion of the task. [9]

Intentionality: the idea that every act of consciousness is correlated with an object (Sokolowski, p. 8); intending means "the conscious relationship we have to an object" of which we are conscious. Our interpretations of what happens in our life is framed within our own understanding. [14]

Inter-rater reliability: It refers to the process of multiple researchers comparing their codes for a given piece of data before coding the remainder to ensure that they share similar codes and definitions. [4]

Item nonresponse: This indicates a situation in which a respondent answers some or most survey items but does not respond to one or more items. [19]

Iteration: Iteration is the repetition of a process or procedure to try to move closer to a goal. [17]

Longitudinal: It refers to repeated study of the same subjects over a period of time. [18]

Learning goal: A learning goal is a capability to be developed through an educational program. [9]

Learning objective: A learning objective refers to an intended state (what you hope students will learn). [9]

Learning outcome: Learning outcome expresses a present or observed state (what students actually have learned and/or what attitudes, skills, and competencies (knowledge) the learner has actually attained. [9]

Methodology: It refers to the theoretical underpinning for understanding which method, set of methods, or best practices can be applied to a specific research endeavor. Research methods are used to enact research methodologies; "methodology" and "method" are not synonymous. [5]

Mixed methods matrix: It is a data integration strategy that takes place at the analysis phase in which researchers create a matrix that organizes data summaries by cases and data collection methods. [21]

Multiphase design: multiple methods are used in multistages. [21]

Nonresponse error: It refers to error in survey findings that arises because some individuals in the population or sample do not respond to the survey. [19]

Norming: Norming, also known as calibration, is "a process that brings a group of faculty raters together to decide how to assess student work in a consistent way" (Washington State University 2013). [8]

Open-ended questions: These are questions that require interpretation or longer responses and cannot easily be answered in a single phrase (e.g., "Tell me about a time when you had a successful literacy program in your library"). [4]

PICO framework: This is a framework for developing quantitative research questions that includes population, intervention, comparison, and outcome. [3]

Pilot testing: It refers to a trial run of your interview, focus group, or other data collection tool, typically with a very small number of people. [4]

***Post facto* naturalistic case:** It refers to a case that was not designed or managed using a design theory, and that is being studied only after it happened. [10]

Practical research problems: These, as practice-based problems, originate from issues or concerns found in real-world settings, such as schools, libraries, or communities (Wildemuth, 2009). [2]

Primary documents: Primary materials are created at or very near the time of the events by eyewitnesses. They include official correspondence, annual reports, minutes of meetings, budgets, newspaper articles, diaries, journals, and personal letters. [6]

Probing: It refers to following up on a statement in an interview or focus group to gather more information (e.g., "You mentioned that your circulation is down, but the picture book collection is frequently used in the library. Can you tell me more about that? Why do you think that is?"). [4]

Problem statement: This is a specific and explicit statement of the problem to be studied that will guide the remaining steps of the research process (Connaway and Powell 2010). [2]

Prompts: Question or statements to elicit a response are called prompts. [18]

Prompting: Similar to probing, providing a redirect to keep your participant on subject (e.g., "We were talking about changes in circulation, but we didn't get to your interpretation of why the numbers have changed. Can you tell me about that?"). [4]

Protocol: A protocol is a plan for conducting research. [3] It refers to the text of introduction, questions, and statements that the researcher uses in an interview or focus group. [4]

Purposive sample: A purposive sample is a "non-probability sample that is selected based on characteristics of a population and the objective of the study" (Crossman 2017). [8]

Qualitative research: In contrast to quantitative research, qualitative research attempts to reach conclusions based on the examination of nonnumerical data or evidence. [11]

Quantitative research: It focuses on "hard" numerical data and the analysis of such data, typically using established computational techniques. The data used may be "freshly" collected by the researcher, or may be preexisting ("archived") data. [11]

Random assignment: It refers to the process of assigning participants to different groups (control group or experimental group) using a random procedure. [13]

Random sample: It refers to a batch of participants randomly selected from the larger population to be included in the study; each participant has an equal chance of being selected. [13]

Reflective listening: It refers to carefully listening with the goal of understanding the participant's perspective and sharing back your interpretation to either obtain clarification or deepen the conversation (e.g., "I heard you say that many of the newer families appear reluctant to speak with staff, is that correct?"). [4]

Reliability: Reliability is the trustworthiness of the results of an assessment, the degree to which results are stable, consistent, and replicable. [11]

Research questions: These questions narrow the problem statement to the specific questions you seek to answer and are usually found at the end of the problem statement. [2]

Research-based problems: These problems come from research and theory in a given field and are often based on gaps, conflicting or disputed findings, or the need to extend the research or theory to other areas or populations (Connaway and Powell 2010; Creswell 2012; Wildemuth 2009). [2]

Research-derived evidence: It refers to evidence found in the corpus of scholarship of the field and its allied disciplines, school librarian-observed evidence and local user-reported evidence, that is interpreted and integrated in order to shape and direct professional practice. [12]

Rich (thick) data: It refers to providing a level of detail about the situation, phenomenon, or observation such that patterns and relationships are clarified and can be considered in light of both the study in question and other situations. [4]

Rounds: The Delphi iterative process is conducted in rounds, also identified as sequential questionnaires. [20]

Rubric: A scheme for characterizing the levels of attainment of a learning objective [9]

Sample survey: Survey that collects information from a subgroup of a population is called sample survey. [19]

Scale: Scale refers to an ascending sequence of levels of attainment of a learning objective. [9]

Semi-structured interview: An interview organized around a series of prompts that elicit responses and open further conversation is called a semi-structured interview. [18]

Secondary documents: Secondary materials are created after the time that the events took place and are based on primary sources. They include the author's explications and judgments of the primary materials on which they are based, so that the values and judgments are from a different perspective than the primary sources. [6]

Situational factors (or situationality): Situational factors influence the outcomes of one or more methods and therefore the preferability of the method(s). [10]

Skip logic: It is a feature of survey software in which a respondent is presented with certain survey items based on his or her responses to prior items. [19]

Social desirability bias: It refers to bias in survey findings that arises when respondents provide answers that are hoped to please the researcher or place the respondent in a favorable light. [19]

Social learning: attitude change through learning from direct personal experience. [17]

Stakeholders: Individuals who have an interest in the findings of research or are affected by those findings are called stakeholders. [19]

Summative assessment: Assessment that is carried out when instruction has been completed and there is no longer a possibility of forming or informing an educational program for currently participating learners. [9]

Surveys: Surveys are questionnaires administered to a group of participants. [18]

Systematic review: A systematic review is an overview of primary research studies, on a specific question, conducted according to an explicit and reproducible methodology to give a summary answer. **[3]**

Systematic scoping review: Systematic scoping reviews seek to provide in-depth and broad results, and take an iterative and reflexive approach (Arksey and O'Malley 2005). **[3]**

Testing and tests: Aggregating the results of assessments of disparate learning objectives into an overall score. [9]

Themes: Themes are not codes. A theme is considered the outcome or result of coding, not that which is coded. The code is the label that is given to particular pieces of the data that contribute to a theme. Themes are longer than codes and reflect more conceptual depth (Saldaña 2013). [15]

Theoretical proposition: It refers to a preliminary prediction to guide the design of the case and facilitate the development of the theory being constructed. [15]

Traditional narrative literature review: This review is a synthesis of existing research that places the current study within the context of what has previously been published. **[3]**

Treatment: It refers to a change or condition that is under investigation, also called manipulation or intervention. [13]

Triangulate: It refers to comparing findings between sources and data collection strategies to determine whether codes and findings are present in multiple places. [4]

Triangulation: It is a data integration strategy that takes place at the interpretation phase of mixed methods research, after analyzing each data set, in which researchers display all relevant findings in one place and see if the findings agree, complement, diverge, or disagree. [4] [22]

Validity: An assessment is valid if it accurately provides evidence of the extent to which a learning goal has been attained. [7] It refers to how well a test, survey, or other measurement tool measures that which it purports to measure. [11]

Variables: Variables are factors that can "vary" from one participant or context to another; researchers can measure, manipulate, and control for variables. [13]

Bibliography

Adams, Robin S. 2001. *Cognitive Processes in Iterative Design Behavior.* Ph.D. Dissertation, University of Washington.

Adams, Robin S. 2002. "Understanding Design Iteration: Representations from an Empirical Study." Paper presented at the International Conference of the Design Research Society.

Adler, Michael, and Erio Ziglio. 1996. *Gazing into the Oracle: The Delphi Method and Its Application to Social Policy and Public Health.* London: Jessica Kingsley Publishers.

Ahn, June, Mega Subramaniam, Elizabeth Bonsignore, Anthony Pellicone, Amanda Waugh, and Jason Yip. 2014, April. "'I Want to Be a Game Designer or Scientist': Connected Learning and Developing Identities with Urban, African-American Youth." Paper presented at the International Conference of the Learning Sciences 2014. Accessed June 23, 2017. http://ahnjune.com/wp-content/uploads/2014/04/ICLS2014-Sci-Dentity-camera-ready.pdf.

ALA. 2017. "LLAMA Foundational Competencies—White Paper." Accessed June 29, 2017. http://www.ala.org/llama/sites/ala.org.llama/files/content/LLAMA%20Foundational%20Competencies%20-%20White%20Paper.pdf.

American Association of School Librarians [AASL]. 2014, December. *Causality: School Libraries and Student Success.* National Research Forum, White Paper. http://www.ala.org/aasl/sites/ala.org.aasl/files/content/researchandstatistics/CLASSWhitePaperFINAL.pdf.

American Library Association [ALA]. 2009, January. *ALA's Core Competencies of Librarianship. Final Version."* Accessed June 1, 2017. http://www.ala.org/

educationcareers/sites/ala.org.educationcareers/files/content/careers/corecomp/ corecompetences/finalcorecompstat09.pdf.

Anderson, Terry, and Julie Shattuck. 2012. "Design-Based Research: A Decade of Progress in Education Research?" *Educational Researcher* 41 (1): 16–25.

Antell, Karen. 2004. "Why Do College Students Use Public Libraries? A Phenomenological Study." *Reference & User Services Quarterly* 43 (3): 227–236

Archibald, Sarah. 2006. "Narrowing in on Educational Resources that Do Affect Student Achievement." *Peabody of Journal of Education* 81 (4): 23–42.

Arnold, John. 2000. *History: A Very Short Introduction.* Oxford: Oxford University Press.

Arnone, Marilyn P., Ruth V. Small, Sarah A. Chauncey, and H. Patricia McKenna. 2011. "Curiosity, Interest and Engagement in Technology-Pervasive Learning Environments: A New Research Agenda." *Educational Technology Research and Development* 59 (2): 181–198. doi: 10.1007/.

Arter, Judith A., and Jay McTighe. 2001. *Scoring Rubrics in the Classroom: Using Performance Criteria for Assessing and Improving Student Performance.* Thousand Oaks: Corwin Press.

Banathy, Bela H. 1987. "Instructional Systems Design." In *Instructional Technology: Foundations* edited by Robert M. Gagne, 85–113. New York: Routledge.

Barab, Sasha, and Kurt Squire. 2004. "Introduction: Design-Based Research: Putting a Stake in the Ground." *The Journal of the Learning Sciences* 13 (1): 1–14.

Bates, Marcia J., and Mary Niles Maack. 2010. *Encyclopedia of Library and Information Sciences.* Boca Raton, FL: CRC Press.

Bernier, Rosemarie. 2004. "Making Yourself Indispensable by Helping Teachers Create Rubrics." *CSLA Journal* 27 (2): 24–25.

Best, Samuel J., and Chase H. Harrison. 2009. "Internet Survey Methods." In *The SAGE Handbook of Applied Social Research Methods* edited by Leonard Bickman and Debra J. Rog, 413–435. Thousand Oaks, CA: SAGE Publications, Inc.

Birnholtz, Jeremy P., Daniel B. Horn, Thomas A. Finholt, and Sung Joo Bae. 2004. "The Effects of Cash, Electronic, and Paper Gift Certificates as Respondent Incentives for a Web-Based Survey of Technologically Sophisticated Respondents." *Social Science Computer Review* 22 (3): 355–362. doi: 10.1177/0894439304263147.

Black, Paul, and Dylan Wiliam. 2003. "'In Praise of Educational Research': Formative Assessment." *British Educational Research Journal* 29 (5):623–637.

Black, Paul, and Dylan Wiliam. 2009. "Developing the Theory of Formative Assessment." *Educational Assessment, Evaluation and Accountability* 21 (1): 5–31. doi: 10.1007/s11092-008-9068-5.

Bloom, Benjamin S. 1956. *Taxonomy of Educational Objectives: The Classification of Educational Goals.* New York: Longmans, Green.

Bloom, Benjamin S. 1969. "Some Theoretical Issues Relating to Educational Evaluation." In *The 68th Yearbook of the National Society for the Study of Evaluation Part I,* edited by R. W. Taylor, 26–50. Chicago: University of Chicago Press.

Bolliger, Doris U. 2006. "Creating Constructivist Learning Environments." In *Educational and Media Technology Yearbook 2006,* edited by Michael Orey, Vivianne Jo McClendon and Robert Maribe Branch, 119–126. Westport, CT: Libraries Unlimited.

Booth, Andrew. 2002. "From EBM to EBL." *Medical Reference Services Quarterly* 21 (3):51–64. doi: 10.1300/J115v21n03_04.

Booth, Andrew, and Anne Brice. 2003. "Clear-Cut?: Facilitating Health Librarians to Use Information Research in Practice." *Health Information & Libraries Journal 20*: 45–52. doi: 10.1046/j.1365-2532.20.s1.10.x.

Bowler, Leanne, and Andrew Large. 2008. "Design-Based Research for LIS." *Library & Information Science Research* 30 (1): 39–46. doi: 10.1016/j.lisr.2007.06.007.

Bresciani, Marilee J., Carrie L. Zelna, and James A. Anderson. 2004. *Assessing Student Learning and Development: A Handbook for Practitioners.* Washington, DC: NASPA.

Brettle, Alison. 2009. "Systematic Reviews and Evidence Based Library and Information practice." *Evidence Based Library and Information Practice* 4(1): 43–50. doi: 10.18438/B8N613

Brettle, Alison, and Denise Koufogiannakis. 2016a. "Articulate." In *Being Evidence Based in Library and Information Practice,* edited by Denise Koufogiannakis and Alison Brettle, 19–26. London: Facet.

Brettle, Alison, and Denise Koufogiannakis. 2016b. Assess. In *Being Evidence Based in Library and Information Practice,* edited by Denise Koufogiannakis and Alison Brettle, 45–57. London: Facet.

Brettle, Alison, and Michelle Maden. 2015. What Evidence Is There to Support the Employment of Professionally Trained Library, Information and Knowledge Workers? A Systematic Scoping Review of the Evidence. Salford, University of Salford.

Brettle, Alison, Michelle Jenkins Maden, Lucy Anderson, and Rosalind McNally. 2011. "Evaluating Clinical Librarian Services: A Systematic Review." *Health information and Libraries Journal 28* (1): 3–22. doi: 10.1111/j.1471-1842.2010.00925.x.

Brown, Ann L. 1992. "Design Experiments: Theoretical and Methodological Challenges in Creating Complex Interventions in Classroom Settings." *Journal of the Learning Sciences* 2 (2): 141–178. doi: 10.1207/s15327809jls0202_2.

Brown, Jennifer Diane, and Thomas Scott Duke. 2005. "Librarian and Faculty Collaborative Instruction: A Phenomenological Self-Study." *Research Strategies* 20 (3): 171–190. doi: 10.1016/j.resstr.2006.05.001.

Budd, John M. 2005. "Phenomenology and Information Studies." *Journal of Documentation* 61 (1): 44–59. doi: 10.1108/00220410510578005.

Budd, John M. 2011. "Meaning, Truth, and Information: Prolegomena to a Theory." *Journal of Documentation* 67 (1): 56–74. doi: 10.1108/00220411111105452.

Burns, C. Sean, and Jenny Bossaller. 2012. "Communication Overload: A Phenomenological Inquiry into Academic Reference Librarianship." *Journal of Documentation* 68 (5): 597–617. doi: 10.1108/00220411211255996.

Bush, Gail, and Jami L. Jones. 2010. "Exploration to Identify Professional Dispositions of School Librarians: A Delphi Study." *School Library Research, 13*. Accessed June 29, 2017. http://www.ala.org/aasl/sites/ala.org.aasl/files/content/aaslpubsandjournals/slr/vol13/SLR_ExplorationtoIdentify.pdf.

Busha, Charles H., and Stephen P. Harter. 1980. *Research Methods in Librarianship: Techniques and Interpretation.* Orlando: Academic Library Press.

Callison, Daniel. 2000. "Rubrics." *School Library Media Activities Monthly* 17 (2): 34.

Cibangu, Sylvain K., and Mark Hepworth. 2016. "The Uses of Phenomenology and Phenomenography: A Critical Review." *Library & Information Science Research* 38 (2): 148–160. doi: 10.1016/j.lisr.2016.05.001.

Cilesiz, Sebnem. 2009. "Educational Computer Use in Leisure Contexts: A Phenomenological Study of Adolescents' Experiences at Internet Cafes." *American Educational Research Journal* 46 (1): 232–274.

Clapham, Kathleen, Claire Manning, Kathryn Williams, Ginger O'Brien, and Margaret Sutherland. 2017. "Using a Logic Model to Evaluate the Kids Together Early Education Inclusion Program for Children with Disabilities and Additional Needs." *Evaluation and Program Planning* 61: 96–105. doi: 10.1016/j.evalprogplan.2016.12.004.

Clarke, Rachel I. 2015. "Beyond Buildings: A Design-Based Approach to Future Librarianship." In *Leading the 21st-Century Academic Library: Successful Strategies for Envisioning and Realizing Preferred Futures* edited by Bradford E. Eden, 39–55. Lanham: Rowan & Littlefield.

Cobb, Paul, Jere Confrey, Andrea diSessa, Richard Lehrer, and Leona Schauble. 2003. "Design Experiments in Educational Research." *Educational Researcher* 32 (1): 9–13. doi: 10.3102/0013189X032001009.

Cobb, Paul, Jere Confrey, Andrea diSessa, Richard Lehrer, and Leona Schauble. 2003. "Design Experiments in Educational Research." *Educational Researcher* 32 (1): 9–13. doi: 10.3102/0013189X032001009.

Collins, Allan. 1992. "Toward a Design Science of Education." In *New Directions in Educational Technology*, edited by Eileen Scanlon and Tim O'Shea, 15–22. Berlin, Heidelberg: Springer Berlin Heidelberg.

Collins, Allan, Diana Joseph, and Katerine Bielaczyc. 2004. "Design Research: Theoretical and Methodological Issues." *Journal of the Learning Sciences* 13 (1): 15–42. doi: 10.1207/s15327809jls1301_2.

Connaway, Lynn S. and Ronald R. Powell. 2010. *Basic Research Methods for Librarians*. 5th ed. Westport: Libraries Unlimited.

Craig, Peter, Paul Dieppe, Sally Macintyre, Susan Mitchie, Irwin Nazareth, Mark Petticrew, Anderson and Groves. 2008. "Developing and Evaluating Complex Interventions: The New Medical Research Council Guidance." *BMJ: British Medical Journal* 337 (7676): 979–983.

Creswell, John. 2012. *Educational Research: Planning, Conducting, and Evaluating Quantitative and Qualitative Research*. 4th ed. Boston: Pearson.

Creswell, John W. 2007. *Qualitative Inquiry and Research Design: Choosing among Five Approaches*. Thousand Oaks: Sage Publications.

Creswell, John W. 2007. *Qualitative Inquiry and Research Design: Choosing among Five Approaches*, 2nd ed. Thousand Oaks: Sage.

Creswell, John W. 2013. *Research Design: Qualitative, Quantitative, and Mixed Methods Approaches*. Thousand Oaks: Sage.

Creswell, John W. 2013. *Research Design: Qualitative, Quantitative, and Mixed Methods Approaches*. 4th ed. Thousand Oaks: Sage Publications, Inc.

Creswell, John W. 2014. *A Concise Introduction to Mixed Methods Research*. Thousand Oaks, CA: Sage Publications, Inc.

Creswell, John W., and Valerie L. Plano Clark. 2011. *Designing and Conducting Mixed Methods Research*. 2nd ed. Thousand Oaks: Sage Publications, Inc.

Crossman, Ashley. 2017. "Understanding Purposive Sampling." Accessed June 24, 2017. https://www.thoughtco.com/purposive-sampling-3026727.

Crowley, Bill. 2005. *Spanning the Theory-Practice Divide in Library and Information Science*. Lanham: Scarecrow Press.

Csikszentmihalyi, Mikaly. 1975. *Beyond Boredom and Anxiety: Experiencing Flow in Work and Play*. San Francisco: Jossey-Bass.

Csikszentmihalyi, Mihaly, Rathunde, Kevin, and Whalen, Samuel. 1993. *Talented Teenager: The Roots of Success and Failure*. New York: Cambridge University Press.

Dalkey, Norman C. 1969. *The Delphi Method: An Experimental Study of Group Opinion* (RM-5888-PR). Santa Monica, CA: RAND. Accessed June 29, 2017. http://www.rand.org/content/dam/rand/pubs/research_memoranda/2005/RM5888.pdf.

Dalkey, Norman C., and Olaf Helmer. 1962. *An Experimental Application of the Delphi Method to the Use of Experts*. (RM-727/1-Abridged). Santa Monica: RAND. Accessed June 29, 2017. https://www.rand.org/content/dam/rand/pubs/research_memoranda/2009/RM727.1.pdf.

Delbecq, Andre L., Andrew H. Van de Ven, and David H. Gustafson. 1975. *Group Techniques for Program Planning: A Guide to Nominal Group and Delphi Processes Group & Organization Studies*. Glenview: Scott, Foresman.

Denzin, Norman, and Yvonna S. Lincoln. 1998. *The Landscape of Qualitative Research.* Thousand Oaks: Sage.

DePaul University Teaching Commons. 2017. "Types of Rubrics." Accessed June 17, 2017, https://resources.depaul.edu/teaching-commons/teaching-guides/feedback-grading/rubrics/Pages/types-of-rubrics.aspx.

Design Based Research Collective. 2003. "Design-Based Research: An Emerging Paradigm for Educational Inquiry." *Educational Researcher* 32 (1): 5–8. doi: 10.3102/0013189X032001005.

Dick, Walter and Lou Carey. 1990. *The Systematic Design of Instruction.* Glenview: Scott, Foresman.

Dow, Steven P., Alana Glassco, Jonathan Kass, Melissa Schwarz, Daniel L. Schwartz, and Scott R. Klemmer. 2012. "Parallel Prototyping Leads to Better Design Results, More Divergence, and Increased Self-efficacy." In *Design Thinking Research: Studying Co-Creation in Practice*, edited by Hasso Plattner, Christoph Meinel and Larry Leifer, 127–153. Berlin, Heidelberg: Springer Berlin Heidelberg.

Dowling, Maura. 2007. "From Husserl to van Manen. A Review of Different Phenomenological Approaches." *International Journal of Nursing Studies* 44 (1): 131–142. doi: 10.1016/j.ijnurstu.2005.11.026.

Dunn, Karee E., and Sean W. Mulvenon. 2009. A Critical Review of Research on Formative Assessment: The Limited Scientific Evidence of the Impact of Formative Assessment in Education. *Practical Assessment, Research & Evaluation.* Accessed June 24, 2017. http://pareonline.net/pdf/v14n7.pdf.

Eccles, Jacquelynne, Allan Wigfield, Rena D. Harold, and Phyllis Blumenfeld. 1993. "Age and Gender Differences in Children's Self- and Task Perceptions during Elementary School." *Child Development* 64 (3): 830–847. doi: 10.2307/1131221.

Eccles, Jacquelynne S, and Allan Wigfield. 2002. "Motivational Beliefs, Values, and Goals." *Annual Review of Psychology* 53 (1):109–132.

Edelson, Daniel C. 2002. "Design Research: What We Learn When We Engage in Design." *Journal of the Learning Sciences* 11 (1): 105–121. doi: 10.1207/S15327809JLS1101_4.

Eder, Donna, and Laura Fingerson. 2003. "Interviewing Children and Adolescents." In *Inside Interviewing: New Lenses, New Concerns*, edited by James A. Holstein and Jaber F. Gubrium, 33–53. Thousand Oak: SAGE.

Edwards, LeondraE. 2013. *Phenomenological Investigation of African American Women in Information Technology Upper Management.* Master's Thesis, UNC Chapel Hill. Accessed June 29, 2017. https://cdr.lib.unc.edu/indexable content/uuid:dee43a7f-8c9c-4634-bb3f-277747ccc9dd?dl=true

Eisenhardt, Kathleen M. 1989. "Building Theories from Case Study Research." *The Academy of Management Review* 14 (4): 532–550. doi: 10.2307/258557.

Elger, Tony. 2010. "Bounding the Case." In *Encyclopedia of Case Study Research*, edited by Albert J. Mills, Durepos, Gabrielle, and Elden Wiebe, 55–59. Thousand Oaks: Sage Publications.

ERIC. n.d. "Critical Incidents Method." Accessed June 29, 2017. http://eric.ed.gov/?qt=critical+incidents+method&ti=Critical+Incidents+Method.

Evans, Joel R., and Anil Mathur. 2005. "The Value of Online Surveys." *Internet Research* 15 (2): 195–219. doi: 10.1108/10662240510590360.

Feret, Blazej, and Marzena Marcinek. 2005. The Future of the Academic Library and the Academic Librarian: A Delphi Study Reloaded." *Proceedings of the IATUL Conferences, Chania, Greece.* Accessed June 29, 2017. http://docs.lib.purdue.edu/iatul/2005/papers/10.

Fischer, David Hackett. 1970. *Historians' Fallacies: Toward a Logic of Historical Thought.* New York: Harper Perennial.

Fischer, Russell G. 1978. "The Delphi Method: A Description, Review, and Criticism." *Journal of Academic Librarianship* 4 (2): 64–70.

Fisher, Shelagh, and Tony Oulton. 1999. "The Critical Incident Technique in Library and Information Management Research." *Education for Information* *17:* 113–125.

Fivars, Grace, and Robert Fitzpatrick. 2001. "12/15/01 Critical Incident Technique Bibliography." Accessed June 22, 2017. https://www.apa.org/pubs/databases/psycinfo/cit-full.pdf.

Fivars, Grace, and Robert Fitzpatrick. (n.d.). "The Critical Incident Technique Bibliography." Accessed June 22, 2017.http://lig-pimlig.imag.fr/sites/default/files/cit-intro.pdf.

Flanagan, John C. 1954. "The Critical Incident Technique." *Psychological Bulletin 5* (4): 327–358.

Frey, Bruce B. 2014. *Modern Classroom Assessment.* Thousand Oaks: SAGE.

Furtak, Erin Marie, and Maria Araceli Ruiz-Primo. 2008. "Making Students' Thinking Explicit in Writing and Discussion: An Analysis of Formative Assessment Prompts." *Science Education* 92 (5): 799–824. doi: 10.1002/sce.20270.

Gaddis, John Lewis. 2002. *The Landscape of History: How Historians Map the Past.* Oxford: Oxford University Press.

Galesic, Mirta, Roger Tourangeau, Mick P. Couper, and Frederick G. Conrad. 2008. "Eye-Tracking Data: New Insights on Response Order Effects and Other Cognitive Shortcuts in Survey Responding." *The Public Opinion Quarterly* 72 (5): 892–913.

Gallin-Parisi, Alexandra. 2015. "The Joy of Combining Librarianship and Motherhood." *The Journal of Academic Librarianship* 41 (6): 839–846. doi: 10.1016/j.acalib.2015.09.002.

Gardois, Paolo, Nicoletta Colombi, Gaetano Grillo, and Maria C. Villanacci. 2012. "Implementation of Web 2.0 Services in Academic, Medical and

Research Libraries: A Scoping Review." *Health Information & Libraries Journal* 29 (2): 90–109. doi: 10.1111/j.1471-1842.2012.00984.x.

Giorgi, Amedeo. 2012. "The Descriptive Phenomenological Psychological Method." *Journal of Phenomenological Psychology* 43 (1): 3–12.

Glaser, Barney G. 1978. *Theoretical Sensitivity: Advances in the Methodology of Grounded Theory.* Mill Valley: Sociology Press.

Glaser, Barney G. 1992. *Emergence vs. Forcing: Basics of Grounded Theory Analysis.* Mill Valley: Sociology Press.

Glaser, Barney G. 1998. *Doing Grounded Theory: Issues and Discussions.* Mill Valley: Sociology Press.

Glaser, Barney G. 2001. *The Grounded Theory Perspective: Vol. 1. Conceptualization Contrasted with Description.* Mill Valley: Sociology Press.

Glaser, Barney G. 2003. *The Grounded Theory Perspective: Vol. 2. Description's Remodeling of Grounded Theory.* Mill Valley: Sociology Press.

Glaser, Barney G., and Anselm Strauss. 1967. *The Discovery of Grounded Theory: Strategies for Alternative Research.* Chicago: Aldine.

Glynn, Lindsay. 2006. "A Critical Appraisal Tool for Library and Information Research." *Library Hi Tech* 24 (3): 387–399. doi: 10.1108/07378830610692154.

Greenhalgh, T. 1997. How to Read a Paper: Papers That Summarise Other Papers (Systematic Reviews and Meta-Analyses). *British Medical Journal 315* (672): 672–675. doi: http://dx.doi.org/10.1136/bmj.315.7109.672.

Gregory, Ian. 2003. *Ethics in Research.* London: Continuum.

Groenewald, Thomas. 2004. "A Phenomenological Research Design Illustrated." *International Journal of Qualitative Methods* 3 (1): 42–55. doi: 10.1177/160940690400300104.

Guba, Egon G., and Yvonna S. Lincoln. 1981. *Effective Evaluation.* San Francisco: Jossey-Bass.

Guest, Greg, Arwen Bunce, and Laura Johnson. 2006. "How Many Interviews Are Enough?" *Field Methods* 18 (1):59–82. doi: 10.1177/1525822X05279903.

Hafner, John, and Patti Hafner. 2003. "Quantitative Analysis of the Rubric as an Assessment Tool: An Empirical Study of Student Peer-Group Rating." *International Journal of Science Education* 25 (12): 1509–1528.

Hall, Hazel. 2010. "Promoting the Priorities of Practitioner Research Engagement." *Journal of Librarianship and Information Science* 42 (2): 83–88. doi: 10.1177/0961000610363978.

Hatch, J. Amos. 2002. *Doing Qualitative Research in Education Settings.* Albany: State University of New York Press.

Heidegger, Martin. 1962. *Being and Time.* London: SCM Press.

Heidi, Julien, and K. Genuis Shelagh. 2009. "Emotional Labour in Librarians' Instructional Work." *Journal of Documentation* 65 (6): 926–937. doi: 10.1108/00220410910998924.

Hernon, Peter, and Candy Schwartz. 2007. "What Is a Problem Statement?" *Library & Information Science Research* 29 (3): 307–309. doi: 10.1016/j.lisr .2007.06.001.

Hernon, Peter, and Candy Schwartz. 2016. "Research May Be Harder to Conduct than Some Realize." *Library & Information Science Research* 38 (2): 91–92. doi: 10.1016/j.lisr.2016.05.003.

Hidi, Suzanne, and K. Ann Renninger. 2006. "The Four-Phase Model of Interest Development." *Educational Psychologist 41* (2): 111–117.

Hirsch, E.D. 2006. "Building Knowledge: The Case for Bringing Content into the Language Arts Block and for a Knowledge-Rich Curriculum Core for All Children." *American Educator* 30 (1): 8–17.

Hoadley, Christopher M. 2002. "Creating Context: Design-Based Research in Creating and Understanding CSCL." Paper presented at the Computer Support for Cooperative Learning Conference (CSCL) 2002, Boulder, CO.

Hoadley, Christopher M. 2004. "Methodological Alignment in Design-Based Research." *Educational Psychologist* 39 (4): 203–212. doi: 10.1207/ s15326985ep3904_2.

Holmes, Claire, and Megan Oakleaf. 2013. "The Official Rules for Norming Rubrics Successfully." *Journal of Academic Librarianship* 39 (6): 599.

Holsapple, Clyde W., and K. D. Joshi. 2002. "A Collaborative Approach to Ontology Design." *Communications of the ACM* 45 (2): 42–47. doi: 10.1145/ 503124.503147.

Howell, Martha, and Walter Prevenier. 2001. *From Reliable Sources: An Introduction to Historical Methods.* Ithaca: Cornell University Press.

Husserl, Edward. 1931. *Ideas.* London: George Allen & Unwin.

Husserl, Edward. 1970. *Logical Investigations*, Vol.1. New York: Humanities Press.

Israel, Mark. 2015. *Research Ethics and Integrity for Social Scientists: Beyond Regulatory Compliance.* 2nd ed. London: Sage.

Ito, Mizuko, Gutierrez, Kris, Livingstone, Sonia, Penuel, Bill, Rhodes, Jean, Salen, Katie, Schor, Juliet, Sefton-Green, Julian, and S. Craig Watkins. 2013. "Connected Learning: An Agenda for Research and Design." Accessed June 29, 2017. https://dmlhub.net/publications/connected-learning-agenda-for-research- and-design/.

Johnson, Ben 2012. "How Do We Know When Students Are Engaged?" *Edutopia.* Accessed June 29, 2017. https://www.edutopia.org/blog/student-engagement- definition-ben-johnson.

Johnson, Mauritz. 1967a. "Definitions and Models in Curriculum Theory." *Educational Theory* 17 (2): 127–140. doi: 10.1111/j.1741-5446.1967.tb00295.x.

Johnson, Mauritz. 1967b. "Schema for Curriculum." *Educational Theory 17*: 127–140.

Johnson, Mauritz. 1976. Needed Research: Emphasis on the Future. *Educational Leadership 33* (7): 505.

Johnson, Mauritz. 1977. *Intentionality in Education: A Conceptual Model of Curricular and Instructional Planning and Evaluation.* Albany, NY.

Kelle, Udo. 2005. ""Emergence" vs. "Forcing" of Empirical Data? A Crucial Problem of "Grounded Theory" Reconsidered." *Forum Qualitative Sozialforschung / Forum: Qualitative Social Research; 6* (2): *Qualitative Inquiry: Research, Archiving, and Reuse.* doi: 10.17169/fqs-6.2.467.

Kendrick, Kaetrena Davis, and Ione T. Damasco. 2015. "A Phenomenological Study of Conservative Academic Librarians." *Behavioral & Social Sciences Librarian* 34 (3): 129–157. doi: 10.1080/01639269.2015.1063952.

Kloda, Lorie Andrea. 2008. "Asking the Right Question." *Evidence Based Library and Information Practice 3* (4). doi: 10.18438/B8B030.

Koufogiannakis, Denise, and Alison Brettle. 2015. "Systematic Reviews in LIS: Identifying Evidence and Gaps for Practice." Poster presented at the *8th International Evidence Based Library and Information Practice Conference,* Brisbane, Australia Accessed June 29, 2017. https://era.library.ualberta.ca/files/nk322d79d#.Vl3Tm1WrS70.

Koufogiannakis, Denise, and Natasha Wiebe. 2006. "Effective Methods for Teaching Information Literacy Skills to Undergraduate Students: A Systematic Review and Meta-Analysis." *Evidence Based Library and Information Practice* 1 (3): 33–43. doi: 10.18438/B8MS3D. doi:http://dx.doi.org/10.18438/B8MS3D

Koufogiannakis, Denise, Andrew Booth, and Alison Brettle. 2006. "ReLIANT: Reader's Guide to the Literature on Interventions Addressing the Need for Education and Training." *Library and Information Research 30* (94): 44–51.

Koufogiannakis, Denise. 2012. "The State of Systematic Reviews in Library and Information Studies." *Evidence Based Library and Information Practice* 7 (2): 91–95. doi: 10.18438/B8Q021.

Krosnick, Jon A. 1991. "Response Strategies for Coping with the Cognitive Demands of Attitude Measures in Surveys." *Applied Cognitive Psychology* 5 (3): 213–236. doi: 10.1002/acp.2350050305.

Kuhlthau, Carol, Jannica Heinström, and Ross J. Todd. 2008. "The 'Information Search Process' Revisited: Is the Model Still Useful?" *Information Research* 13 (4). Accessed June 29, 2017. http://InformationR.net/ir/13-4/paper355.html

Kuhlthau, C. C., L. Maniotes, and A. Caspari. 2012. *Guided Inquiry Design: A Framework for Inquiry in Your School.* Santa Barbara: Libraries Unlimited.

Kuhlthau, Carol, Leslie Maniotes, and Ann Caspari. 2012. *Guided Inquiry Design: A Framework for Inquiry in Your School.* Santa Barbara: Libraries Unlimited.

Kuhlthau, Carol, Leslie Maniotes, and Ann Caspari. 2015. *Guided Inquiry: Learning in the 21st Century*, 2nd ed. Santa Barbara: Libraries Unlimited.

Law, Margaret. 2005. The Systematic Review: A Potential Tool for Research-Grounded Library Management. *Proceedings of the Annual Conference of the Canadian Association for Information Science*. Accessed June 29, 2017. http://www.cais-acsi.ca/ojs/index.php/cais/article/view/209/670.

Levinas, Emmanuel. 1969. *Totality and Infinity: An Essay on Exteriority.* Duquesne: Duquesne UP.

Lewin, Kurt. 1946. "Action Research and Minority Problems." *Journal of Social Issues* 2 (4): 34–46. doi: 10.1111/j.1540-4560.1946.tb02295.x.

Lewis, Marianne W., and Andrew J. Grimes. 1999. "Metatriangulation: Building Theory from Multiple Paradigms." *The Academy of Management Review* 24 (4): 672–690. doi: 10.2307/259348.

Lincoln, Yvonna S., and Egon G. Guba. 1985. *Naturalistic inquiry.* Newbury Park: Sage Publications.

Linstone, Harold A., and Murray Turoff. 1975. "Introduction." In *The Delphi Method: Techniques and Applications*, edited by Harold A. Linstone, and Murray Turoff, 3–12. Reading: Addison-Wesley.

Loertscher, David. 2000. *Taxonomies of the School Library Media Program*, 2nd ed. Salt Lake City: Hi Willow Research and Publishing.

Ludwig, Logan, and Susan Leigh Starr. 2005. "Library as Place: Results of a Delphi study." *Journal of Medical Library Association 93* (3), 315–326.

Maxwell, Joseph A. 2005. *Qualitative Research Design: An Interactive Approach*, 2nd ed. Thousand Oaks: Sage Publications.

McKenney, Susan, and Thomas C. Reeves. 2013. "Systematic Review of Design-Based Research Progress." *Educational Researcher* 42 (2):.97–100. doi: 10.3102/0013189X12463781.

McKibbon, K. A. 2006. Systematic reviews and librarians. *Library Trends 55* (1): 202–215.

McMillan, James H. (Ed.) 2013. *The SAGE Handbook of Research on Classroom Assessment.* Thousand Oaks: SAGE.

McMillan, James H., and Sally Schumacher. 2010. *Research in Education: Evidence-Based Inquiry,* 7th ed. Boston: Pearson.

Merleau-Ponty, Maurica. 1962. *Phenomenology of Perception.* New York: Routledge.

Merriam, Sharan B. 1988. *Case Study Research in Education: A Qualitative Approach.* San Francisco: Jossey-Bass.

Methley, Abigail M., Stephen Campbell, Carolyn Chew-Graham, Rosalind McNally, and Sudeh Cheraghi-Sohi. 2014. "PICO, PICOS and SPIDER: a comparison study of specificity and sensitivity in three search tools for qualitative systematic reviews." *BMC Health Services Research 14*:579-588. doi: 10.1186/s12913-014-0579-0.

Meyers, Eric M., Karen F. Fisher, and Elizabeth E. Marcoux. 2009. "Making Sense of an Information World: The Everyday-Life Information Behavior of Preeteens." *Library Quarterly* 79 (3): 301–341.

Miles, Matthew B., and A. Michael Huberman. 1984. *Analyzing Qualitative Data: A Source Book for New Methods*. Beverly Hills: Sage Publications.

Miles, Matthew B., Huberman, A. Michale, and Johnny Saldaña. 2014. *Qualitative Data Analysis: A Methods Sourcebook*. 3rd ed. Thousand Oaks: Sage Publications.

Millar, Morgan M., and Don A. Dillman. 2011. "Improving Response to Web and Mixed-Mode Surveys." *Public Opinion Quarterly* 75 (2): 249–269. doi: 10.1093/poq/nfr003.

Montiel-Overall, Patricia. 2015. "Toward a Theory of Collaboration for Teachers and Librarians." *School Library Media Research, 8.* Accessed June 29, 2017. http://www.ala.org/aasl/sites/ala.org.aasl/files/content/aaslpubsandjournals/slr/vol8/SLMR_Theoryofollaboration_V8.pdf.

Moskal, Barbara M. 2000. "Scoring Rubrics: What, When and How?" *Practical Assessment* 7 (3): 1–5.

Moustakas, Clark. 1994. *Phenomenological Research Methods*. Thousand Oaks: Sage.

Nakhoda, Maryam, and Samaneh Rahimian. 2015. "Factors Affecting Empowerment of Female Librarians, Views of Female Managers of Tehran Public Libraries." *Library Management* 36 (8/9): 663–672. doi: 10.1108/LM-09-2015-0059.

National Center for Education Statistics. 2015. *Digest of Education Statistics: 2015.* Accessed June 29, 2017. http://nces.ed.gov/programs/digest/d15/.

Neuman, Delia. 1995. "High School Students' Use of Databases: Results of a National Delphi Study." *Journal of the American Society for Information Science* 46 (4): 284–298. doi: 10.1002/(SICI)1097-4571(199505)46:4<284::AID-ASI5>3.0.CO;2-J.

Nitko, Anthony J. 1996. *Educational Assessment of Students*. Englewood Cliffs, NJ: Prentice Hall.

O'Cathain, Alicia, Elizabeth Murphy, and Jon Nicholl. 2010. Three Techniques for Integrating Data in Mixed Methods Studies. *BMJ 341.* doi:10.1136/bmj.c4587.

Oakleaf, Megan. 2007. "Using Rubrics to Collect Evidence for Decision-Making: What Do Librarians Need to Learn?" *Evidence Based Library and Information Practice* 2 (3): 27–42.

Oakleaf, Megan. 2008. "Dangers and Opportunities: A Conceptual Map of Information Literacy Assessment Approaches." *Portal: Libraries and the Academy* 8 (3): 233–253.

Oakleaf, Megan. 2009a. "The Information Literacy Instruction Assessment Cycle: A Guide for Increasing Student Learning and Improving Librarian Instructional Skills." *Journal of Documentation* 65 (4): 539–560.

Oakleaf, Megan. 2009b. "Using Rubrics to Assess Information Literacy: An Examination of Methodology and Interrater Reliability." *Journal of the American Society for Information Science and Technology* 60 (5): 969–983.

Oakleaf, Megan. 2009c. "Writing Rubrics Right: Avoiding Common Mistakes in Rubric Assessment." Presentation at the ACRL National Conference, Seattle, WA, March 12–15.

Oakleaf, Megan, and Lisa Hinchliffe. 2009. "Assessment Cycle or Circular File: Do Academic Librarians Use Information Literacy Assessment Data?" *Proceedings of the Library Assessment Conference*. Seattle, Association of Research Libraries: 159–164.

Okoli, Chitu, and Suzanne D. Pawlowski. 2004. "The Delphi Method as a Research Tool: An Example, Design Considerations and Applications." *Information & Management* 42 (1): 15–29. doi: 10.1016/j.im.2003.11.002.

Otter, Sue. 1992. *Learning Outcomes in Higher Education: A Development Project Report.* Accessed June 29, 2017. http://files.eric.ed.gov/fulltext/ED354397.pdf.

Parliament of the Commonwealth of Australia. 2011. "School Libraries and Teacher Librarians in 21st Century Australia. Canberra: Commonwealth of Australia." Accessed June 29, 2017. http://www.aph.gov.au/ Parliamentary _Business/Committees/ House_of_Representatives Committees?url=ee/ schoollibraries/ report.htm.

Patton, Michael Quinn. 2002. *Qualitative Research & Evaluation Methods,* 3rd ed. Thousand Oaks: Sage.

Patton, Michael Quinn. 2015. *Qualitative Research & Evaluation Methods: Integrating Theory and Practice,* 4th ed. Thousand Oaks: Sage.

Pellegrino, James W. 2014. A Learning Sciences Perspective on the Design and Use of Assessment in Education. In *Cambridge Handbook of the Learning Sciences,* 2nd ed., edited by R. Keith Sawyer, 233–252. New York: Cambridge University Press. doi: 10.1017/CBO9781139519526.015.

Phelps, Sue F., and Nicole Campbell. 2012. "Systematic Reviews in Theory and Practice for Library and Information Studies." *Library & Information Research* 36 (112): 6–15. Accessed June 27, 2017. http://www.lirgjournal.org.uk/lir/ojs/ index.php/lir/article/view/498/546.

Phenomenology Online. 2011. Accessed June 29, 2017. "Edward Husserl." http:// www.phenomenologyonline.com/scholars/husserl-edmund/.

Pohjanen, Aira Maria, and Terttu Anna Maarit Kortelainen. 2015. "Transgender Information Behaviour." *Journal of Documentation* 72 (1): 172–190. doi: 10.1108/JD-04-2015-0043.

Popham, W. James. 2003. *Test Better, Teach Better: The Instructional Role of Assessment*. Alexandria, Association for Supervision and Curriculum Development.

Popham, W. James. 2014. *Classroom Assessment: What Teachers Need to Know*, 7th ed. Boston: Pearson.

Powell, Catherine. 2003. "The Delphi Technique: Myths and Realities." *Journal of Advanced Nursing* 41 (4): 376–382. doi: 10.1046/j.1365-2648.2003.02537.x.

Presser, Stanley, and Johnny Blair. 1994. "Survey Pretesting: Do Different Methods Produce Different Results?" *Sociological Methodology* 24: 73–104. doi: 10.2307/270979.

Presser, Stanley, Mick P. Couper, Judith T. Lessler, Elizabeth Martin, Jean Martin, Jennifer M. Rothgeb, and Eleanor Singer. 2004. "Methods for Testing and Evaluating Survey Questions." *Public Opinion Quarterly* 68 (1): 109–130. doi: 10.1093/poq/nfh008.

Preston, Carolyn C., and Andrew M. Colman. 2000. "Optimal Number of Response Categories in Rating Scales: Reliability, Validity, Discriminating Power, and Respondent Preferences." *Acta Psychologica* 104 (1): 1–15. doi: 10.1016/S0001-6918(99)00050-5.

Rabina, Debbie. 2013. "Reference Materials in LIS Instruction: A Delphi Study." *Journal of Education for Library and Information Science* 54 (2): 108–123.

Radford, Marie L. 2006. "The Critical Incident Technique and the Qualitative Evaluation Connecting Libraries and Schools Project." *Library Trends 55* (1): 46–64.

Ravindranath, Sindhu. 2016. "Soft Skills in Project Management: A Review." *IUP Journal of Soft Skills 10* (4): 16–25.

Rawson, Casey, and Sandra Hughes-Hassell. 2015. "Research by Design: The Promise of Design-Based Research for School Library Research." *School Libraries Worldwide 21* (2): 11–25.

Reigeluth, C. M., and T. W. Frick. 1999. Formative Research: A Methodology for Improving Design Theories. In C. M. Reigeluth (Ed.), *Instructional-Design Theories and Models: A New Paradigm of Instructional Theories* (Vol. 2). Mahwah, NJ: Lawrence Erlbaum Associates.

Reigeluth, Charles M., and Theodore W. Frick. 1999. Formative Research: A Methodology for Creating and Improving Design Theories. In *Instructional-Design Theories and Models, Volume II: A New Paradigm of Instructional Theory*, edited by Charles M. Reigeluth, 633–651. Mahwah: Lawrence Erlbaum.

Reigeluth, Charles M., and Yun-Jo An. 2006. "Functional Contextualism: An Ideal Framework for Theory in Instructional Design and Technology." *Educational Technology Research and Development* 54 (1):,49–53.

Reigeluth, Charles M., and Yun-Jo An. 2009. "Theory Building." In *Instructional-Design Theories and Models, Volume III: Building a Common Knowledge Base,* edited by Charles M. Reigeluth and Alison Carr-Chellman, 365–386. New York: Routledge.

Reja, Urša, Manfreda, Katja Lozar, Valentina Hlebec, and Vasja Vehovar. 2003. "Open-Ended vs. Close-Ended Questions in Web Questionnaires." *Developments in Applied Statistics* 19 (1): 160–117.

Renninger, K. Ann, and Suzanne Hidi. 2002. "Student Interest and Achievement: Developmental Issues Raised by a Case Study." In *The Development of Achievement Motivation* edited by Allan Wigfield and Jacquelynne S. Eccles, 173–195. New York: Academic Press.

Renninger, K. Ann, Carol Sansone, and Jessi L. Smith. 2004. "Love of Learning." In *Character Strengths and Virtues: A Classification and Handbook*, edited by Christopher Peterson and Martin E. P. Seligman, 161–176, New York: Oxford University Press.

Rhoades, Ellen A. 2011. "Commentary on Literature Reviews." *Volta Review 111* (3): 353–368.

Ricoeur, Paul. 1975. Phenomenology and Hermeneutics. *Noûs*, 85–102.

Rowe, Gene, and George Wright. 1999. "The Delphi Technique as a Forecasting Tool: Issues and Analysis." *International Journal of Forecasting* 15 (4): 353–375. doi: 10.1016/S0169-2070(99)00018-7.

Rubric Assessment of Information Literacy Skills (RAILS). 2017a. "Preparing 125 Artifacts of Student Learning for RAILS Scoring." Accessed June 17, 2017. http://railsontrack.info/media/documents/2014/8/Preparing_Your _Artifacts_for_Scoring.pdf.

Rubric Assessment of Information Literacy Skills (RAILS). 2017b. "Rubrics." Accessed June 29, 2017. http://railsontrack.info/rubrics.aspx.

Rubric Assessment of Information Literacy Skills (RAILS). 2017c. "Top 5 Barriers that May Impede You from Assessing IL Using This Rubric." Accessed June 17, 2017. http://railsontrack.info/media/documents/2014/8/individualbarriers.pdf.

Sackman, Harold. 1974. *Delphi Assessment: Expert Opinion, Forecasting, and Group Processes* (R-1283-PR). Santa Monica, RAND. Accessed June 29, 2017. http://www.rand.org/content/dam/rand/pubs/reports/2006/R1283.pdf.

Sadler, D. Royce. 1989. "Formative Assessment and the Design of Instructional Systems." *Instructional Science* 18 (2): 119–144. doi: 10.1007/BF00117714.

Saldaña, Johnny. 2013. *The Coding Manual for Qualitative Researchers*, 2nd ed. Thousand Oaks: Sage Publications.

Sampson, Margaret, Raymond Daniel, Elise Cogo, and Orvie Dingwall. 2008. "Sources of Evidence to Support Systematic Reviews in Librarianship (EC)." *Journal of the Medical Library Association* 96: 66–69.

Sartre, Jean Paul. 1992. *Being and Nothingness*. New York: Washington Square Press.

Scheibe, Mark Henry, Margaret Skutsch, and Jerry Schofer. 1975. Experiments in Delphi Methodology. In *The Delphi Method: Techniques and Applications*, edited by Harold A. Lintone and Murray Turoff, 262–287. Reading: Addison-Wesley.

Schmidt, Roy C. 1997. "Managing Delphi Surveys Using Nonparametric Statistical Techniques." *Decision Sciences* 28 (3): 763–774. doi: 10.1111/j.1540-5915.1997.tb01330.x.

Scholastic 2016. *School Libraries Work: A Compendium of Research Supporting the Effectiveness of School Libraries*. New York: Scholastic: Accessed June 29, 2017. http://www.scholastic.com/SLW2016/.

Scriven, M. 1967. "The Methodology of Evaluation." In *Perspectives of Curriculum Evaluation, Volume I* edited by Ralph W. Tyler, Robert M. Gagne, and Michael Scriven, 39–83. Chicago: Rand McNally.

Shavelson, Richard J., Maria Araceli Ruiz-Primo, and Edward W. Wiley. 2005. "Windows into the Mind." *Higher Education* 49 (4): 413–430. doi: 10.1007/s10734-004-9448-9.

Shoket, Mohd. 2014. "Research Problem Identification and Formulation." *International Journal of Research* 1(4): 512–518.

Skulmoski , Gregory J., Francis T. Hartman, and Jennifer Krahn. 2007. "The Delphi Method for Graduate Research." *Journal of Information Technology Education* 6, 1–21.

Sokolowski, Robert. 2000. *Introduction to Phenomenology*. Cambridge University Press.

Stake, Robert E. 1995. *The Art of Case Study Research*. Thousand Oaks: Sage.

Stake, Robert E. 2005. "Qualitative Case Studies." In *The SAGE Handbook of Qualitative Research*, 3rd ed., edited by Norman K. Denzin and Yvonna S. Lincoln, 443–466. Thousand Oaks: Sage Publications.

Stefl-Mabry, Joette, and William E. J. Doane. 2014. "Teaching to Assess: Lessons Learned When Faculty and Preservice Educators Learn to Assess and Assess to Learn." Paper presented at the American Educational Research Association Annual Meeting, Philadelphia, PA.

Stevens, Dannelle D., and Antonia J. Levi. 2004. *Introduction to Rubrics: An Assessment Tool to Save Grading Time, Convey Effective Feedback and Promote Student Learning*. Stylus Publishing, LLC.

Stokes, Donald E. 1997. *Pasteur's Quadrant: Basic Science and Technological Innovation*. Washington, DC: Brookings Institution Press.

Strauss, Anselm. 1987. *Qualitative Research for Social Scientists*. Cambridge, Cambridge University Press.

Strauss, Anselm, and Jeremy Corbin. 1990. *Basics of Qualitative Research: Grounded Theory Procedures and Techniques*. Newbury Park: Sage.

Subramaniam, Mega. 2016. "Designing the Library of the Future for and with Teens: Librarians as the 'Connector' in Connected Learning." *The Journal of Research on Libraries and Young Adults 7* (2). Accessed June 29, 2017. http://www.yalsa.ala.org/jrlya/2016/06/designing-the-library-of-the-future-for-and-with-teens-librarians-as-the-connector-in-connected-learning/.

Suh, Nam P. 2013. "On Design of Large Complex Systems." ICAD 2013 Keynote Speech. Worcester Polytechnic Institute, Worcester, Massachussetts.

Thangaratinam, Shakila, and Charles W. E. Redman. 2005. "The Delphi Technique." *The Obstetrician & Gynaecologist 7* (2): 120–125. doi: 10.1576/toag.7.2.120.27071.

Todd, Ross J., Carol Gordon, and Ya-Ling Lu. 2011. "One Common Goal: Student Learning. Report of Findings and Recommendations of the New Jersey School Library Survey Phase 2." Accessed June 29, 2017. http://cissl.rutgers.edu/images/stories/docs/njasl_phase%20_2_final.pdf.

Todd, Ross J., and Carol Kuhlthau. 2005. "Student Learning through Ohio School Libraries, Part 1: How Effective School Libraries Help Students." *School Libraries Worldwide 11* (1): 89–110.

Urquhart, Christine. 2010. "Systematic Reviewing, Meta-Analysis and Meta-Synthesis for Evidence-Based Library and Information Science." *Information Research 15* (3). Accessed June 29, 2017. http://www.informationr.net/ir/15-3/colis7/colis708.html.

Vagle, Mark D. 2014. *Crafting Phenomenological Research*. Walnut Creek: Left Coast Press.

van den Akker, Jan. 1999. "Principles and Methods of Development Research." In *Design Approaches and Tools in Education and Training*, edited by Jan van den Akker, Robert Maribe Branch, Kent Gustafson, Nienke Nieveen and Tjeerd Plomp, 1–14. Dordrecht: Springer Netherlands.

van Manen, Max. 2014. *Phenomenology of Practice*. Walnut Creek: Left Coast Press.

van Veen, Floris van, Anja S. Göritz, and Sebastian Sattler. 2015. "Response Effects of Prenotification, Prepaid Cash, Prepaid Vouchers, and Postpaid Vouchers." Social Science Computer Review 34 (3): 333–346. doi: 10.1177/0894439315585074.

VanScoy, Amy. 2013. "Fully Engaged Practice and Emotional Connection: Aspects of the Practitioner Perspective of Reference and Information Service." *Library & Information Science Research 35* (4): 272–278. doi: 10.1016/j.lisr.2013.09.001.

Wang, Feng, and Michael J. Hannafin. 2005. "Design-Based Research and Technology-Enhanced Learning Environments." *Educational Technology Research and Development* 53 (4): 5–23. doi: 10.1007/BF02504682.

Warriner, Keith, John Goyder, Heidi Gjertsen, Paula Hohner, and Kathleen McSpurren. 1996. "Charities, No; Lotteries, No; Cash, Yes: Main Effects and Interactions in a Canadian Incentives Experiment." *The Public Opinion Quarterly* 60 (4): 542–562.

Washington State University. 2016. "Quick Guide to Norming on Student Work for Program-Level Assessment." Accessed June 16, 2017. https://atl.wsu.edu/documents/2015/03/rubrics-norming.pdf

Weijters, Bert, Elke Cabooter, and Niels Schillewaert. 2010. "The Effect of Rating Scale Format on Response Styles: The Number of Response Categories and Response Category Labels." *International Journal of Research in Marketing* 27 (3): 236–247. doi: 10.1016/j.ijresmar.2010.02.004.

Wiggins, Grant. 1996. "Creating Tests Worth Taking." In *A Handbook for Student Performance in an Era of Restructuring*, Edited by Robert E. Blum and Judith Arter, 1–6. Alexandria, VA: Association for Supervision and Curriculum Development.

Wiggins, Grant P. 1998. *Educative Assessment: Designing Assessments to Inform and Improve Student Performance*. San Francisco: Jossey-Bass.

Wijayaratne, Anusha Lakmini, and Diljit Singh. 2015. "Developing an Academic Library Website Model, a Designer's Checklist, and an Evaluative Instrument: A Delphi Method approach." *The Electronic Library* 33 (1): 35–51. doi: 10.1108/EL-11-2012-0115.

Wildemuth, Barbara M. 2009. *Applications of Social Research Methods to Questions in Information and Library Science*. Westport: Libraries Unlimited
.Arksey, Hilary, and Lisa O'Malley. 2005. "Scoping Studies: Towards a Methodological Framework." *International Journal of Social Research Methodology* 8 (1): 19–32. doi: 10.1080/1364557032000119616.

Willis, Gordon B., and Kristen Miller. 2011. "Cross-Cultural Cognitive Interviewing." *Field Methods* 23 (4): 331–341. doi: 10.1177/1525822X11416092.

Wilson, Virginia. 2013. "Formalized Curiosity: Reflecting on the Librarian Practitioner-Researcher." *Evidence Based Library and Information Practice* 8 (1): 111–117. doi: 10.18438/B8ZK6K.

Woolsey, Lorette K. 1986. "The Critical Incident Technique: An Innovative Qualitative Method of Research." *Canadian Journal of Counselling and Psychotherapy* 20 (4): 242–254.

Worthen, Blaine, and James R. Sanders. 1987. *Educational Evaluation: Alternative Approaches and Practical Guidelines*. New York: Longman.

Yin, Robert K. 1984. *Case Study Research Design and Methods*. Beverly Hills: Sage Publications.

Yin, Robert K. 2014. *Case Study Research: Design and Methods.* Thousand Oaks: Sage Publications. Kotter, John. 1996. *Leading Change.* Cambridge: Harvard University Press.

Zhang, Yin, and Athena Salaba. 2009. "What Is Next for Functional Requirements for Bibliographic Records? A Delphi Study." *The Library Quarterly: Information, Community, Policy* 79 (2): 233–255. doi: 10.1086/597078.

Zheng, Lanqin. 2015. "A Systematic Literature Review of Design-Based Research from 2004 to 2013." *Journal of Computers in Education* 2 (4): 399–420. doi: 10.1007/s40692-015-0036-z.

About the Editors and Contributors

EDITORS

Ruth V. Small is Laura J. and L. Douglas Meredith Professor and Director of the Center for Digital Literacy at the School of Information Studies, Syracuse University. Her research focuses on the motivational aspects of information use in learning contexts and the role of the school librarian in providing motivationally supportive learning environments. For her research, she received the 2001 Carroll Preston Baber Research Award from the American Library Association and the 1997 Highsmith Research Award from the American Association of School Librarians.

Marcia A. Mardis is an Associate Professor of Information Science, Assistant Dean for Interdisciplinary Research and Education, Coordinator for Educational Informatics, and Co-Director of the Information Institute at Florida State University. Her research intersects learning resources, high-speed networking, and digital libraries with particular emphases in K–12 education, curation, STEM learning, data mining, and learning analytics. She is an experienced author, researcher, K–12 teacher, and school librarian.

CONTRIBUTORS

Chapter Authors

MARILYN P. ARNONE is a Professor of Practice in the School of Information Studies at Syracuse University. Her research explores motivation and learning in formal and informal and face-to-face and cyberlearning environments, and she has a keen interest in the influence of intellectual curiosity, perceived competence, autonomy, and social relatedness on student achievement.

ALISON BRETTLE is Professor of Health Information and Evidence Based Practice at the University of Salford, United Kingdom. She has specialist expertise in literature searching, systematic review methodology, evidence-based practice, and the evaluation of health information services.

JENNY BOSSALLER is an Associate Professor at the School of Information Science & Learning Technologies at the University of Missouri—Columbia. Her research focus broadly encompasses constraints on information flow, including aspects of information policy, history, and related social and technological phenomena.

MARIA CAHILL is an Associate Professor with a joint appointment in the School of Information Science College of Communication and Information and Department of Educational Leadership College of Education at the University of Kentucky. Her research interests include school librarianship, literacy, and education.

AUDREY P. CHURCH is a Professor in the College of Education & Human Services, Longwood University. Her research interests center on school librarianship in the areas of stakeholder perceptions and both program and performance assessment.

LESLEY FARMER, Professor at California State University Long Beach, coordinates the librarianship program at her university and manages the CSU ICT Literacy Project. Her research interests include school librarianship (including international aspects), information literacy, digital citizenship, program assessment, data analytics, and educational technology (particularly gender issues).

KRISTEN GREGORY is a doctoral candidate in Curriculum and Instruction: Literacy Leadership at Old Dominion University. Her research interests center on disciplinary literacy, adult literacy, and mobile learning.

MELISSA GROSS is a Professor in the School of Information at Florida State University. Her research is in the areas of information-seeking behavior, information literacy, library program and service evaluation, information resources for youth, and teacher–librarian collaboration.

JANNICA HEINSTRÖM is an Associate Professor in Information Studies at Åbo Akademi University, Finland, and a docent at the University of Borås, Sweden.

Her research investigates psychological aspects of information interaction, particularly the role of personality, motivation, and emotion.

SANDRA HUGHES-HASSELL is a Professor at the School of Information and Library Science at the University of North Carolina at Chapel Hill. Her research focuses on social justice issues in youth library services, diverse youth literature, and the role of school librarians in education reform.

JAMI JONES is Associate Professor in the College of Education at East Carolina University. Her research focuses on creativity and resiliency in the multiple roles of the school librarian.

MINKYOUNG KIM is an instructional consultant in the College of Education at Texas Tech University. Her research interests center on instructional design theories related to the learner-centered paradigm, personalized learning, and collaborative learning in a task-based learning environment.

DENISE KOUFOGIANNAKIS is Associate University Librarian at the University of Alberta (Canada) Libraries. Her research focuses on evidence-based library and information practice.

CAROL COLLIER KUHLTHAU is Professor Emerita of Library and Information Science at the School of Communication and Information, Rutgers University. Her research is on the Information Search Process and for the ISP model of affective, cognitive, and physical aspects in six stages of information seeking and use and on the use of guided inquiry for facilitating learning.

DABAE LEE is an Assistant Professor in the Teachers College at Emporia State University. Her areas of research interest include personalized learning, student collaboration in Problem-Based Learning, roles of technology in personalized learning, learner-centered paradigm, active learning spaces, and research methods in instructional technology.

KYLE A. LEE is an Adjunct Professor at the University of Kentucky. His research interest focus on individual and collective teacher efficacy, educational leadership, and teacher retention.

LESLIE MANIOTES is a Curriculum/ Instructional Specialist and Educational Consultant for BLV Consulting, Colorado. Her research focuses on discourse analysis in classrooms looking at the Third Space for learning, as well as inquiry-based learning.

NELSON MAYLONE is a Professor in the College of Education at Eastern Michigan University. His research interests include student assessment and public education policy.

MEGAN OAKLEAF is an Associate Professor in the School of Information Studies at Syracuse University. Her research interests include library value and impact, outcomes assessment, evidence-based decision making, information literacy instruction, information services, and digital librarianship.

SHANA PRIBESH is an Associate Professor at the Darden College of Education, Old Dominion University. Her research focuses on the structural aspects of educational inequality.

CHARLES REIGELUTH is Professor Emeritus, School of Education, Indiana University. His research centers on instructional design theories and models and on systemic change in education.

SUSAN ROTHWELL is a postdoctoral education researcher for the EMPOWER STEM Workforce Development Project at the Rochester Institute of Technology. Her research focuses on the interaction of people, cultures, science, and technology.

SUZANNE STAUFFER is Associate Professor at the School of Library and Information Science, Louisiana State University. She conducts historical research on the American public library as a social and cultural institution, on children's services in public libraries, on the professionalization of librarianship, and on gender issues in the American public library.

JOETTE STEFL-MABRY is an Associate Professor in the Department of Information Science and an Associate Research Professor at the State University of New York at Albany. Her research focuses on educational assessment and evaluation and documenting evidence of practice PreK–12 through higher education.

MEGA SUBRAMANIAM is an Associate Professor at the College of Information Studies and Associate Director for the Information Policy and Access Center at the University of Maryland. Her research focuses on enhancing the role of libraries in fostering the mastery of information and new media literacies that are essential to STEM learning among underserved young people.

REBECCA TEASDALE is a doctoral candidate in Educational Psychology at the University of Illinois at Urbana–Champaign. Her research interests focus on developing methodologies for evaluating informal science learning.

ROSS J. TODD is Associate Professor in the School of Communication and Information and Director of the Center for International Scholarship in School Libraries, Rutgers. His current research focuses on how students learn in digital information environments and how school librarians can engage with evidence-based practices to ensure the ongoing development of school libraries to meet the needs of students in 21st-century schools.

AMANDA WAUGH is a doctoral candidate at the University of Maryland. Her research interests focus on the information behavior of teens in online communities and the impact of school libraries in school communities.

Scenario Writers

MOLLY BROWN is User Experience and Outreach Librarian and Assistant Professor at the DuPont Ball Library at Stetson University, as well as an editor and contributor for the International Librarians Network website. She has worked in academic libraries for 13 years and has research interests in the areas of 21st-century libraries, including improving the user experience, library instruction and information literacy, assessment, outreach, and international librarianship.

ANGELA BRANYON is an Assistant Professor in the College of Education at the University of West Georgia. Her research interests center on intellectual freedom, library advocacy, and the development of partnerships between universities and K–12 school systems in the field of library science.

SARAH A. CHAUNCEY is Director of Instructional Technology & Curriculum Development in the Student Services Division of the Rockland County (NY) Board of Cooperative Educational Services. She conducts research on a multiplicity of factors supporting learning in formal and formal settings that serve students with emotional, behavioral, cognitive, and physical learning disabilities.

MIRAH J. DOW is a Professor and Director of the PhD Program in the School of Library and Information Management at Emporia State University. She conducts research on interdisciplinary coteaching that includes school librarians and multiple content area teachers who together use guided inquiry strategies to prepare children and youth for careers in STEM fields.

LYNN HOFFMAN is Director of Operations at the Somerset County Library System of New Jersey. As an experienced public library administrator, she has a particular interest in organizational development, developing lasting patron relationships, and implementing big ideas on the front lines.

ANNE LEDFORD is the Youth Services Department Head at Douglas County Libraries at Lone Tree, Colorado. Her research interest is school and public library collaboration.

CRYSTAL LONG is Head of Reference, Eugene P. Watson Memorial Library at Northwestern State University. Her focus is new media and how it is leveraged for outreach, instruction, and management.

H. PATRICIA MCKENNA is the President of AmbientEase in Victoria, Canada. Through the UrbanitiesLab, an initiative of AmbientEase, Patricia explores social media and other aware technologies affecting information interactions, engagement, creativity, and learning in 21st-century cities.

HEIDI NELTNER is a Digital Learning Coach and Certified School Librarian for Fort Thomas Independent Schools in Kentucky. She is interested in children's use of technology for learning, makerspaces, design thinking, and project-based learning and is the recipient of several state awards for her professional work, including the 2016 Kentucky Society for Technology in Education's Outstanding Teacher Award, KASL 2016 Outstanding Library Media Specialist, 2016 NKASL Outstanding Library Media Specialist, and a Google Certified Innovator.

CHARLES O'BRYAN is Director of the James M. Milne Library at the State University of New York at Oneonta. His research interests include collaborative space, institutional alignment, social capital, and change leadership.

BREE L. RUZZI is a doctoral candidate in the Darden College of Education at Old Dominion University. Her research focuses on STEM resources for learning in the school library.

Index